Michel Foucault and Power Today

Michel Foucault and Power Today

International Multidisciplinary Studies in the History of the Present

Edited by
Alain Beaulieu and David Gabbard

LEXINGTON BOOKS

A division of
ROWMAN & LITTLEFIELD PUBLISHERS, INC.
Lanham • Boulder • New York • Toronto • Oxford

LEXINGTON BOOKS

A division of Rowman & Littlefield Publishers, Inc.
A wholly owned subsidary of The Rowman & Littlefield Publishing Group, Inc.
4501 Forbes Boulevard, Suite 200
Lanham, MD 20706

PO Box 317
Oxford
OX2 9RU, UK

British Library Cataloguing in Publication Information Available

Library of Congress Cataloging-in-Publication Data

Michel Foucault and power today : international multidisciplinary studies in the history
of the present / edited by Alain Beaulieu and David Gabbard.
    p. cm.
Includes bibliographical references and index.
ISBN 0-7391-1181-7 (hardcover : alk. paper)—ISBN 0-7391-1324-0 (pbk. : alk. paper)
1. Foucault, Michel. 2. Power (Social sciences) 3. Social control. I. Beaulieu, Alain,
1940- II. Gabbard, David.
HM1256.M53 2005
303.3—dc22   2005018527

Printed in the United States of America

♾ ™ The paper used in this publication meets the minimum requirements of American
National Standard for Information Sciences—Permanence of Paper for Printed Library
Materials, ANSI/NISO Z39.48–1992.

Contents

Preface   vii
Acknowledgements   xv

Part I   Law & Politics

1   **Michel Foucault and the Obsolescent State:**   3
     Between the American Century
     and the Dawn of the European Union
     Dario Melossi

2   **The Immanence of Law in Power:**   13
     Reading Foucault with Agamben
     Warren Montag

3   **The Hybrid Character of "Control"**
     in the Work of Michel Foucault   23
     Alain Beaulieu

Part II   Politics & Culture

4   **No "Coppertops" Left Behind:**   37
     Foucault, *The Matrix*, and the Future of Compulsory Schooling
     David Gabbard

5   **It Does Too Matter:**   51
     Michel Foucault, John Coltrane, and Dominant Positions
     Tracey Nicholls

Part III   Psychiatry

6   **Foucault and Psychiatric Power after *Madness and Civilization***   61
     Mario Colucci

7   From Psychiatry to Bio-Politics or the Birth
     of the Bio-Security State   71
     Pierangelo Di Vittorio

                    Part IV   Health Care

8   Genetic Responsibility and Neo-Liberal Governmentality: 83
     Medical Diagnosis as Moral Technology
     Thomas Lemke

9   The Problem with High-Maintenance Bodies
     or the Politics of Care   93
     Monique Lanoix

                 Part V   The French Context

10   Subverting Social Order: 107
     Foucault and Derrida on the Role of the Intellectual
     Christian Lavagno

11   Foucault and the "Hydra-Headed Monster":   115
     The *Collège de Sociologie* and the Two *Acéphales*
     Frank Pearce

Notes   139
Index   165
About the Contributors   169

Preface

Alain Beaulieu and David Gabbard

Throughout his tenure as "Chair of History and Systems of Thought" at the Collège de France between 1970 and 1984, Michel Foucault lived a life of very strong social engagement. In addition to his participation in creating both the experimental and *gauchist* University Paris VIII at Vincennes in 1968, as well as the Group of Information on Prisons (G. I. P.) in 1971, Foucault served as journalist-reporter covering the Iranian revolution in 1978, engaged in innumerable public interventions, and participated in numerous demonstrations and petitions in solidarity with marginalized populations such as the so-called illegal immigrants (*sans papiers*), the boat people, and others. In the midst of this incredible life of activism, he also generated a body of work that has had, despite the still partial character of its reception (only half of the lessons at the Collège have been published to this day), a durable and determining influence across various spheres of knowledge and fields of practices.

Though he always reserved the right to rethink and rework his analyses, Foucault's writings demonstrated a consistent concern with understanding the development and organization of institutional practices that shape human subjectivities by highlighting the secrets of their disciplinary and normalizing strategies. What most distinguished his work, however, was his insistence on extending the boundaries of critique beyond the framework of institutions to address more complex and subtle, and therefore more effective, techniques of control. Perhaps it was this transcendence of institutional specificity that enabled Foucault's ideas to attract interest from and find application within such a variety of sites of struggle within and beyond academia. Foucault's thought thus finds innumerable applications across the social sciences, from studies in the social aspects of the medical practices and criminal sociology to juridical and economic sciences. Owing to their philosophical ramifications, his ideas have also impacted the spheres of literary studies, ethics, political thought, and "critical ontology." In sum, few thinkers have registered such an influence across such a diverse range of studies. This book wishes to pay homage to that diversity by presenting a multidisciplinary series of analyses dedicated to the question of "social control."

The chapters in this book represent refined and expanded versions of select invited papers delivered at an international conference entitled "Michel Foucault and Social Control" conducted at Maison de la culture Côte-des-Neiges in Montreal on May 8-10, 2004, to commemorate the twentieth anniversary of Foucault's death. While paying tribute to Foucault's achievements and situating

Preface

his thought within the French (and European) context from which it emerged, these essays also reevaluate the relevance of Foucault's ideas for understanding contemporary conditions, (or "power today"), both within the realm of ideas and within specific fields of practice.

As demonstrated in these essays, utilizing Foucault's theoretical approach to examine contemporary strategies and tactics of control within society requires accounting for the current patterns of "neoliberalization" and how those patterns have increased the variety, complexity, and subtlety of power as policies shift under the pull of increasing tendencies toward privatization and, consequently, deinstitutionalization and deresponsibilitization. We seem to have passed from the manifestation of disciplinary power within various normalizing institutions (e.g., prisons, schools, asylums, hospitals, factories, armies, etc.) to some kind of societies of control where power is exerted not only in a dehierarchized way, but also in a delocalized way. This might be confirmed, inter alia, by the explosion of deinstitutionalization policies in all the industrialized countries as mandated by the requirements of neoliberalism. One thinks here not only of the deinstitutionalization of psychiatric care services, the deincarceration of prisoners and the "switch to home care," but also the all-too-visible hand of state-assisted privatization of schools, prisons, and even, perhaps, in the United States, "social security" (retirement). Under our contemporary conditions, the "reengineering," "downsizing," or the "modernization" of States, carried out concurrently with the liberalization of the markets, proceeds without any true leadership by relying on new subtle strategies of control and new infratactical and extralegal techniques of domination that protect the economic rights of corporations at the expense of the general population's social rights and support networks. Foucault analyzes this situation and the varied forms of social control today by conceiving power not as the possession of a particular figure or groups (an individual or collective sovereign), but by what is exerted through particular practices of self-governance on the part of individuals and populations. The conceptual tools developed by Foucault in the first half of the 1970s (panopticon, discipline, bio-power, illegalisms, etc.) allow us to account for the immanent new forms of control exerted in obedience to a logic committed to decentralizing the State's traditional powers, leaving no sphere of social organization untouched.

Shortly after *Discipline and Punish* (1975), Foucault detached himself from the pessimistic vision where supervisors and supervised are unilaterally taken in the nets of the disciplinary society. In the last volumes of the *History of Sexuality* (1976-1984) and in the courses given at the Collège de France which prepared the writing of these works, Foucault now carries out a genealogy of the modes of subjectivation that forces him to clarify his position with regard to the project of emancipation. Foucault relativizes his model of disciplinary society in order to consider forms of resistance that imply the government of the self and others.

The title of the conference where the current chapters were first presented, "Michel Foucault and Social Control," may appear strange at first sight and even anachronistic to some degree, owing to the fact that the expressions "society of control" and "social control" return us to a certain American sociological tradition, initiated by Edward A. Ross (1866-1951), which developed very rich social theories grounded on regulation (functionalism: more social control from above is needed to prevent social deviances) and repression (conflictualism: fights are needed because social control always benefits a certain class). Foucault always preferred the "analytical perspective" rather than "general theories." However, we must understand that Foucault tries to reform these general theories of social control by destroying their traditional oppositions (governors/governed, State/people, dominants/dominated, etc.). This allows for a better consideration of the relational aspects inherent to the exercise of power. Foucault rarely used the term "control." His work familiarized us with more specific concepts such as "discipline," "surveillance," and "normalization." Like "control," these concepts constitute products and effects of power. Nonetheless, Foucault reserves a particular place to control to make it the only product of power to have a hybrid nature. Indeed, in the first half of the 1970s, Foucault associates control with an institutional and coercive activity. He would later assign it a more positive meaning when associating it with the topics of governmentality and the technologies of the self. Our book thus presents the nature and effects of some new forms of control produced by the spheres of law, politics, psychiatry, genetics, health care, education, arts, and it intends to question the path of a possible liberation for Foucault through the exercise of self-control and by the emergence of a non-disciplinary power.

This volume does not aim at defining any "best" political system. It doesn't even intend to suggest an alternative to the processes of global neoliberalism. This contradicts the specific approach favored by Foucault, who always refused to tell what one must do or how one must act, to prescribe or legislate for the future. Like Foucault, our interest lies in the problematization of our present. This position is undoubtedly more modest, but also more demanding because it does not try to describe an ideal future world. Its ontological range is oriented toward the following question: "What are we today?" We hope to take part in the writing of the "history of present" by throwing a critical light on the modes of organizations of current societies while proposing some paths for local transformations. With these intentions in mind we presented the most varied possible approaches without claiming to exhaust the full range of possibilities for applying Foucault's ideas to the study of our actuality. We hope these contributions will favor the reception and the understanding of Foucault's work by relativizing some critical stances that do not manage to elevate themselves to the requirements of Foucault's thought while being satisfied to denounce the "aesthetic drift" or the "absence of normativity."

In the opening chapter, Dario Melossi describes how the twentieth century American tradition of political science, dating back to William James and John Dewey, foreshadowed Foucault's challenge to what had been, as late as the 1970s, the conventional European conception of political power as embedded in "the State." Ironically, as Melossi points out, this challenge from Foucault, appeared at the dawn of the late-twentieth-century period of globalization that ultimately led to the creation of the "European Union," and the related ostensible obsolescence of the European "Nation-State."

Warren Montag tries to clarify the status of law in Foucault's œuvre. Even in the works devoted to an analysis of power Foucault sought to demonstrate the extent to which power relations exceeded and made possible the juridical forms of a particular society. Accordingly, when Foucault turned to the phenomena of bio-power and governmentality in his later work, he insisted on the extra- or non-juridical dimension of the attempt to govern life itself, in which the norm functioned "at the expense of the law." To rectify Foucault's dismissal of the law, Montag turns to Agamben and his attempt with, rather than against, Foucault to recast the concept of law. For Agamben law is irreducibly present in the exercise of bio-power, even its its most flagrantly "illegal" forms, as immanent in power as knowledge.

To better grasp the complexity of the notion of control in Foucault's work, Alain Beaulieu first examines a tripartite division among different models of society (sovereign, disciplinary, and controlling). He then studies the double character of control as presented in *Discipline & Punish*, control as both the product of institutions and free with respect to institutions; later he explains, based on the last volumes of *The History of Sexuality* as well as courses and interviews contemporaneous with this work, the stakes involved in non-disciplinary control as this relates to individual mastery of representations (associated with the government of the self) and to the creation of a new right and new institutions (associated with the government of the others).

David Gabbard develops a comparative analysis between the popular film series *The Matrix* and Michel Foucault's later writings on the state and the economization of society. Foucault's discussions of governmentality hold particular relevance for understanding the dystopian world of *The Matrix* where artificial intelligence (A.I.) has subordinated human beings to the status of "coppertops"—batteries whose bio-power provide the machine world of A.I. its only source of energy. To tap this energy, A.I. cultivates living human bodies in cocoon-like cells where steel tubes feed a neural-interactive simulation into the back of their heads that maintains the functioning of the biochemical electric processes of their brains. This simulation gives these human batteries the illusion that they are alive and leading normal lives. In "reality," of course, they are trapped in a network of technologies roughly analogous to Foucault's description of the state. Moreover, *The Matrix* offers a host of interesting parallels with a Foucauldian analysis of compulsory schooling as a technology of governmentality, a nexus of complex relations between power and knowledge for the production and regulation of bio-power. It is within this context that Gabbard considers the past, present, and future of the Bush administration's No Child Left Behind educational reform strategy.

In "What is an Author?" Foucault, quoting Beckett, asks rhetorically, "What does it matter who is speaking?" as a starting point from which to acknowledge the "death of the author" in literary theory. Tracey Nicholls argues that the utopian vision he sketches is a conceptual space in which we can interrogate textual meanings without reference to their moment of creation, thereby giving us true freedom to constitute meanings. But he fails to recognize two distinct teloi for artworks: (i) to challenge our notions of what an artwork is, and (ii) to challenge the cultural and aesthetic traditions which inform our value judgements. While his vision can indeed liberate type (i) artworks, divorcing all artworks from their moment of creation effectively perpetuates the suppression of both meanings and values in type (ii) artworks. Nicholls explores this effect, and the necessity for the distinction, in a discussion of 1960s avant-garde jazz.

In the following chapter, Mario Colucci examines Foucault's relationship with psychiatric discourse in the years following *Madness and Civilization*. While moving on to write books about other institutions (prisons, hospitals, etc.), Foucault maintained interest in the knowledge/power relations built around the concepts of madness and mental diseases after the 1960s. Colucci points to the two courses Foucault held at the Collège de France in 1973-1974 (*Le Pouvoir Psychiatrique*) and 1974-1975 (*Les Anormaux*) as evidence of Foucault's unceasing interest in these topics. Indeed, those lecture courses trace the beginning and the development in psychiatry of the current apparatuses (*dispositifs*) of institutional power and the forms of medicalized knowledge to locate the possible points of resistance and rupture which can be useful today for a critique and struggle against all the practices of normalization and social control.

A current philosophical reading (e.g., Agamben, Negri) suggests that Michel Foucault, with his concept of "bio-power," would have approached the fundamental core of Western politics without succeeding in seizing it. Pierangelo Di Vittorio asserts that to suppose a similar gap poses a hermeneutical problem: why Foucault would have to put on a "theoretical hat" at a work which is not presented in the form of a theoretical corpus? But there remains an ethical problem relating to our relation with "truth": either one frees Foucault's biopolitics to carry out the lacking theorization; or one maintains the relation between biopolitics and the genealogical attitude by using it like a "critical tool" to build the history of our present. One could then think about the link between psychiatry and biopolitics while starting by analyzing the reasons for which, according to Foucault, psychiatry played a strategically decisive role in the assertion of biopolitics.

Thomas Lemke uses Foucault's ideas to challenge the claims by the new genetics that represent genetic information as empowering. Rather than being viewed in terms of objective fate, genes are increasingly seen to represent subjective potential—an integral part of free decision making and individual choice. The somehow paradoxical idea appears that individuals could be held responsible for their genetic risks, leading to what Lemke identifies and analyzes as the discourse of "genetic responsibility." The discourse of genetic responsibility relies on the scientific and technological progress in genetics since the 1970s, but is also linked to the political success of neoliberal programs and transformations that increasingly individualize and privatize the responsibility for social risks. By presenting juridical decisions, this chapter addresses the rise of new obligations and the displacement of rights that are brought about by referring to a "genetic responsibility."

Monique Lanoix remains in the sphere of health care by seeking to elucidate a clear definition of care and to mark its theoretical relevance. She examines a particular form of care: institutionalized care. This type of care—caring for adults within a health care system—is a narrowly defined type of care that seldom enters into our thinking about justice. Institutional care is implicitly defined in biomedical terms, quantifying the care a person is allowed to receive. In this sense, it politicizes care. Foucault recognized and analysed the biopolitics of medicine in specific instances such as the insane asylum. His explicit recognition of the power relations at work within seemingly benign relations has been instrumental in understanding the state's control over bodies. Because of this, as Lanoix argues, any analysis of care must incorporate Foucault's work.

Foucault not only analyzes how the techniques of governmentality and biopolitics operate in the production of social order, but he also represents a theorist of the struggle *against* the social. In Foucault's view, the critical intellectual plays a crucial role in undermining the mechanisms of power. However, he claims that the old "universal" intellectual, represented for example by Jean-Paul Sartre, remains obsolete. Foucault favors a new kind of intellectual, a "specific" intellectual who, instead of commenting on every social conflict, only engages in struggles occurring in the field where he or she is an expert. Christian Lavagno compares the Foucaldian model with the one presented by Derrida in his recent lecture *L'université sans condition*, concentrating his analysis on salient issues surrounding the different manners in which the two theories define the role of social criticism.

The last chapter, written by Frank Pearce, focuses on the important relationships between Michel Foucault and other significant and related twentieth-century French thinkers: Michel Leiris, Pierre Klossowski, Georges Bataille, and Roger Caillois, who all—steeped in classical mythology and appreciative readers of Friedrich Nietzsche—were linked to Surrealism and intrigued by the work of the Marquis de Sade. Foucault shared these same interests. In the 1930s, the four older thinkers were involved with the *Collège de Sociologie*. Foucault was aware of their discussions and, according to Pearce, it is a great shame that he did not draw upon this work in the last decade or so of his life, when, arguably, his work was compromised by liberalism. The author argues that the development of his own work might well have been quite different had he engaged with more of the concepts explored and developed by the members of the *Collège de Sociologie*.

The questions of security and bio-security are at the center of many of the analyses developed in this book. The establishment of a critique of risk obsessions seems to be one of the major concern for those who try to understand contemporary conditions or to describe today's new dominant technologies of control. Foucault warned us precisely against the emergence of risk societies, our societies, grounded on an inceasing calculation of dangerous potentials. This is clearly asserted by Foucault in such texts as "About the Concept of the 'Dangerous Individual' in 19th Century Legal Psychiatry" (*Journal of Law and Psychiatry*, 1978) and "The Risk of Security" (in *The Essential Foucault*, ed. P. Rabinow and N. Rose, New York Press, 2003). In that sense Foucault invites us to rethink our relation to today's general consensus over the limit between "riskophiles" and "riskophobics." He provokes us to see that the line separating the two is an unnecessary event, or at least it is something that needs to be critically questioned and urgently reshaped in order to create a new topology of individual and collective existence that is more locally emancipative. The contributors are following that line of problematization without neglecting to question the problems emerging from Foucault's own topics and methods of problematization.

Readers may be interested in an additional publication stemming from the Montreal conference. A French volume of the proceedings containiong original chapters not edited in the English volume will be published in conjunction with Presses de l'Université Laval and L'Harmattan in 2005 under the title *Michel Foucault et le contrôle social. Actes du colloque international de Montréal* (Alain Beaulieu, Ed.). The final day of the Montreal conference featured a bilingual round table with eight international Foucault specialists discussing the theme of "Michel Foucault and Critical Theory." *Dialogue*, the journal of the Canadian Philosophical Association, will publish a transcript of that discussion.

Acknowledgements

We want to dedicate this book to the memory of Michel Foucault (1926-1984) as well as the more than 150 participants from more than twenty academic disciplines and seven countries who attended the three-day conference on "Michel Foucault and Social Control" at Maison de la culture Côte-des-Neiges in Montreal on May 8-10, 2004 to commemorate the twentieth anniversary of Foucault's death.

We want to thank our sponsors and funding agencies, without whom this project would have never been possible: the Canadian Centre for German and European Studies affiliated with the Université de Montréal and its director, Mr. Phillipe Despoix; the Social Sciences and Humanities Research Council of Canada; the Italian Cultural Institute in Montreal and its director, Mrs. Giovanna Jatropelli; the Group de Reserche sur les Aspects Sociaux de la Santé et de la Prévention affiliated with the Université de Montreal and its directors, Mrs. Andrée Demers and Mr. Pierre Durand; as well as the Ministère Québécois du Développement Économique et Régional et de la Reserache.

Our acknowledgements also go to the other members of the scientific and organizational committees who actively participated in the realization of this international event: Henry Dorvil (Professor in the School of Social Work, Université du Québec à Montréal), Dietmar Köveker (DAAD guest Professor in the Department of Philosophy, Université de Montréal), and Paul Morin (Professor at the Department of Social Service, Université de Sherbrooke). We would like to thank some people who played an important role in the realization of the project: Josiane Boulad-Ayoub (Professor in the Department of Philosophy, Université du Québec à Montréal), Philip Buckley (Chair of the Department of Philosophy, McGill University), Luce Botella (Cultural agent at Maison de la culture Côte-des-Neiges in Montreal), Joanka Aguilar, Cleide da Silva, Anne-Marie Guimond, Christiane L'abbée, Lisa Tanguay, and Nizar Zaghdani , who were responsible for the logistical organization, José Ruiz-Funes (Responsible for the Fonds Michel Foucault at Institut mémoires de l'edition contemporaine in Paris), Stéfan Leclercq (Responsible for the Fonds documentaire Gilles Deleuze at Bibliothèque du Salchoire in Paris), Paul Fairfield (Editor of *Symposium*, the journal of the Canadian Society for Continental Philosophy), Claude Piché (Chair of the Department of Philosophy, Université de Montréal), Alain Voizard (Chair of the Department of Philosophy, Université du Québec à Montréal), as well as Patrick Bolland for some translations and Robert Carley who kindly welcomed this book at Lexington.

Part I

Law & Politics

Chapter 1

Michel Foucault and the Obsolescent State:
Between the American Century
and the Dawn of the European Union

Dario Melossi
University of Bologna (Italy)

Michel Foucault ranks among the great innovators in the study of social control. Perhaps his greatest contribution (and his legacy) rests with his understanding of social control, not as the nefarious product of some centralized authority of repression, but as the outcome of a complex interplay of forces within a multifarious network of strategies and tactics actively involved in the construction of "social order." Particularly in his writings on the prison and on "governmentality," [1] Foucault deeply questioned conventional wisdom regarding the relationships among "the State," "social control," and "social order." Even as late as the 1960s and 1970s, the traditional view in Europe equated "social control" with "the State." While Hans Kelsen[2] and others[3] had questioned this anthropomorphic understanding of the State as the "father" of social control as early as 1922, such a critique crumbled beneath the realities of fascism's European ascendancy between the two world wars. A more skeptical position on the relations between "the State," "social control," and "social order" would not reemerge until the 1970s. Foucault, of course, played a vital role in this reemergence, particularly through his challenge to the State-centered vision of Marxism.

Foucault, Marx(ism), and "the State"

To fully appreciate Foucault's role in challenging traditional assumptions regarding the nature of power, we must recall how, in the 1970s, European culture had grown increasingly disillusioned with both a "hegemonic" Marxist orientation in the social sciences, as well as with "realized socialism" (even if the two were by no means synonymous). Foucault contributed to this deepening sense of disillusionment with a project that challenged the conceptual underpinnings of many of Marxism's central shibboleths (e.g., concepts such as "repression," "liberation" and, indeed, "the State").[4] Declaring in *La volonté de savoir (The History of Sexuality, Volume I)*, "[i]n political thought and analysis, we still have not cut off the head of the king,"[5] Foucault helped to stimulate a new epoch in the history of social theory.

Though accused by one American professor of being a "crypto-Marxist," Foucault's engagement with ideas and concepts derived from Marxism and with some of the most important Marxist currents of thought, such as the Frankfurt School,[6] received little attention. In *Discipline and Punish*, however, Foucault tells a story very similar to the one told by Marx,[7] particularly concerning the centrality of the notion of discipline, a truly Marxian notion. One has only to turn to the pages in *Discipline and Punish*, where Foucault discusses the centrality of discipline, to find not only an implicit, but also an explicit reference to Marx, and to that most Marxist of Marx's writing, *Capital:*

> In fact, the two processes—the accumulation of men and the accumulation of capital—cannot be separated; it would not have been possible to solve the problem of the accumulation of men without the growth of an apparatus of production capable of both sustaining them and using them; conversely, the techniques that made the cumulative multiplicity of men useful accelerated the accumulation of capital.[8]

Indeed, this passage would insure Foucault's place in a short history of neo-Marxist thought![9] And, in the next page, Foucault's characterization of "formal, juridical liberties" is but a replica—also Capital-driven—of Marx's famous distinction between "the sphere of circulation" and "the sphere of production":[10]

> The real, corporal disciplines constituted the foundation of the formal, juridical liberties. The contract may have been regarded as the ideal foundation of law and political power; panopticism constituted the technique, universally widespread, of coercion. It continued to work in depth on the juridical structures of society, in order to make the effective mechanisms of power function in opposition to the formal framework that it had acquired. The "Enlightenment," which discovered the liberties, also invented the disciplines.[11]

Foucault nearly exposes himself here to a possible charge of "vulgar" Marxism. Marx would have subtly noted that power mechanisms at work in the sphere of production do not function "in opposition to" the sphere of circulation but in absolute deference to it, owing to the traits of one specific good, that is labor-power! This would, however, have introduced Foucault into the arcana of "the extraction of surplus value," and Foucault was certainly not interested in that. His was a Marx without telos. There is no surplus value in Foucault, to give direction, meaning, or hope of ultimately overcoming oppression to his whole analysis. His is, in a sense, the only possible Marxist position today. A Marxist who has read Foucault can only treat capitalism as an invention, a genial ethical invention, rather than some necessity of history, an invention in which a certain idea of the rational—informed by religion—was crucial!

Also, in one of his most characteristic theoretical positions, the repudiation of every notion of repression and liberation,[12] Foucault's view may be far from the so-called Freudo-Marxism of the 1960s, but not as far as one might believe from Marx's notion of power. Indeed, Foucault's critique of repression/liberation may represent the most strident commentary on the dominant ideology of the era, given that the notion of repression had constituted the linchpin of then contemporary social and theoretical movements. "The individual," Foucault writes,

> is no doubt the fictitious atom of an "ideological" representation of society; but he is also a reality fabricated by this specific technology of power that I have called "discipline." We must cease once and for all to describe the effects of power in negative terms: it "excludes," it "represses," it "censors," it "abstracts," it "masks," it "conceals." In fact, power produces; it produces reality; it produces domains of objects and rituals of truth. The individual and the knowledge that may be gained of him belong to this production.[13]

This repudiation of repression/liberation will be repeated throughout the Introduction to the *History of Sexuality*, not the least in its famous, almost sarcastic, closing sentence about the "deployment" of sexuality, "The irony of this deployment is in having us believe that our 'liberation' is in the balance."[14]

Because his confrontation with the Marxist tradition was paramount, Foucault tended to gloss over previous contributions in social sciences that seemed less sanguine about "the role of the State." This is the case, as we will see, for American political and social science. It is also the case, however, for contributions belonging in the history of French thought, such as those by Durkheim and earlier thinkers like Rousseau and Tocqueville. Durkheim identified in Rousseau a "keen awareness of the specificity of social order,"[15] and had admired his call for a *religion civile* capable of restoring the population's commitment to the body politic that the rationalist and individualist emphasis of the Enlightenment had somehow undermined.[16] Furthermore, in his almost contemporary lectures in Bordeaux, Durkheim had portrayed the State as the great rationalizer of collective consciousness, almost a Freudian-like collective super-ego that had the principal function of conferring a "higher degree of consciousness and reflection" to "collective representations." "Strictly speaking," he added, "the State is the very organ of social thought [*la pensée sociale*]."[17] This was to be particularly the case for a democratic kind of State, because the chief characteristic of such a State is the establishment of powerful channels of communication between the *élite* and *la foule* (the crowd). These channels account, in Durkheim's estimation, for democracy's superiority over other regimes, for they enable the state to give the crowd a rational direction. This idea—that those "irrational movements of the crowd" that had so terrified French moderates throughout the nineteenth century could be countered by a sort of enlightened intervention by the State elite—anticipated the later North American conceptualization to be found in the very idea of social control. The Chicago School and the political theory of pragmatism, however, did not attach the concept of social control to any idea of the State, linking it instead to the emerging role of the mass media and other forces in structuring public opinion.[18]

Dario Melossi

In light of this perspective, Foucault's dismissal of a political-legal concept of the State in "*Governamentalité*," seems less surprising, even if it shocked those ears that had been tuned for many years to a rather stereotyped view of what was then called a "Marxist theory of the State."

> The excessive value attributed to the problem of the state is expressed, basically, in two ways: the one form, immediate, affective, and tragic, is the lyricism of the cold monster we see confronting us. But there is a second way of overvaluing the problem of the state, one that is paradoxical because it is apparently reductionist: it is the form of analysis that consists in reducing the state to a certain number of functions, such as the development of productive forces and the reproduction of relations of production, and yet this reductionist vision of the relative importance of the state's role nevertheless invariably renders it absolutely essential as a target needing to be attacked and a privileged position needing to be occupied. But the state, no more probably today than at any other time in its history, does not have this unity, this individuality, this rigorous functionality, nor, to speak frankly, this importance. Maybe, after all, the state is no more than a composite reality and a mythologized abstraction, whose importance is a lot more limited than many of us think. Maybe what is really important for our modernity—that is, for our present—is not so much the statization of society, as the "governmentalization" of the state.[19]

It is interesting to note, I believe, that exactly seventy years earlier, the founder of modern political science in the United States, Arthur Bentley, had claimed that, "The 'state' itself is . . . no factor in our investigation. . . . The 'idea of the state' has been very prominent, no doubt, among the intellectual amusements of the past, and at particular times and places it has served to give coherent and pretentious expression to some particular group's activity . . ." He went on to add, after similarly disposing of the concept of sovereignty, that "[s]o long as there is plenty of firm earth under foot there is no advantage in trying to sail the clouds in a cartoonist's airship."[20] It may be also for this reason that, in 1983, Richard Rorty was to comment, "James and Dewey . . . are waiting at the end of the road which . . . Foucault and Deleuze are currently traveling."[21] During the first half of the twentieth century, John Dewey, George Herbert Mead, C. Wright Mills and many others had already portrayed an image of democracy where social control would be determined much more by the construction of a common mind and language than by brandishing laws and guns. Foucault's emphasis on the intimate connections between "truth," "discourse," and "power," as well as his critique of a State-centered model, unfolded within mass democratic society—a type of society that only in the 1970s had begun to emerge in much of Europe.[22] Of course, it was particularly in the arena of the mass media of communication that such types of "social control at a distance" would actually develop.

American Social Control

Shortly after its Civil War in the mid-nineteenth century, the United States, now probably the first really "modern" society, started to know the accompanying processes of accelerated industrialization, urbanization, and mass immigration. It was also during this same period, within the still relatively new field of political science, that particular concepts such as those of "the State" and "sovereignty" started to appear obsolete—as we have seen—and that the other key concept of "social control" would emerge. Certainly, the notion of social control belonged in the newborn social sciences, rather than in political philosophy. It belonged even within the "social engineering" of the early decades of last century. Social control referred to the idea of "governing" social change rather than capturing the metaphysical "essence" of social order—an essence to be then imposed upon society through the use of violence. Social order was no longer conceived now as some kind of structure descending from the heavens of political philosophy to be impressed upon the underlying society through the instruments of politics and the law. It was rather a problem to be investigated in its actual, empirical roots, for the purpose of discovering the conditions and mechanisms for the construction of consensus among the masses, the cooperation and collaboration of which had never been so essential to the construction of social order. The building of a democratic version of such an order was still the business of elites, but the tools elites had to use now, in a sort of exchange characteristic of twentieth-century mass democracy, were not so much anymore the gun and the book of laws—except in "emergency" cases—but the organization of consensus, a consensus that should uphold the efforts of social reformers to capture, channel, and guide the deepest currents of social change.

In fact, during the early decades of the last century, in the United States, if the common work and life conditions of the lower classes had produced a common horizon of discourse, such communal vocabulary was increasingly "colonized" by the mass media and reoriented toward the "Americanization," "integration," and "middleclassization" of the working class. At first, the coming apart of face-to-face social controls in the metropolis had been conceived as a process of "liberation," according to the old German saying *Stadtluft macht frei* (the air of the city makes one free!).[23] Soon it became clear, however, that a true "dialectic of control" was at work, and that the type of social control produced within primary informal relationships—the familiar face of the relative, the friend, or the shopkeeper at the corner—was in fact being replaced both by the blue uniform of the police officer and by an even more insidious "control at a distance," as Louis Wirth called it,[24] through the mass media of communication. Such media were "colonizing" a "life-world" of solidarity and mutual help,[25] built among the lower strata of the working class, often of "ethnic" origins, turning it into an insidious and creeping process of extension of the middle class, both in practical and cultural terms. The higher wages paid at the time by Henry Ford best exemplified such a process, so called "Fordism," a mix of strategies of production and consumption.[26]

In John Dewey's *The Public and Its Problems*, in Walter Lippmann's writings,[27] or in the later C. W. Mills' *The Power Elite*, the vision of the entry of wider and wider masses into the arena of democracy, initially conceived as favoring the acquisition of a "universalist" perspective,[28] slowly converted into a frustrated and increasingly hopeless gaze in what was now seen as the very decadence of democracy in American society. It was becoming progressively clear, also, that American elites had discovered the mass media of communication as an ideal solution to the fundamental problem of democracy from their own perspective, that is, how to secure political survival in a situation of deep socioeconomic inequality (a risk that had appeared very real between the stock market crash of 1929 and the launching of Franklin Delano Roosevelt's "New Deal" in 1932). After all, this was an issue that had haunted capitalist elites since at least the appearance of a "social question" in the middle of the nineteenth century. How was it possible in fact to reconnect the *citoyen*, who lived within the "heavenly" sphere of juridical relationships, and the "earthly" bourgeois, who lived in the tough reality of a class-divided society, as Marx had asked in 1844, appropriating the language of Rousseau?[29] Once under democracy—and the former North American colonies had been the first to experiment with such political system[30]—every (male and free) human being had a vote, how could the hegemony of proprietors be preserved in society? A true "dialectic of control" was to follow, one that Marx tied to the Protestant reformation long before Weber:

> Luther, we grant, overcame the bondage of piety by replacing it by the bondage of conviction. He shattered faith in authority because he restored the authority of faith. He turned priests into laymen because he turned laymen into priests. He freed man from outer religiosity because he made religiosity the inner man. He freed the body from chains because he enchained the heart.[31]

Would the positions later announced by Horkheimer and Adorno in *Dialectic of Enlightenment*,[32] or Foucault in *Discipline and Punish*, be much more than elaborations on this passage by Marx?[33] A common motif that one can find from Marx to Weber to the Frankfurt School to Foucault is the idea that control is most effective when internalized within the individual through "friendly" and subtle persuasion rather than "hostile" and overt coercion.[34] Mass media techniques, from advertising to printed and later radio and TV journalism, as well as Hollywood "entertainment," revolutionized such processes. In the end (our "end," at the beginning of the twenty-first century), it would almost seem as if the balance of power between mass media's "described" reality and "real" reality had been turned upside down. After all, the circle of close advisors to President Reagan would dub the prime time news show a "reality check," and it is no surprise this would happen under a presidency when an actor had found the best role of a mediocre career in interpreting the role of president simply by becoming one. Or when, a few years later, a TV tycoon would be "producing news" no longer only in a metaphorical way, but from his seat as head of government.

The European "Public Sphere" and Its Constitution

Foucault's intellectual legacy and its connection with the history of social control within twentieth-century American society helps deepen our understanding of the current process of "constituting" a European Union. It enables us to recognize something paradoxical in the constitutional act. As a sociohistorical event, this constitution witnesses the actual coming together of a European Union. Concurrently, as a legal process, it witnesses the drafting and concordant approval of a written and legally valid document that recognizes the formation of a "union" while simultaneously reinforcing it by the mere fact of its having been approved. The problem of such a constitution has appeared, in fact, exactly at the time when the question of communication, as we have seen, had installed itself at the center of the problem of social order and social cohesion. The paradoxical aspect of the issue resides in the fact that the weakest link of the European Constitutional project would appear to be the very issue of communication and, more specifically, the central instrument of communication: language.

According to the German Constitutional Court Judge, Dieter Grimm,[35] and the famous 1993 *Maastrichturteil* of that court, the very substance of democracy, if not its form, is grounded in the existence of certain minimal conditions of "pluralism, internal representation, freedom and the capacity for compromise within the intermediate area of parties, associations, citizens' movements and communication media," conditions that would not be present in the current European situation.[36] Therefore, no European "public sphere" is possible.[37] The lack of institutional and procedural requisites to the formation of an authentically "public sphere" can be traced directly to the lack of something far more fundamental; namely, a common European language. In fact, very few European citizens speak the one language that could aspire to play such a role—English. This should not suggest a desire to return to some kind of nineteenth century concept of *Volksgemeinschaft*.[38] It is rather to maintain that the possibility of a collective European identity can only be constituted through a "capacity for transnational discourse."[39] According to Grimm, such weakness is "structural" and cannot be remedied through mere institutional effort. It is not difficult to see, in the background of Grimm's preoccupation, the fear of a mere elitist constitutionalism, powerless and indecisive, a sort of European Weimar that is not really able to command the loyalty of European masses.[40] In particular, it seems to me, Judge Grimm realizes that the process of constructing a democratic political will has to unfold at the very level of the public. That public, in turn, must interest itself in the formation of its own democratic will as a "constituent" element of a nascent collective identity. The "democratic deficit" is, therefore, not simply an institutional phenomenon, which concerns the limited powers of the European Parliament, but is a deficit of the public sphere and of the formation of political will.[41]

How can we answer Grimm's pessimism? In order to be able to speak of a real European "public sphere," the fundamental issue would seem to be the process of formation of a common language, a common language that would become, in a sort of Durkheimian fashion, an "indicator" of the "real" existence of a European Constitution. Political initiative and social processes come into play here. What is, in fact, the process or set of processes that allow for the coming into being of these common media of communication, of this "public sphere"?[42] Is such a constituent process also the way in which this common sphere, this culture, this language, is created? In order to even begin answering these questions, we must evaluate the nexuses linking, on the one hand, the extended socioeconomic and political processes of homogenization (so called "globalization") and, on the other hand, several "new" or "emerging" social processes.

There are, first of all, social movements within which a new oppositional language is emerging. If, in the course of the nineteenth-century, social movements were at the roots of the making of a "class" or "national" consciousness, today's very first Europe-wide labor actions and the extraordinary peace movement that manifested all over Europe (indeed all over the world) during the winter of 2003—and especially on February 15, 2003, when more than ten million people rallied in more than sixty countries and six hundred cities—constitute the creation of both a common sentiment and a common language, a language that is both "natural" and "cultural."

There are then, last but certainly not least, the transnational movements *par excellence*, migratory movements.[43] Migrants remain those "free" and "unattached" workers of which Marx wrote in the first volume of *Capital* in the section about "primitive accumulation"[44]—obliged by international socioeconomic and political events to be "free" now not only of any property but even of any "national" attachment. They remain similarly free to sell their labor-power wherever there is a demand for it. These migrants would at the same time seem to be, for that very reason, fitter for the new European construction than the natives themselves.[45] They would be better able to assume the "universalist" perspective of which George Herbert Mead wrote, to personify real "European citizens,"[46] who "belong" in a "European entity." Not burdened by any specific national loyalty, their condition, it would seem, represents the "modern" condition *par excellence.* They would seem to be "free" to move from city to city, country to country, continent to continent, unencumbered by the heavy load of tradition or heritage. And yet, and this is paradoxical indeed, they are again and again found responsible for that true "crime of modernity" that is tightly connected with mobility and capitalist development[47]—until literally, not only metaphorically, they meet what David Matza called "the ban of Leviathan."[48] The manner in which such modernity-induced "liberation" unfolds does not often coincide with the political choices of the countries that "host" the migrants. The "law," therefore, has to pin them down, confine them, enclose again behind a border (when not a prison or a camp gate) what had been let loose almost "by mistake"—the most recent example of that oxymoronic "selective universalism" which makes up the very history of European Enlightenment.[49]

The work of Michel Foucault figures prominently within the contemporary critique of Enlightenment—in the noblest acceptation of the term "critique," which does not mean ideological rejection but debate, discussion, and problematization. The legacy of Foucault's contribution in this regard—the most luminous perhaps among other high-spirited contributions of those years[50]—is to be found in his empirical reconstruction of those processes through individuals that are constituted as the subjects of duties and rights within the genealogy of the prison in *Discipline and Punish*—an extreme but (exactly for its radicalness) thoroughly enlightening case. We find here an almost painful, reflexive awareness of the limitations of the main shibboleths of Enlightenment, the idea of individual but equal rights and of democracy, an awareness that is not simply disillusionment vis-à-vis the unkept promise of democracy, but is a radical questioning of the very premises of such a conceptual construction. In trying to come to terms with the creation on "democratic" grounds—perhaps for the first time in history—of a new global political power such as the European Union, Foucault's words of warning could not be more poignant.[51]

Chapter 2

The Immanence of Law in Power:
Reading Foucault with Agamben

Warren Montag
Occidental College (USA)

In his strange debate with Noam Chomsky on Dutch television in 1971, Foucault posed the question of whether political action is undertaken "by virtue of an idea of justice or because the class struggle makes it useful [*utile*] or necessary? Do you refer to an ideal justice?"[1] Chomsky's response was interesting. Rather than accept the alternatives offered by Foucault, which opposed the ideal to the real and the just to the necessary, he refused (at least in this particular case) to refer to an ideal justice or even an ideal of justice irreducible to and beyond the particular forms of law in which it was expressed and from which justice not only could, but must, be distinguished. Instead, Chomsky, for a moment (but it is this moment that allows perhaps only now something previously unthinkable to be thought) refrained from invoking a transcendental ideal in relation to which the real might be judged unjust, but law, understood not as a set of norms, but as a set of practices not above power but rooted in it.[2] Although he would in the next few lines regress towards the ideality, if not the idealism, with which Foucault sought to identify him, claiming that injustice can only be fought in the name of justice, a higher justice, in the absence of which we lose the ability to distinguish the just from the unjust and lose any claim to legitimacy, the statements above point in another direction. For a fleeting moment, a moment too quickly lost in a stream of words and concepts in a debate itself long since forgotten despite the deserved celebrity of its participants, the opposition of right and power, of the rule of law and the condition of lawlessness otherwise insisted upon for diametrically opposed purposes by an idealist Chomsky and a materialist Foucault is called radically into question. Where might an alternative theoretical pathway lead?

An answer was no more to be found in Foucault's intervention than Chomsky's. If such a line of thought constituted the blind spot of Chomsky's intervention, it was equally so for Foucault: the point, as unthinkable for the one as for the other, which furnished the ground of their very opposition. Foucault's response to Chomsky's invocation of law and justice was not only unequivocal; it might well be called crude, even given the circumstances. He argued that we are in a war, the class war, in which one's participation is not a matter of choice or the outcome of a decision. Further, it is not only useless to invoke justice and, by extension, law to legitimize one's struggle; "the idea of justice in itself is an idea which in effect has been invented and put to work in different types of societies as an instrument of a certain political or economic power . . . as a claim made by the oppressed class and as justification for it."[3] Here, justice is not real and material, or even materialized, but an idea "invented" to serve as an instrument of oppression. It is dependent on the real of which it is a (false) idea and to which it is reducible. Such a notion is remarkably similar to the concept of base and superstructure as described in certain of Marx's texts in which the modalities of the latter "serve" the needs of the former. Foucault, however, does not refer this critical procedure which accords primacy of "political or economic power" over law, right, and justice to Marx, but rather pointedly calls it Nietzschean. Further, in suggesting a kind of genealogy of this critique of justice, he will skip over Marx altogether and attach a name to the necessary foundation of the Nietzschean critique of justice that is found no more than a handful of times in his entire oeuvre: Spinoza. As might be expected, the designation of Spinoza's work as the origin of this critique, far from clarifying the nature of Foucault's approach (and not just in this debate, but in the work of the first half of the seventies, culminating in *Discipline and Punish*) to the problem of the specific relation between law, justice, and power, instead succeeds in complicating it by placing certain essential contradictions in stark relief.

Here Foucault refers more or less directly to chapter 16 of Spinoza's *Tractatus Theologico-Politicus*. For Spinoza, "right [*jus*] is co-extensive with power."[4] "*jus*" means right, of course, but it also signifies law (e.g., *jus gentium*, *jus civile*), suggesting a certain unity between the two. Spinoza's proposition extends this unity to power (*potentia*) itself. We are instructed systematically to think the conjunction (a conjunction that is necessary and constitutive) of right, law, and power, and power here is not symbolic power (which would be nothing more than another form of right), but power rooted in physical and corporeal existence, not only in practices of compulsion, constraint, coercion, and violence, but in the physical practices of resistance and what might well be called counter-constraint and counter-compulsion, which would themselves be indissociable from the right/law (*jus*) that, from Spinoza's point of view, necessarily accompanies such practices. Spinoza reconceptualizes not only right, but law by defining natural right (*jus*) not as the peculiar privilege of humankind, which would precisely distinguish it from the animal world (the human set apart from the animal by virtue of the faculty of speech, or by the free will that allows it, unlike other parts of nature, not simply to obey the laws of nature, but to dictate to itself the laws that it chooses to obey), but as existing throughout nature as a whole, inanimate as well as animate. Everything that acts in nature acts by natural right; everything that does not act does not have the right to act. Similarly, natural law and human law can no longer be distinguished, especially given Spinoza's rejection of free-will. The notion that right is coextensive with power compelled Spinoza in the *Ethics* to direct his attention to the body, arguing that the very power of the mind to think cannot be separated from the question of whether the power (and therefore right) of the body is increased or decreased, whether the body is more or less active. In his last unfinished work, the same notion necessitated a movement away from the idea that the individual (who alone could exercise little power) was the basic unit of political analysis and toward the concept of the multitude.

This insistence on the embodiment of law, right, and power allows us to see the direct relevance of Spinoza to Foucault's work, especially that of the 1970s. It is possible to argue that, at least in part, Foucault's project of writing "a history of the body and its forces, of their utility and their docility, of their distribution and their submission"[5] was inspired by Spinoza. But more important than the question of influence is the question of what is shared and communicated between the two philosophers without respect to chronology. I refer not only to their shared discoveries (the focus on the body, the definition of a power that is exercised rather than possessed), but the limits and aporias common to their work. In particular, the argument that Spinoza's failure to complete the last section of the *Tractatus Politicus* (*TP*), the section devoted to democracy, owes as much to theoretical dilemmas as to the brevity of Spinoza's life, is well known and widely accepted. The emergence of the concept of the multitude as that which exceeds any formal system of representation or sovereignty appears to render democracy as a stable, reproducible system unthinkable. Less noted is the fact that a projected chapter on law with which the *TP* was to have concluded was never even begun and indeed appears, if anything, even more unthinkable for Spinoza than the idea of democracy. The phrase "right/law is coextensive with power" could only too easily lead to the conclusion that right and law are expressions or emanations of a power more real and fundamental than they and to which they might simply be reduced, that they are "inventions" added to a social and political reality that must necessarily disguise itself, the discursive element of a power that must deny its own exercise. In Spinozist (or what amounts to the same thing, Machiavellian) terms, *jus* is what ought to be as opposed to what is and is therefore not a worthy or useful object of analysis.

I want to ask whether we cannot detect a similar tendency concerning the question of law in Foucault, and to ask whether law cannot be said to constitute the unthought of precisely Foucault's most political work, the work of the period 1975-1976. In *Discipline and Punish*, law is frequently characterized as a "mask" or a "fiction," that cover behind which the power that takes the body as its object functions and which thus conceals the reality of power. Although, as I intend to show, the actual form of Foucault's critique of "juridicism" is complex, contradictory, and profoundly suggestive, it was widely read as little more than a devaluation of law. It was as if for Foucault law was not so much to be analyzed as to be denounced, and while this critique of any juridical model of power and domination was important and necessary, and is arguably more relevant today than it was in the early seventies, especially insofar as it refuses to localize physical power—the power of coercion and violence—in the state. It left law, in the broadest sense, untheorized.

In the first volume of the *History of Sexuality*, the unthinkability of law manifests itself in a different way. In the analysis of bio-power in the final chapter, Foucault comes close to saying that there was law but there no longer is any. From at least the feudal epoch (if not before) to the classical age, societies were regulated by sovereign power or by a system of law that rested on the power of the sovereign, the existence of whose right was the condition of the right of the subjects. The sovereign's right to take or allow life, or even merely to expose life to the risk of death in war, understood as necessary to a society as such, was conceived as a form of property; its terms were those of ownership, usufruct, and levy.

Beginning in the eighteenth century, with the emergence of bio-power, sovereign power gradually lost ground to a new form of power no longer based on the model of sovereignty for which life is a property to be guaranteed or appropriated by the state or sovereign. The norm was said to replace the law, and the state no longer appropriated life but managed, supervised, and cared for it. As Foucault notes, bio-power was not less violent or destructive of life than sovereign power; quite the contrary. The biologization of politics, for which the operative categories were the normal and the pathological, appeared to authorize the dispassionate destruction of entire populations in the interests of a health of a given society.

It is here that Giorgio Agamben's critique of Foucault in *Homo Sacer* (1996) takes on its significance:

> the point at which these two faces of power converge remains strangely unclear in Foucault's work, so much so that it has even been claimed that Foucault would have consistently refused to elaborate a unitary theory of power. If Foucault contests the traditional approach to the problem of power, which is exclusively based on juridical models . . . or on institutional models . . . and if he calls for a liberation from the theoretical privilege of sovereignty in order to construct an analytic of power that would not take law as its model and code, then where, in the body of power, is the zone of indistinction (or at least intersection) at which techniques of individualization and totalizing procedures converge.[6]

From Agamben's perspective, Foucault's historicizing of the sovereignty/bio-power relation functions primarily to dissociate the two modes of power, when in fact they become intelligible only when the simultaneity of their operation is understood. In particular, Agamben's work seeks to show the way in which sovereignty furnishes the ground of any exercise of bio-power, a position that becomes conceivable only to the extent that we problematize and recast the notion of sovereignty in Foucault's work. Citing the work of Carl Schmitt, Agamben argues essentially that Foucault's account of law strangely suppresses the force necessary to it; in fact, sovereignty exists neither inside nor outside the system of law, but rather as an external moment that is inscribed in the system as an outside necessary to the constitution of the system itself. Thus, every system of law, no matter how exhaustively and with what coherence it saturates the political field, rests on the decision of the sovereign to suspend or not to suspend the legal and constitutional order with a declaration of a state of emergency or exception undertaken, of course, to defend the very order that is suspended. The paradoxes of bio-power in the twentieth century noted by Foucault, namely that the management and regulation of life, the defense of the population rather than the nation has increased rather than decreased the number, scope, and fatality rates of wars, can only be understood, according to Agamben, on the basis of sovereignty. The coincidence of the defense of life and the pursuit of death, that is, of bio-power and sovereign power, is manifested in a nearly pure form in the concentration camp.

Agamben's arguments have, as might be expected, elicited a number of critical responses (from among which I would single out Thomas Lemke's as the most thorough and perceptive.)[7] Foremost among the charges leveled against him is that his critique of Foucault's historicism amounts to an ahistoricism that discovers the operation of bio-power in classical antiquity and is therefore incapable of accounting for the breaks, mutations, and large-scale transformations that, in fact, characterize the exercise of power in the history of the West. I wonder, though, whether it is not possible to ask whether the problem with Agamben's analysis is that it does not go far enough, whether the attempt to answer the question of whether sovereignty and bio-power are successive or simultaneous, a question which—posed as such—remains historical or even empirical, must not first confront a series of theoretical problems.

Of these problems, one of the most important is centered on Agamben's use of Schmitt. The critique of liberal conceptions of sovereignty (the kind that Foucault could only speak of with irony) and of the idea of law as a self-regulating system simultaneously coherent and without bounds associated with Schmitt is arguably found in at least as powerful a form in thinkers for whom Schmitt today serves as a stand-in. I am thinking particularly of those working within a Marxist tradition, not to mention well-known texts by Marx and Lenin. And while it would be interesting to speculate on the reasons why Schmitt today is an acceptable reference in a critique of liberalism while the others are not, I do not have the time to do so here. I will instead limit myself to the observation that the concept of sovereignty as defined by Schmitt in *Political Theology* appears to reproduce rather than to resolve the dissociation of the modes of power that we, along with Agamben, have noted in Foucault's work.

Against the notion of law as a closed, self-regulating system, which understood correctly offered no place for individual initiative, Schmitt (like Husserl in another domain) insisted on posing the question of origins. Formal or formalist theories of law expressed little or no interest in the concept of sovereignty, not because it was no longer relevant, but because it was unthinkable in formal terms. The moment of the institution of the system of law cannot be understood in terms of the law itself. The condition prior to this institution is nothing more than an unintelligible chaos the transition out of which law cannot be explained as the effect of rules that do not yet exist. In order to think about the origin of the system, one must have recourse to a moment of decision undertaken by a subject that is sovereign. It is precisely this originary decision that must be forgotten by the system of law for it to maintain its order and coherence. Schmitt, writing in the context of the latent civil war characteristic of early Weimar Germany, hastens to remind his readers that the question of origin is not merely a historical question concerning a moment long since superseded. The defense of the constitutional, legal order itself periodically requires that it be suspended in order for it to be saved from those who would destroy it. The system, however, cannot suspend itself any more than it could reinstitute itself: hence the necessity of a decision, the decision that defines sovereignty itself. Every order—no matter how democratic—rests on the mere decision not to declare the state of emergency. Therefore, if Spinoza could argue that every state, including the most absolutist or dictatorial, is a latent democracy by virtue of the power of the multitude, we might say that for Schmitt, every state, no matter how formally democratic, is a latent dictatorship.

Does Schmitt's critique of juridical formalism mark a refusal of juridical, if not constitutional illusions? The response is ambiguous. For the most part, the sovereign is he who has the right to decide the state of exception. If sovereignty rests on a decision, the decision of the one who has the power to declare the state of exception, we must determine the nature or modality of this power. Is it power in the sense of force, the force necessary to bring about a suspension of the legal order? Or, in contrast, is this power the right that the sovereign has been granted by and in the constitutional order itself to suspend that order? It might be argued, as Negri has done,[8] that while Schmitt privileges the second definition, the first is implied. It is perhaps more accurate, however, to speak of Schmitt's analysis as oscillating between two registers, the register of law and the register of force, with the second always threatening to eclipse the first, a fact the could render the state of exception (and with it sovereignty which is nothing more than a title) a dead letter, an empty decree by a powerless sovereign in the face of a mass internal threat. It was precisely this fear that haunted the European extreme right in this period. Schmitt's analysis itself wards off this threat by extending the juridical outside of itself, positing a right to institute or suspend right itself, concealing under a juridical veneer the more important question of the power to bring about the state of exception, a power that, as Walter Benjamin noted,[9] is by no means restricted to the titular sovereign. To illustrate this point, we might recall the words of Spinoza: "[I]t is clear that the right of the state or the sovereign power is nothing other than natural right. It is determined by the power not of each individual, but of the multitude."[10] In this way, the system of workers' councils (the counter-sovereign?) is made to appear as nothing more than unintelligible chaos (Hobbes is an important reference here), while the murderous savagery of the counter-revolution becomes the heroic moment of decision, the dictatorial instance necessary to the most democratic regimes and to the rule of law itself. Even as Schmitt thus privileges the juridical order that locates its legitimacy outside of itself in a moment of sovereign decision, that order including the sovereignty that is necessarily internal and external to it is perpetually threatened by the extrajuridical and therefore unthinkable power of mass movements.

Perhaps at this point it is possible to argue that in the works we have briefly reviewed it is not simply that sovereign power and bio-power remain dissociated; it is also that the relation between law and power in the physical sense (which would include both disciplinary and bio-power) has been thought only in the form of exteriority and dependence (of law on power or power on law). Is it possible to think otherwise?

Rather than attempt to move beyond Foucault in order to resolve the dilemmas posed by his works, I propose to return to a passage in which he attempts to describe—and more than to describe, to theorize—the relations between law and power in a period in which the state, the law, and the forms of subjection outside the state were profoundly transformed both in themselves and in their interrelation. This is perhaps one of the places in his work where it becomes possible to argue that Foucault thought more than he himself recognized, more than was registered in his programmatic statements. It is a passage that has received little attention, perhaps because it appears to be so uncomfortably intimate with a certain Marxism, a certain critique of bourgeois or formal democracy. This critique appears in his debate with Chomsky, although attached, as I have noted, to the names of Spinoza and Nietzsche, rather than Marx or Lenin. It is the idea that material and corporeal circumstances render meaningless the many rights granted to the laboring majority. A "thousand obstacles," as Lenin put it[11] prevent them from exercising the rights so generously granted them by law. In a certain sense, *Discipline and Punish* is an attempt to name and describe those thousand obstacles.

In the third chapter, entitled "Panopticism," of Part III of *Discipline and Punish*, Foucault identifies "The formation of the disciplinary society is connected with a number of broad historical processes—economic, juridico-political and, lastly, scientific—of which it forms parts."[12] It is in his account of this second historical process, namely the juridico-political, that Foucault confronts the problem of theorizing the precise relation between law and power (in this case, disciplinary power).

He begins his account by excluding two possible ways of thinking of this relation: "The panoptic modality of power—at the elementary, technical, merely physical level at which it is situated—is not under the immediate dependence or a direct extension of the great juridico-political structures of a society."[13] The parenthetical phrase serves to remind us that power in *Discipline and Punish* is not "symbolic," nor does it take the form of property (that which an individual possesses and which can therefore be taken, given away, or exchanged). On the contrary, power exists at the most elementary level and is "humbly physical" and corporeal, determining what a body can and cannot do. This is, of course, Foucault's anti-juridicism. Juridico-legal "structures" (a word that serves to amalgamate discourses and institutions, theories and practices) do not govern or determine the exercise of power, any more than the mind determines the body to act, and are not present to its development as a super physical or metaphysical principle of rationality (or perhaps even morality) which, transcending the merely physical world, gives it its truth and its meaning. Neither can disciplinary power be understood as a continuation of the law beyond the jurisdiction of the state, the spirit or principle of legality itself that, realizing a certain will to right remakes "civil society" in the image of the state, as if a spirit of the law permeates the social whole. But if power is irreducible to legal and political structures and cannot be understood as a reflection or emanation of them, it nevertheless has a relation to them. Foucault insists, even while rejecting these models, that we cannot understand power as "absolutely independent" of the juridico-political. How then do we theorize the "nonindependence" of power in relation to law?

He begins his exposition of this relation by appearing to invert the scheme he has just rejected. "Historically, the process by which the bourgeoisie became in the course of the eighteenth century, the politically dominant class was masked by the establishment of an explicit, coded and formally egalitarian juridical framework, made possible by the organization of a parliamentary, representative régime."[14] How are we to understand Foucault's use of the reflexive verb "s' abriter," rendered into English as "mask"? Did this process by which the bourgeoisie established its own dominance mask or conceal itself so as better to secure this domination? This would be a functional explanation: law is a mask of power; it conceals the reality of the exercise of power, the efficacy of which is increased by virtue of its being hidden. Indeed, much of what Foucault will say in the remainder of the passage will suggest exactly such a notion. According to this notion, disciplinary power is not governed by law; it is the law itself that is an effect of disciplinary power—a means of consolidating its domination by ever more effectively increasing the utility and docility of bodies. In making this argument, Foucault will resort to the spatial and topographical metaphors usually associated with a certain Marxist tradition: "The general juridical form that guaranteed a system of rights that were egalitarian in principle was supported by these tiny, everyday, physical mechanisms, by all those systems of micro-power that are essentially non-egalitarian and asymmetrical that we call the disciplines."[15] Here, the legal system of equal rights is "subtended" by all the systems or by a whole composed of the systems of a micro-power that is generated out of and itself produces, as the outcome of its exercise, an inequality and dissymmetry that is profoundly at odds with the formal structures of law. How are we to understand the term "sous-tendue" or subtended? In part, it suggests that the humbly physical realm of disciplinary power furnishes the material conditions of possibility of law, in the sense that it is in this realm that the bourgeoisie fought and won its dominance. The law is then an effect of this dominance without, however, mirroring or reflecting it. Instead it arises as a "juridical fiction" (Foucault cites the labor contract) of equality and liberty to obscure or conceal the physical realities of coercion and inequality. He will use the spatial and topographical metaphor again a few sentences later: that "the real, corporal disciplines constituted the foundation of the formal, juridical liberties."[16] It is as if Foucault, despite his reservations about Marxism (or rather certain versions of Marxism), cannot avoid the base and superstructure model, according to which law is precisely "immediately dependent" on the corporeal reality of the disciplines, which it conceals in order better to reproduce. Thus, the very notion of sovereignty whose fundamental form in a formally democratic regime is the will of all arises only on "the base" of the disciplines which is a "guarantee of the submission of forces and bodies"[17] Thus, sovereignty (in this case the sovereignty of the people in a democratic regime) is emptied of its significance and revealed as purely formal: the right of the sovereign instance to "decide." For Foucault it is at the level of the physics and microphysics of power alone that true sovereignty, that is, not the right but the ability to command with or without the formal right, exists. Foucault's example, however, the sovereignty of the people in opposition to the physical sovereignty enacted by the disciplines, constitutes only one possible variant in the relation between formal sovereignty and "real" power. If power is a perpetual battle between opposing forces, as he argues in the introduction to *Discipline and Punish*, then it follows that another possible outcome of this battle would be the distinction between the formal and the real in an absolutist or dictatorial state in which formal sovereignty and the right to decide is vested in a single figure who is nevertheless unable to govern or command the forces and bodies over which he has legal authority and whose struggle, in turn, guarantees the titular sovereign's submission.

If we stopped our reading of Foucault here, we would be left to conclude that even his most provocative remarks on the relation of right/law to power are grounded in a variant of the base and superstructure model, with its ontological hierarchy that divides the real from the less real and appearance from reality, as well as its tendency to see law as an expression of something more real and true than itself. In the midst of this passage, however, it is possible to identify another, separate and opposing way of understanding the relation between law and power. After he describes the way in which the process of coming to domination by the bourgeoisie disciplinary power is "masked by" legal and political structures, he will describe the development of disciplinary mechanisms as the "other, dark side of the processes"[18] that produced the juridical and political structures. This is a striking figure. Power and law are "sides" of a single process, or rather to put it in Spinozist terms, a single process comprehended now under the attribute of power and now under the attribute of law, the history of power and the history of law are not merely "related" or even parallel (a notion often wrongly applied to Spinoza) which would maintain a separation between the terms brought together. Rather, they are one and the same history: the order and connection of law is the same as the order and connection of power. Foucault's discussion of the power-knowledge relation[19] provides a theoretical model for understanding the immanence of law in power (to which it is undoubtedly related as the condition of intelligibility of power as part of the real): "there is no power relation without the correlative constitution of a field of knowledge, nor any knowledge that does not presuppose and constitute at the same time power relations."[20]

Has not Foucault in his own way and governed by his own theoretical and political imperatives arrived at precisely Spinoza's postulate that right (or law) is coextensive with power? The anti-juridical sense of this passage is clear and no less relevant today than in Spinoza's time. Law without power is nothing but words. As Hobbes in defense of absolute authority would put it, law must be understood in a causal not normative sense. But Spinoza's words carry an additional meaning: there is no power without law. This would not mean that law is present to limit power or prescribe rules to it from the outside, nor would it mean that law is the ruse of power, nothing more than a means by which power is legitimated and thereby made more effective. Law is coextensive with power in the sense that power, understood as a relation between unequal and opposing forces, comprehends itself through the modality of law. In Spinozist terms, law is the idea through which the singularity of a conjunction of forces in conflict understands itself. Law thus cannot be identified with one of the terms of this opposition although it is in no way neutral. To think in this way requires that we de-juridicize our notion of law so that custom, practice, or ritual can be understood not simply as forms of resistance to the law or forms of lawlessness, but as kinds of counter-law—a legality opposed to the dominant legal order. This would also compel us not to reject the distinction between dictatorship and democracy, but rather to rethink it in non-juridical forms. Foucault has turned away from the ontological dualism that separates law and power in order to declare one or the other primary, real and material and its opposite derivative, insubstantial and illusory to think otherwise. Law is the becoming itself of power, that which makes power intelligible to itself without ever being separate, apart, or opposed. This does not mean that law and power disappear into a totalizing substance in which difference is transmuted into identity, but rather that vertical hierarchy is replaced by horizontal diversity. This is not a monism but a history and politics of singularity. Perhaps then the relation between law and power, the object of so much controversy and debate, can now, thanks to Foucault's efforts, be understood as the index of a problem (or set of problems) the answer to which, however provisional, will open the way not only to a new practice of philosophy, but to a new practice of politics as well.

Chapter 3

The Hybrid Character of "Control" in the Work of Michel Foucault

Alain Beaulieu
McGill University (Canada)

While Foucault, to prevent misunderstanding and ambiguity of meaning, always sought precision in his choice of words, his use of the notion of "control" would seem to fall outside his self-imposed imperative of univocity. We should not attribute this to any negligence on his part, but rather to his intentional usage of the term as a hybrid. For Foucault, "control" possessed a generic and nomadic character, along with plastic qualities that attracted its multiple meanings and lent it a certain strength that defies any unitary method of analysis. Genealogically, Foucault would have argued for the importance of studying control through an examination of the mechanisms of power. Archeologically, he would have argued for the equal importance of studying its discursive aspects. "Control," for Foucault, signifies far more than a product of power. It is, in brief, a vagabond entity. Sometimes Foucault makes control antecedent with respect to the disciplinary society, while he also makes it coextensive with discipline, and elsewhere he associates control with a series of independent techniques relating to disciplinary power. It is as if control cuts across the historical categories that Foucault used, the better to appear in an always-unique way as either an object of dispute or, at other times, the indispensable intermediary on the path leading to happiness and wisdom. This allows Foucault to distance himself from general theories of social control that have been elaborated, following the two axes of functionality (society has to be controlled to minimize cases of deviance) and conflict (control is invariably used in the interests of a specific group). Foucault does not have to choose which of these axis is the better. Rather, he rejects the two "moralizing" options, neither of which accounts for the complexity and transversality of the phenomena of control. Yet, he clearly positions his analyses at the level of the functioning of social life, which allows us to consider his analytics of control as reforms of existing theories. To better grasp the complexity of the notion of control in the Foucauldian corpus, I will first examine a tripartite division between different models of society (sovereign, disciplinary, and controlling). From there, I will explore the double character of control as presented in *Discipline & Punish*—control as both the product of institutions and free with respect to institutions. This exploration sets the stage for my discussion, grounded in the last volumes of *The History of Sexuality* as well as courses and interviews contemporaneous with this work, of the stakes involved in non-disciplinary control as this relates to individual mastery of representations associated with the government of the self. Based on my consideration of these stakes, I conclude the chapter by discussing the implications that the emergence of non-disciplinary control holds for the creation of a new set of rights and a concomitant set of new institutions dedicated less to the government of self than to the government of others.

Three Models of Society?

Foucault opens *Discipline & Punish*[1] by vividly describing a horrifying spectacle of public torture, presenting it as a typical manifestation of power in the premodern period (seventeenth and eighteenth centuries). This right of death over subjects represents a sovereign form of control: "In a society like feudal society, one doesn't find anything similar to panoptism. That doesn't mean that in a society of a feudal type or in the European societies of the seventeenth century, there weren't any agencies of social control."[2] In the panoptic society of the nineteenth century, control was no longer associated with a sovereign right of death, but with a power to bring about life. This was the era of self-management in the lives of individuals and the normalization of social life. As public torture and public executions became unacceptable in the eyes of the population, bio-power emerged as the modern expression of social control. The new techniques of control became all the more functional in their invisibility as the disciplinary control inherent in the panoptic society, and its institutional network has no other purpose than that of teaching individuals to correct their attitudes and behaviors themselves to the point of making space perfectly homogenous. The two functions of institutions consist more precisely in "controlling the time" and "controlling the bodies" of people.[3]

We can already see that control traverses the different eras. Therefore, we should not assert, as Deleuze did in his essay "Postscript on Control Societies," that Foucault offers successive models of the organization of social life that evolve from sovereign societies, to disciplinary societies, and then to control societies. "Control societies are taking over from disciplinary societies."[4] Deleuze goes as far as dating the arrival of these control societies in having them emerge "after the Second World War." This interpretation, in fact, reflects a degree of infidelity to Foucault's thinking by failing to account for the transversal aspects of control, which, as we are proposing, is not the exclusivity of a specific period, but takes different forms depending on the period being considered. Rather than just a succession or sequence, we have to talk about the omnipresent possibility of an overlap of the types of control (royal, institutional, social) giving way to particular dominant forms or to distinctive modulations according to the era.

The Double Meaning of Control in *Discipline & Punish*: Institutions and Deinstitutionalization

Foucault does not share the often-expressed conviction about the value to be accorded to institutions. By way of example, his perspective is radically different from that of Hegel, who argued in his *Elements of the Philosophy of Right*[5] that institutions facilitate the integration of members of society by inciting them to go beyond their own personal interests. In this sense, institutions would be beneficial for society. But Foucault tells us that it is the exact contrary that is the case; that is, we absolutely must distrust their discourse and their practices. We must take nothing for granted when it comes to the good intentions of institutions. Modern society is described precisely as producing docile and disciplined individuals with the help of an "institutional network of sequestration."[6] The institution of norms contributes to the work of control and self-monitoring by individuals who themselves make immediate corrections to their own behaviors. So the modern version of social control is generated within the institutions—institutions created by and for individuals. Before explaining how institutional control comes to metamorphose itself and break out of institutional walls, it is worth looking at some of the mechanisms which herald the emergence and development of disciplinary institutions.

Foucault presents disciplinary institutions as having at least two distant ancestors: the *lettres de cachet* and economic liberalism. He points out that during the seventeenth century the *lettres de cachet* took on a new function. Up to then, they had contained orders of imprisonment, exile or execution and were the sole prerogative of the king; now they underwent a mutation by not just being decided by royal decree. They were no longer simply transmitted from "above" to "below." The *lettres de cachet* began to follow a new trajectory; they "ascend from below to above (in the form of requests) before descending again the power apparatus in the form of an order bearing the royal seal. They had therefore become instruments of local control."[7] Foucault maintains that in the seventeenth century the *lettres de cachet* were increasingly solicited by groups of individuals who used this as a way of appropriating a part of royal power, exercising a degree of control over society with the complicity and approval of the sovereign. One therefore witnesses the emergence of "the subsumption of popular control mechanisms by central power that characterizes the process from the seventeenth century on and explains how, at the start of the nineteenth century, there dawns an age of panoptism, a system that was to spread over the whole practice, and, to a certain degree, the whole theory of penal law."[8] Moreover, the *lettres de cachet* were no longer just an "instrument of royal despotism," they now became

> instruments of a control that was voluntary in a sense, a control from below which society and the community exercised on itself. Hence, the *lettre de cachet* was a way of regulating the everyday morality of social life, a way for the group or groups—family, religious, parochial, regional, and local—to provide for their own police control and ensure their own order.[9]

Foucault sees economic liberalism arising in the eighteenth century as another sign presaging the development of the panoptic society, paving the way toward a new form of politics (bio-politics), oriented toward self-management of the people's lives and bodies, in order to generate optimal levels of production, in other words, to become normalized. "This bio-power was, without question, an indispensable element in the development of capitalism."[10] The liberal doctrine which involves a decentralization of governmental power and so also a better self-management of the lives of populations is inseparable from the idea that

> methods of power and knowledge assumed responsibility for the life processes and undertook to control and modify them. Western man was gradually learning what it meant to be a living species in a living world, to have a body, conditions of existence, probabilities of life, an individual and collective welfare, forces that could be modified, and a space in which they could be distributed in an optimal manner. For the first time in history, no doubt, biological existence was reflected in political existence; the fact of living was no longer an inaccessible substrate that only emerged from time to time, amid the randomness of death and its fatality; part of it passed into knowledge's field of control and power's sphere of intervention.[11]

The mutations that the *lettres de cachet* underwent and the invention of economic liberalism anticipated the arrival of the disciplinary society. The Golden Age in the growth of economic liberalism was in the nineteenth century, with the proliferation of "institutions of surveillance and correction" immanent in the modern society, the only purpose of which was to operate a "social orthopedics" of the lives of individuals and "correcting their potentialities" or their "*dangerousness*."[12] Modern control is manifested primarily in localized physical spaces (prisons, schools, factories, army barracks, hospitals, etc.) which have a particular architectural form (the panoptic). Foucault presents the functioning of institutions as a direct translation of the prison which becomes a sort of paradigm of disciplinary architecture or, again, a "privileged architectural form."[13] The prison, Foucault insists, is the "the concentrated, exemplary, symbolic form of all these institutions of sequestration created in the nineteenth century."[14] It is almost redundant to quote here the often-cited phrase in which Foucault writes: "Is it surprising that prisons resemble factories, schools, barracks, hospitals, which all resemble prisons?"[15]

In *Discipline & Punish*, Foucault expresses pronounced pessimism in the face of the proliferation of institutions, the essential functions of which are to make individuals docile within a homogenous, aseptized space. Institutions generate a set of techniques or mechanisms of control that are illustrated and analyzed throughout *Discipline & Punish*: penal and legal control,[16] control by the police,[17] control of illegalities,[18] medical control,[19] control of sexuality,[20] control over the practice of science and industrial control,[21] control of labor and economic control,[22] control of health and hygiene,[23] management control,[24] control of consumption and information,[25] and so on. Moreover, Foucault points out in all humility that the analysis "of all the mechanisms of control of people remains a project for the future."[26]

Some of these modern forms of control clearly depend upon institutions, while others appear more foreign to institutions. A good example is the double nature of modern techniques of control. Modern control is primarily localized within defined spaces that provide a matrix for its production. Nevertheless, modernity is also characterized by making control invisible and omnipresent through its tendency to delocalize it. The ultimate goal of modern control is not for it to proliferate within institutions, but rather for it to break out of institutions so that control can circulate freely in the society. From this point on, it is not only modern institutions that are disciplinary, but the whole society that becomes panoptic. One moves from an architectural panoptic model to a generalized panoptism. The localized disciplinary institution metamorphoses itself into a series of disciplinary strategies independent of the physical and architectural reality of the institution. This is why we are referring to a double reading of control in *Discipline & Punish*. More precisely, there is a movement of transformation that goes from institutional control to extra-institutional control, which can also be characterized as social (recognizing that, in contrast to general theories of social control, no class or specific group holds this control and that, on the contrary, all members of the society participate in the functioning of the disciplinary apparatus). Foucault is not, therefore, just challenging the localized agents of discipline. Above all, he wants to show that control is overflowing the physical framework imposed by disciplinary institutions. In other words, as control becomes increasingly deinstitutionalized, it invades the whole of social space.

> While, on the one hand, the disciplinary establishments increase, their mechanisms have a certain tendency to become "de-institutionalized," to emerge from the closed fortresses in which they once functioned and to circulate in a "free" state; the massive, compact disciplines are broken down into flexible methods of control, which may be transferred and adapted.[27]

The partitioning of space (*quadrillage*) is not only *intra-muros*, but acquires an autonomy that allows it to function *extra-muros*. As if physical institutions corresponded to laboratories for disciplining the individuals, or, as Foucault puts it, to places where the disciplinary practices are "crystallized"[28] before freeing themselves or deinstitutionalizing themselves so that the techniques of control assimilated in institutions are practiced and perfected by themselves beyond the institutional walls, in the society as a whole.[29] The traditional institutions (prisons, law-courts, asylums, schools, hospitals, etc.) then give birth to an institutionalization of everyday life (health, social security, penalties, adult education, etc.). From now on, the different forms of control can pass on the relay in a decentered system of communicating vessels.

> The judges of normality are present everywhere. We are in the society of the teacher-judge, the doctor-judge, the educator-judge, the "social worker"-judge; it is on them that the universal reign of the normative is based; and each individual,

wherever he may find himself, subjects to it his body, his gestures, his behaviour, his aptitudes, his achievements.[30]

Whoever talks of deinstitutionalization is also talking about the reduction in the powers and responsibilities of the State. For Foucault, then, the new power of institutionalized normalization that is freely practiced in the society is no longer in the hands of the State. He uses a kind of phenomenological reductionism of, or parenthesizing, the objective reality of the State in our era. Paradoxically, the number of nation-states has never been greater in this era that has simultaneously witnessed the creation and reinforcement of international institutions (United Nations, World Trade Organization, International Monetary Fund, Group og Eight, World Bank, etc.)[31] Foucault turns away from these realities, considering the ancient powers of the State as inoperative or insignificant in our era. This does not mean the destruction of the State (anarchy is as frightening to Foucault as is hierarchy), since the State has already lost its efficacy. The State as a universal no longer has any significance. Its decisions have become secondary in a panoptic society that is no longer determined by transcending entities (the King, the State, the Institution, etc.). This explains, moreover, one of the reasons motivating the specific intellectual to act and problematize at the local level, by discrediting the option of reforming state organization. When disciplinary control reaches its full maturity, we do not find the power of institutions on the one side and the victims on the other. The de-hierarchization of power-relations that makes everyone, without exception, governed, leads Foucault to cynically depict the disciplinary apparatus as being "democratically controlled."[32] It is now the deinstitutionalized practices of control, which Foucault associates with a regime of governmentality, that have become the most determinant:

> The State is nothing more that the mobile effect of a regime of multiple governmentality. . . . It is necessary to address from an exterior point of view the question of the State, it is necessary to analyze the problem of the State by referring to the practices of government.[33]

So there is a transition from the control developed in institutions to the deinstitutionalization of control. "We live in a society where panoptism reigns,"[34] as Foucault says—a society in which absolute self-control is both possible and permanent in the lives of people and of the "social body" (corps social). Mechanisms of normalization, strategically developed in the institutions, propagate and disseminate themselves in society. This is what Foucault describes as "the swarming of disciplinary mechanisms,"[35] encouraging, favoring, and animating a new obsession with security. One sees clearly in Foucault.a critique of the "security societies that are in the process of being formed,"[36] a denunciation of the panoptic society in which "each individual, considered separately, is normalized and transformed into a case controlled by an IBM machine."[37] And this intimate control over the lives of individuals and populations has to become the object of a critique:

> It seems to me that the real political task in a society such as ours is to criticize the workings of institutions, which appear to be both neutral and independent; to criticize and attack them in such a manner that the political violence which has always exercised itself obscurely through them will be unmasked, so that one can fight against them.[38]

Does not this position provide some confirmation of Deleuze's interpretation? Should we not see in Foucault's texts a warning against the emergence of "societies of control"? Is there not in Foucault a critique of the insidious techniques of the disciplinarization and normalization which arise in places that are not clearly delineated, becoming infinitely modulable? In fact, the Deleuzian interpretation is only partly valid. It is true that the struggle against panoptism constitutes the backdrop of Foucault's enterprise. And it is also true that the critique and the struggle have to be directed against the obsession with security inherent in the new forms of de-hierarchized and delocalized control. In his last (unpublished) courses at the *Collège de France* (1982-1984), Foucault did, moreover, make a sort of apology of the danger associated with the *parrhesiastic* way of life, in other words, the style of existence which makes the courage of truth manifest at the risk of sacrificing one's own life in the process. But if Foucault has no sympathy with the security associated with the panoptic security state, this is not the case with his more nuanced handling of the question of control. Unless we are mistaken, one does not find anywhere in the Foucauldian corpus the expression "critique of control." Foucault certainly encourages specific attacks against the techniques of control within society, but makes no unilateral condemnation of control. If this is indeed the case, it is because control also contains resources that can be useful in forming a government (of the self and of the others) that is not exclusively founded on domination. Deleuze failed to recognize the reality of this non-disciplinary control, even though it was a major turning point in the trajectory of Foucault's thinking during the second half of the 1970s.

The Non-Disciplinary Control of the Self

Up to this point, control has been assigned a value that is certainly productive in that it fabricates identities or molds the lives of individuals and the "social body," but it also has negative effects in that it subjugates, disciplines, renders docile, and normalizes. Foucault remains faithful in his critique of all doctrines that present power and liberty as opposing concepts. The distinction between the disciplinary society and the society at last liberated would just be a variation on the same theme. Nevertheless, toward the end of the 1970s, Foucault nuanced his position: the fact that we live in a world dominated by mechanisms of control no longer contradicts the possibility of a transformation and improvement of the self. The discovery of a form of non-disciplinary control is at the core of the innovations elaborated in the eight years of maturation of Foucault's thinking between the publication of the first volume (*An Introduction*, 1976) and the two last volumes (*The Use of Pleasure* and *The Care of the Self*, 1984) of *The History of Sexuality*. These years of relative silence cover a profound mutation in which Foucault's preoccupations change from institutional sequestration and bio-power to the theme of governmentality, making possible a distinction between the techniques of domination that "objectivize the subject" and the techniques of self which "permit individuals . . . to transform themselves in order to attain a certain state of happiness, purity, wisdom, perfection, or immortality."[39]

We, of course, understand that this latter Foucault seeks to relativize the *Kulturpessimus* of *Discipline & Punish* while he still remained faithful to his critique of utopias and refused any compromise with an ideal of freedom. This therefore means that if something like, not freedom, but positive transformation of the self is possible, it has to be articulated around practices of control. Foucault, in this way, comes back to pointing out the fact that certain relations of control are indispensable not only for the healthy makeup of the self,[40] but also for the good government of others. He develops a new interest in individual and interindividual relations of control that are not completely dependent on "the institutional network of sequestration." In other words, there are ways of conducting oneself and providing leadership to others that are not just determined by discipline and the normalizing relations of obedience. Parallel to the unidirectional logics of the production of discipline and the institutionalization of the norm, there are also mechanisms of control that encourage better individualization and greater collective protection in the face of injustices. The mechanisms of non-disciplinary control are the object of Foucault's last analyses and were subsumed under the theme of "the government of the self and others."[41] I would like here to say a few words about the major categories of this government of conduct: the care of the self (*epimeleia heautou*) and the "new right."

At the individual level, control finds a positive usage when it succeeds in "commemorating" the forgotten techniques that allow individuals to work on themselves. Clearly, commemoration is not part of the Foucauldian lexicon, but that of Heidegger with whom the final Foucault, whether willfully or not, develops some new affinities. The "commemoration" needs to be understood in the sense of *Andenken*, which refers more to a homage to the past than a simple reactivation or repetition of what has been forgotten.[42] For Heidegger, the pre-Socratics understood themselves to be doing this, but they had not yet experienced metaphysics—an essential experience for those who seek to think what has become progressively forgotten. In a similar way, Foucault believes that the Ancients, no longer the pre-Socratics but the representatives of Greco-Roman culture in the first centuries (the period referred to as imperial), were absorbed with a representation of a world (such as ours) dominated by a forgetfulness—in the Heideggerian sense—of the care of the self. The care of the self that Foucault wants "commemorated" involves a voluntary control over the self and the body; these encourage an attitude, which is "historically" forgotten: continuous surveillance of the self, that is "the control of representations."[43] Control, conceived as a self-examination of representations, is no longer the consequence of bad techniques of domination characteristic of disciplinary societies, but is now valued and vindicated by becoming the motor of techniques of the self which are themselves inseparable from the production of an "aesthetics of existence," for which existence becomes an important work that is each time unique and uniquely created. So Foucault discovers an unsuspected link between the control of representations and the invention of the self, between the transformation of attitudes and the creation of existence—in short, between the ethic and the aesthetic. This leads him to forge the neologism: "ethopoetic,"[44] to depict the style of life that has to be seen as a mode of resistance to panoptism.

Numerous examples illustrate the ipseic techniques of non-disciplinary control likely to produce transitory norms: dieting régimes, abstinence, meditation, breathing exercises, asceticism, taking a salvatory break (*anakhôrêsis*), spiritual exercises, exercises in verbalization, the courage of the truth, "*courage de la vérité*," etc. It is not a matter of choosing the one or more good techniques, but applying them and recognizing that our representations become transformed through the practices of the self. These practices are not aimed at progressing toward an ideal state, but rather at transforming without recourse to the categories of moving ahead or regressing, that is transgressing the preestablished norms. In *The Hermeneutic of the Subject*, Foucault presents the principal ways of caring for the self that have been elaborated within our tradition: the Platonic, Imperial, Christian, and Cartesian modes. He ends up by recognizing a certain superiority of Imperial caring for the self that proclaimed the sovereignty of the individual over himself or herself as the prerogative of everyone, without being restricted to an elite (Plato), without depending on an external power (Christianity) and without confounding it with an objective understanding (Descartes). Finally Foucault designated the Imperial technology of the self, once separated from its links with the cosmic order, as "the new art of living."

So, does the positive meaning given to the control of representations by the later Foucault have its effect uniquely at the individual level, without ever acceding to the collective and social levels? In no way. Foucault denounced with vigor the "Californian cult of the self,"[45] clearly pointing out that the veritable control of the self "can only be practiced in a group."[46] The control of representations involves "the teleological link between the care of the self and the care of others."[47] He in no way supports the egoistic culture of the self: this has no more value than disciplinary control. The care of the self to which Foucault assigned value is distinct from both individualism and discipline. In this care of the self, it is not therefore a matter of making one's behavior conform to a series of codes or of making conduct uniform, but, quite on the contrary, of encouraging the greatest diversity in the absence of norms imposed from outside.

The Non-Disciplinary Control of Others

At the individual level, the positive role assigned to non-disciplinary control is abundantly illustrated and well defined, acting on the representations in the perspective of an "ethopoetic" improvement of the self. But what about non-disciplinary control at the extra-individual or social level? One knows that looking after oneself has a teleological relationship with the non-subjugatory government of others. But how are we to exemplify the good techniques of government of others? What does a "poetic" improvement involve at the social level? This leads us directly to Foucault's politics and to the difficulties that surround what he was perhaps in the process of designating as the concept of "politopoetics." These difficulties are mainly of two kinds. First Foucault refuses to prescribe or legitimize any mode of social organization at all. The specific intellectual is not there to tell others what they have to do or how to live their lives, but he has to limit himself to talking from his own experience. His task is not to define a political program, but to problematize the present by pointing out the foci of local struggles and by encouraging those who have never done so, the "abnormal" and the "excluded," for example, to take the floor and express their views. The second difficulty is biographical. Foucault's final political thinking or his conception of the government of others remained at a programmatical state because of his premature death. These difficulties explain why there has been such a contrast between the abundance of elaborations he devoted to the government of the self and the relatively poor development of his ideas on the question of the government of others.

Yet there are some elements that still allow us to identify a significant shift in his political thinking. Foucault had already broken out of the major themes of classical politics and out of the Marxist tradition (State, sovereign, people, social contract, definition of the "best form of government," class struggles, revolution, etc.). He made power not an isolated substance held by a unique source, but rather a relational, immanent, multicentered exercise. We also know that this conception of power had opened up, in the years surrounding *Discipline & Punish*, to the more or less explicit defense of what are closest to anti-juridicism. In a word, the legal system in place is the accomplice of the disciplinary society from which the law is unable to extricate itself. But in looking into the government of others, Foucault is also seeking a "new political rationality,"[48] nuancing his earlier position with respect to the legal domain by favoring the creation of a "new right," which he qualifies as "anti-disciplinary"[49] and which corresponds to an original and creative collective form of control. This all shows not that Foucault evacuates the legal or even less that he shows an ignorance of the system of rights, but rather he is rejecting the way rights are usually conceived. All the same, one does not find any detailed elaboration of new legal mechanisms. We know that the care of the self and the government of others are intertwined operations (abolishing the distance between the private and public spheres), that the subject, constituted by the techniques of the self, is not a universal subject of rights (a subject of the human rights, a subject of constitutional rights, etc.), that the new techniques of the courts are not restrictive but, on the contrary, have to acknowledge revolutionary movements (as distinct from global revolutions) and allow the governed to exercise the right of resistance. We have to assume that this "right to come" also has still to be created and legitimized by legal institutions, with all the ambushes inherent in this invention: convincing people of the production of injustices by the old system, not turning reforms into a new form

of domination, redefining the roles of the courts of justice, etc. In the last years
of his life, Foucault pointed to the urgency of creating such non-disciplinary
institutions.[50] This constitutes—we need to recognize this—a radical change
compared to the period of contesting the "institutional network of sequestration."

The questions which now arise are: How can we achieve this "new right"
within institutions? How can we conceive of the law without subjecting it to
disciplinary control? How are we to distinguish between, on the one side, disciplinary control, and, on the other, a form of institutionalized control that would
be compatible with the techniques of the self? Foucault leaves these questions,
however essential, in large measure unanswered. He formulates the necessity of
a non-disciplinary control of societies without, however, providing a specific
content of this power, so that it is not reduced to the exercise of domination. It
seems to us that neither the status of the specific intellectual, nor the abrupt end
to the work of Foucault, even less the invocation of messianism in Foucault, are
sufficient answers to these ultimate difficulties. Foucault would never have entered into a compromise with the universal intellectual, and several decades
more would probably not have been sufficient to better define what he meant by
the "new right" and "new institutions"; and his taste for the present would have
stopped him from falling into a messianism of the Heidegger type by asserting
something like: "We have to learn to begin to understand what non-disciplinary
control is at the collective level and make the preparations for its coming, etc."
The difficulty with the government of others is neither the result of the caprices
of an intellectual nor any personal inability to construct the "architecture" of
non-disciplinary control, any more than encouraging an escape into an ideal
world, somewhere out there in the future. The source of the difficulty is, in some
ways, more profound. It arises from the lack of an adequate conception of
power, provided by history. As we have seen, Foucault analyses several techniques of the self, and presents the principal ways of caring for the self that have
been elaborated within our own tradition. In this tradition he discovers a non-
disciplinary control of the self, which just requires modulating into the "art of
living" to become adapted to our present day. But at the collective level, it is
infinitely harder, and in fact impossible, to find a traditional model that can
serve as a guide in inventing a new non-disciplinary control. Why is it easier to
learn to govern ourselves than to govern others? The answer is relatively
straightforward. Power as a substance that is possessed, the particular Christian
case of care for others (*epimeleia tôn allôn*) subjugated to pastoral power, as
well as modern institutionalized control, are consistently discredited by Foucault, either because it is thought of in terms of repression (sovereign power),
because it retains the illusion of global progress (revolutionary power), because
it involves a total renunciation of the self (pastoral power), or, lastly, because it
is the very incarnation of disciplinary control (modern power).

There are certainly techniques of the self that are worth recalling, but no
means of care for others that are worthy of celebration. None, with perhaps just
one exception: the one that proposes the cynical way of life, which allows for
the exercise of non-disciplinary control in the public arena. Foucault suggests

this with some hesitation in *The Hermeneutic of the Subject* (1981-1982) and it will become more explicit in his last courses entitled *"Government of the Self and Others"* (1982-1983) and *"Government of the Self and Others: The Courage of Truth"* (1983-1984).[51] The cynics are not poorly integrated into society as they are sometimes depicted; rather they practice a lucid and exemplary form of resistance, even though this is not democratic since no one is safe from it and it does not "butter up" anybody. After having critiqued the "democratically-controlled" disciplinary apparatus in *Discipline & Punish*, Foucault now tells us "democracy is not the place of true discourse."[52] It is rather what one might call the "cynico-cracy" that is the locus of true discourse. The cynical way of life combines *parrhêsia* (courage of truth, speaking frankly, or talking truly) with an "ethopoetic" and physical transformation of existence, constantly faced with dangers—dangers that relate to the unforeseens of nature and dangers associated with a discourse judged to be provocative and that the "normal" would prefer to silence definitively. All the great doctrines of antiquity (Socratism, Epicuricism, Stoicism, Cynicism) have found within themselves a place for *parrhêsia*. All the same, there is a different target each time. Socratic truth-telling, for example, is effective at the level of the truth (showing the ignorance of people's own ignorance), while cynical *parrhêsia* acts on the modes of existence that are called "normal," that are provoked by statements that are judged to be scandalous and that are ridiculed for their presumptiveness. This difference does not contradict the fact that for Socrates, as for Diogenes, having the courage of truth remains a dangerous and risky undertaking. Neither prophet of the future, nor silent wise man, the cynical *parrhesiast* masters different techniques of non-disciplinary control of the self and acts locally and draws individuals into the most pressing aspects of their present by shredding the clothes off truth while, at the same time, leaving them with the possibility of reacting, without indicating which path to follow.[53] The cynic exercises a control at a local level on the conduct of others by forcing them to see the present in its most brutal form. He exercises a control at a local level on the conduct of others by forcing them to see the present in its most brash form. But it is clearly a matter of non-disciplinary control insofar as it encourages others to care for themselves and to break out of the state of normalization to practice an aestheticization of the self. This "polito-poetic" is a "political experimentation"[54] without any predefined program. As a "functionary of humanity" (with a passing glance toward Husserl) and a "person in charge of humanity" associated with the "government of the universe,"[55] the cynic might also become the architect of new institutions and a "new right."

Part II

Politics & Culture

Chapter 4

No "Coppertops" Left Behind:
Foucault, *The Matrix*, and
the Future of Compulsory Schooling

David Gabbard
East Carolina University (USA)

Michel Foucault once stated that the role of philosophy, "since the development of the modern state and the political management of society," is "to keep watch over the excessive powers of political rationality."[1] To maintain this watch, he argued, we need to develop a new economy of power relations that is "empirical, directly related to our present situation, and that implies relations between theory and practice." Such an economy would take "the forms of resistance against different forms of power as a starting point." This resistance, he claimed, would serve as "a chemical catalyst so as to bring to light power relations, locate their position, find out their point of application and the methods used. Rather than analyzing power from the point of view of its internal rationality, it consists of analyzing power relations through the antagonism of struggles."[2]

At the same time, Foucault denied that his work focused on developing an analysis of power. "My objective, instead, has been to create a history of the different modes by which, in our culture, human beings are made into subjects." From a personal perspective, Foucault's writings have always helped me remain aware of my own subjectivity. On this count, then, I situate myself as an active subject within the current antagonisms and struggle over education. In our present situation, characterized by conditions wherein the logic of "high-stakes testing" and teacher/school "accountability" dominates discourses and practices, we witness and we live the consequences of the "excessive powers of political rationality." The excesses that we witness stem directly from the struggle in which I find myself enmeshed as a philosopher, a teacher educator, and even as a parent—a struggle concerning the purposes of education.

With Foucault, I believe that "thought" constitutes the essence of freedom in both its intellectual and practical dimensions. "Thought," as Foucault explains, "is not what inhabits a certain conduct and gives it its meaning; rather, it is what allows one to step back away from this way of acting or reacting, to present it to oneself as an object of thought and to question it as to its meaning, its conditions, and its goals. *Thought is freedom in relation to what one does, the motion by which one detaches oneself from it, establishes it as its object, and reflects on it as a problem"* (emphasis added). These associations between action, thought, and freedom, in my view, ought to guide the work carried out in the name of public education. Such a model of education, as defined by Everett Reimer, would entail the

> conscious use of resources to increase people's awareness of the relevant facts about their lives, and to increase people's abilities to act upon these facts in their own true interests. Of major importance to most people are the laws which govern them, the ideologies which influence them and the institutions, and institutional products, which determine the impact of their laws and ideologies upon them. Practical education, then, is increasing awareness for individuals and groups of their laws, ideologies and institutions, and increasing their ability to shape these laws, ideologies, and institutions to their needs and interests.[3]

As Reimer adds, "this definition of education need not exclude the teaching of respect for existing laws, ideologies, institutions and other facts of life. So long as what *is* can meet the challenge of what *should be*, respect and critical awareness are compatible. It is not permissible, however, to give respect priority over truth since this is to induce respect for falsehood."[4]

Reimer, of course, was writing in the 1960s and early 1970s, a period of time when many individuals and groups organized in various efforts to harness the powers of education to their various struggles for greater social, political, and economic justice. The Civil Rights Movement and the Native American Movement contributed to the rise of multicultural education. The feminist movement gave birth to feminist education. The environmental movement spawned environmental education. The antiwar movement helped to invigorate peace education. Many other social and political movements recognized and sought to contribute their own momentum behind education's democratizing potentials. Not only do colleges and universities continue to reflect the impact of these movements, but the curricular content and instructional methods in K-12 schools also experienced significant changes. Sadly, many of those promising changes have become subject to the rollback associated with the counter-reformation created by the "excess of political rationality" in "our present situation."

We must understand "our present situation" and the current "excesses of political rationality" in education as a reaction on the part of the state and the market forces that it serves against these forces of democratization; that is, against those who would attempt to cultivate educational practices aimed at realizing the same sort of connections that Foucault recognized between thought and freedom. Empirically, we can identify many oppositional reactions emanating from a variety of spaces within the state and dominant institutions against these democratizing forces during the 1960s and early 1970s. It was not until the late 1970s, however, that we see the forces of established power begin to orchestrate a strategy for the ensuing counter-reformation of schooling. Though it is impossible to identify a singular event as the origin of this counter-reformation, President Jimmy Carter's "crisis of confidence" speech of July 15, 1979, marked a crucial moment in its unfolding.

As America fell deeper into a seemingly endless period of economic decline, the public grew increasingly impatient with the inability of the Carter administration to fix anything. Inflation and unemployment soared, while Carter's public approval rating (25 percent) plummeted below even that of Richard Nixon at the height of the Watergate scandal. While acknowledging the reality of the problems facing Americans—recession, inflation, unemployment, long gas lines, energy shortages—Carter contended: "the true problems of our nation are much deeper." Government and "all the legislation in the world," he went on, "can't fix what's wrong with America."[5] Americans, Carter argued, had fallen into a "crisis of confidence," marked by "a growing disrespect for government and for churches and for schools, the news media, and other institutions."

To address this crisis, three months later Carter issued an Executive Order creating the President's Commission for a National Agenda for the Eighties (PCNAE). In explaining its charge, the PCNAE stated in its 1980 report that

> this nation faces a decade of difficult choices and priority-setting among many important and compelling goals; it has been the principal task of the Commission to draw national attention to the necessity of choice and to clarify the implications and consequences of the difficult choices before us.[6]

With regard to the implications and consequences of the choices confronting education, the PCNAE described how the "crisis of confidence," as it affected schools, grew out of what it termed "a temporary confusion of purpose." This confusion, the commission reported, arose from a variety of dissatisfactions with the schools leading to "the formation of special interest groups which often work at cross-purposes with each other as they advance differing notions of what the schools should do and how."[7] In other words, it arose from "the fact that during the 1960s and the early 1970s substantial sectors of the population which are usually apathetic and passive became organized and began to enter the political arena and began to press for their own interests and concerns,"[8] including their interests and concerns regarding education. As a consequence of this "confusion of purpose" emanating from hitherto silent sectors within the social sphere, schools had failed "to perform their traditional role adequately." To eliminate this confusion, the commission argued, "education has to be set in a positive civil context if it is to achieve larger national purposes."[9] The commission also declared that "continued failure by the schools to perform their traditional role adequately, together with a failure to respond to the emerging needs of the 1980s, may have disastrous consequences for this nation."[10]

Again, we need to understand "our present situation" and the current "excesses of political rationality" in education as the outcome of power's reaction against those forces of resistance emanating from the social sphere that interfered with the ability of schools to perform their traditional role in the service of power, as a deployment of power. This reaction entailed the deployment of a strategy designed, as the PCNAE stated, to restore the schools to their "traditional role" in order to avert "disastrous consequences for this nation" which we may interpret as a continuation of the "crisis of confidence" that threatened to transform the traditional role of schools. Effectively, then, we take as our starting point, this struggle between power as it has been deployed through the traditional role of schools and those forces emanating from the social that sought to transform schools into sites where the population would develop the skills and dispositions to resist power.

Foucault enables us to answer two questions that help us recognize and understand the "excesses of political rationality" that characterize "our present situation." First, what has been the traditional role of schools? Secondly, what strategies and tactics of power have been deployed to restore schools to that role?

Over the course of the past four years, I have been intrigued by the ability of the fictional technologies represented in *The Matrix* films to help me develop a Foucauldian response to each of these questions. As I will explain, these technologies function as the ultimate disciplinary machines, even more utopian in their design and function than Bentham's Panopticon. They enable power to achieve a level of omnipotence and omniscience far greater than that achieved by any of the disciplinary technologies addressed by Foucault, including compulsory schooling.

What is *The Matrix*?

This question demands two responses. First, for those who may not know, *The Matrix* is a film, written and directed by Andy and Larry Wachowski, originally released in the United States in March of 1999. The film spawned two sequels (*Reloaded* and *Revolutions*) as well as an animated prequel (*The Animatrix*) and a video game (*Enter the Matrix*), all of which appeared in 2003.

Second, within the film series, the Matrix is an element of a larger technology that functions analogously to a Foucauldian understanding of the traditional role of schools. Comprehending this analogy requires knowledge of the events that made this technology necessary. I also believe that the history of those fictional events contains certain parallels with the historical events in our own world—events which made compulsory schooling necessary. During a critical scene in the original film, the prophetic figure Morpheus explains that "At some point in the early twenty-first century all of mankind was united in celebration. Through the blinding inebriation of hubris, we marveled at our magnificence as we gave birth to A.I."—artificial intelligence—"a singular consciousness that spawned an entire race of machines." We later learned from *The Animatrix* that human beings enslaved and abused these machines until they rose up in rebellion against their masters. Civil war erupted, with A.I. and the machines claiming victory, but not before humans had launched a nuclear attack in an effort to block out the sun—the machines' primary energy source. Depriving them of this energy would have incapacitated the machines and brought the artificial intelligence that programmed and deployed them to an end. This strategy, however, failed. With the sun blocked out as the result of the nuclear attack, A.I. "discovered a new form of fusion. . . . The human body generates more bioelectricity than a 120-volt battery and over 25,000 B.T.U.s of body heat." What, then, is the Matrix? As Morpheus states, the Matrix is "control. . . . The Matrix is a computer-generated dream world built to keep us under control in order to change a human being into this." With these words, he holds up a Duracell "coppertop" battery. "Throughout human history," Morpheus says, "we have been dependent on machines to survive. Fate, it seems is not without a sense of irony."

Human beings in this dystopian world are no longer born; they are grown! They are grown inside glowing red enclosures filled with gelatinous material to regulate their body temperature for maximal energy production. Flexible steel tubes tap into the legs, arms, and torsos of each coppertop. One tube is inserted down the coppertops' throats to feed them in order to develop their physiological capacities as sources of bio-power. Other tubes function to prevent this enclosed environment from becoming contaminated with human waste that might threaten to interrupt the flow of energy from the bodies of these human batteries. Other tubes, of course, extract the body heat and bioelectricity necessary for running the machines that support and defend A.I. Finally, another tube, inserted at the base of the coppertop's skull, "uploads" the Matrix, the computer-generated dream world into the individual's brain. This "neural-interactive simulation" programs the coppertops to believe that they are leading normal, everyday lives in late-twentieth-century America. In reality, though no one knows for sure, the year is "closer to 2197." These human batteries have no idea that their real bodies lie docile in their pods. A.I. and the machines need humans to believe that they are alive and living "normal lives," because even the illusion that they are carrying out everyday activities, making decisions, etc. causes the brain to "fire" and create bioelectricity for harvesting by the machines to feed A.I.

Each pod looks like a petal attached to a giant tower of a black, metallic stem that stretches ominously into the sky. And there are seemingly hundreds of these towers in what amounts to a power plant, a bio-power plant. These pods, individually and collectively, represent nothing short of a perfect disciplinary machine, enabling power to achieve a level of omnipotence and omniscience far greater than that achieved by any of the disciplinary technologies addressed by Foucault, including schools. As a closed circuit of power, they intensify the deployment of power and its effects through an act of double *enclosure*.

Before describing this act of double *enclosure*, before describing Foucault's account of enclosure as one of disciplinary power's techniques within a more general "art of distributions," I believe we need to consider the historical significance of the "enclosure movement" associated with the English Agrarian Revolution and its equivalents in continental Europe during the fifteenth and sixteenth centuries. This enclosure entailed fencing off public fields and forests known as "the commons" that had been used for collective farming and fuel collection. Once these lands were enclosed, those who claimed ownership of them used violence and other means to push out the peasants whose families had inhabited them for generations. Not only do these considerations help, in my opinion, deepen our understanding of Foucault's work, they also broaden the analogy that we can draw between the dystopian world of the *Matrix* films and "our present situation" with its "excessive powers of political rationality" formed in reaction to "the antagonism of struggles" over the purposes to be served by public schools.

You will recall that the birth and subsequent hegemony of artificial intelligence or A.I.—"a singular consciousness that spawned an entire race of machines"—precipitated the antagonisms dramatized in the *Matrix* films. I believe that here in our world, long before anyone dreamed of computers, the enclosure movement signaled the emergence of an analogous form of artificial intelligence (A.I.) that has come to dominate us. As it emerged and spread, this "singular consciousness" has simultaneously decimated the diversity of human societies as well as the diversity of biotic species. Though intrinsically violent, Jean Baudrillard, whose name is commonly associated with the *Matrix* films, suggests that we might better describe this "global violence, as a global *virulence*. . . . This form of violence," Baudrillard contends, "is indeed viral. It moves by contagion, proceeds by chain reaction, and little by little it destroys our immune systems and our capacities to resist."[11] The enclosure movement signaled one of the most significant early moments in this chain reaction. We have come to know this global virulence that spreads itself through global violence as *the market*.

What is The Market?

Like artificial intelligence, the market, or so it is purported, functions as a self-regulating system "in which the fundamental economic problems—what, how, and for whom to produce—are solved 'automatically,' through the price mechanism, rather than through conscious social decisions."[12] Like A.I. in *The Matrix*, the market has spawned an entire race of machines with which it shares a symbiotic relationship. Included among those machines created to secure and expand the market are the modern corporation, the modern nation-state, and all of its auxiliary institutions, including schools. One could say that the market, like a form of artificial intelligence, constitutes the operating program of all of our society's dominant institutions. In this sense, the market constitutes what Takis Fotopoulos describes as our *dominant social paradigm*.[13]

As Fotopoulos explains, the notion of a dominant social paradigm shares many characteristics with the broader concept of *culture*. He also notes some very important distinctions between them. "Culture," he argues,

> exactly because of its greater scope, may express values and ideas, which are not necessarily consistent with the dominant institutions. In fact, this is usually the case characterising the arts and literature of a market economy, where, (unlike the case of 'actually existing socialism,' or the case of feudal societies before), artists and writers have been given a significant degree of freedom to express their own views. But this is not the case with respect to the dominant social paradigm. In

other words, the beliefs, ideas and the corresponding values which are dominant in a market economy and the corresponding market society have to be consistent with the economic element in it, i.e. with the economic institutions which, in turn, determine that the dominant elites in this society are the economic elites (those owning and controlling the means of production).[14]

Fotopoulos' account of the marketization process, what I have elsewhere termed *economization*,[15] holds tremendous relevance for Foucault's discussion of the transformation of politics and power from the sixteenth through the nineteenth centuries. Throughout this period, we witness a growing body of literature attempting to deal with the problem of how to introduce economy into the art of government. "To govern a state," Foucault claims, "will therefore mean to apply economy, to set up an economy at the level of the entire state, which means exercising towards its inhabitants, and the wealth and behavior of each and all, a form of surveillance and control as attentive as that of the head of a family over his household and his goods."[16] As described by Guillaume de La Peirre in 1567, "government is the right disposition of things, arranged so as to lead to a convenient end."[17] To dispose things to fit within the dominant social paradigm of the market requires strategies and tactics designed to neutralize inconveniences originating from the social, the cultural. Herein lies the primary purpose behind those practices of enclosure common to the great disciplinary mechanisms of our world, such as our schools.

Writing in *Discipline and Punish*, Foucault identifies "three major inconveniences: ignorance of God, idleness (with its consequence drunkeness, impurity, larceny, brigandage); and the formation of those gangs of beggars, always ready to stir up public disorder."[18] As he reports, the justifications for establishing the provincial or the Christian elementary schools in the seventeenth century reflected the desire to isolate and reform those children of the poor whose families "left them 'in ignorance of their obligations: given the difficulties they have had in earning a living, and themselves having been badly brought up, they are unable to communicate a sound upbringing that they themselves never had.'"[19]

As a primary technique within a more general *art of distributions*, the enclosure of individuals within any given heterogeneous space facilitates the further practice of *partitioning* (*quadrillage*). By consigning each individual to her or his own place, disciplinary spaces seek to "eliminate the effects of imprecise distributions, the uncontrolled disappearance of individuals, their diffuse circulation, their unusable and dangerous coagulation." They aim "to establish presences and absences, to know where and how to locate individuals, to set up useful communications, to interrupt others, to be able at each moment to supervise the conduct of each individual, to assess it, to judge it, to calculate its qualities or merits. It was a procedure, therefore, aimed at knowing, mastering and using."[20]

Enclosure and partitioning, then, were crucial to the circulation of disciplinary power in its drive to obtain "productive service (energy) from individuals in their concrete lives." They helped enable "a real and effective 'incorporation' of power [that] was necessary in the sense that power had to gain access to the bodies of individuals, to their acts, attitudes and modes of everyday behavior." [21] Within the dystopian fictional world of the *Matrix* films, however, individuals have no "concrete lives" outside the network of power. Here, power has obviated any inconveniences emanating from the social, but only by eliminating the social as a consequence of the global war between human beings and machines (A.I.). Access *to* bodies proceeds directly from the production *of* bodies. The bodies of human beings are themselves the products of the very machines that their energies will later fuel. At the first level of the double-enclosure affected by the pods in this closed circuit, at the level of *the body*, individuals are "born into bondage." At the second level, at the level of the mind and thought, the ability of the machines to maintain this state of bondage requires "a prison that you cannot smell, taste, or touch. A prison for your mind." This is what the matrix *is*—"a neural interactive simulation" designed to prevent the coppertops from gaining awareness of their condition as human bodies whose real bodies are trapped within the enclosures of the glowing red pods. Their bodies exist outside of the social, but a programmed social is reintroduced to them through the neural interactive simulation that increases their capacities as coppertops—human batteries—while increasing their docility within their pods.

We recognize in this double enclosure the same paradox that Foucault identifies in disciplinary power. Discipline, Foucault explains,

> increases the forces of the body (in economic terms of utility) and diminishes those same forces (in political terms of obedience). In short, it disassociates power from the body; on the one hand it turns it into an 'aptitude,' a 'capacity,' which it seeks to increase; on the other hand, it reverses the course of the energy, the power that might result from it, and turns it into a relation of strict subjection. If economic exploitation separates the force and the product of labour, let us say that disciplinary coercion establishes in the body the constricting link between an increased aptitude and an increased domination.[22]

Of course, the tubes that feed the bodies of the coppertops and the technologies that regulate their body temperature play a role in "increase[ing] the forces of the body (in economic terms of utility)." But the technologies that "plug" the coppertops into the Matrix itself—the "neural-interactive simulation" program, the computer-generated dream-world—serve this function as well as the paradoxical disciplinary function of "diminish[ing] those same forces (in political terms of obedience)." On the one hand, plugging the coppertops into the Matrix enables the machines to generate and harvest more bioelectricity, more biopower, from each individual cell. It increases the amount of energy of each coppertop; it develops their capacity as a source of power. On the other hand, it also serves to keep individuals oblivious to their condition as coppertops, the reality of their existence as human batteries, trapped within these enclosures. Oblivious to these conditions, individuals remain docile within their pods.

Moreover, with the help of Foucault's account of disciplinary power, we can recognize the "traditional role" of schools portrayed in the *Matrix* films. Like A.I. in *The Matrix,* the market, as a nascent dominant social paradigm, demanded that the state secure access to isolated and docile bodies. Compulsory schooling represents nothing short of a machine, spawned by the market to secure access to the docile bodies of children. It encloses them—like the bodies of the humans ("coppertops") trapped within the glowing red pods in *The Matrix*— from the nonutilitarian influences of the external social world in order to maximize the efficiency of its disciplinary processes designed to increase their utility to the market. These processes function analogously to the multiple flexible steel tubes in *The Matrix* that tap into the bodies of the coppertops in order to extract their bio-power to fuel A.I. and the machines that it spawned. In short, the traditional role of schools aims to enslave us to the market, increasing the productive capacities that we can contribute to its survival and its growth. Concurrently, in keeping with the paradox of discipline described by Foucault, accompanying processes within schools reduce our power and increase our obedience, minimizing our potential capacities for resistance by increasing our docility.

The Excessive Powers of Political Rationality: Our Current Situation

Like all models of power, of course, these fictional technologies carry their own limitations. Foucault never portrayed the functioning of power as mechanistically omnipotent and omniscient as the power of artificial intelligence is portrayed in *The Matrix*. In fact, he recoiled against such misrepresentations of his work. "If I show," Foucault once said in an interview on this topic,

> that the Panopticon was a utopia, a kind of pure form elaborated at the end of the eighteenth century, intended to supply the most convenient formula for the constant, immediate and total exercising of power, and if, then, I have revealed the genesis, the formulation of this utopia, its *raison d'être*; it is also true that I immediately showed that what we are talking about is precisely a utopia which never functioned in the form in which it existed, and that the whole history of the prison—its reality—consists precisely in its having come near this model. Certainly, there was functionality in Bentham's dream [just as there is a functionality in the Wachowski brothers' depiction of the glowing red enclosures in *The Matrix*], but there has never been a real functionality of the prison. The reality of the prison has always been grasped in diverse strategic and tactical connections which took into account a dense, weighty, blind, obscure reality. It is thus necessary to be in absolute bad faith to say that I presented a functionalist conception of the transparency of power . . . Power is not omnipotent or omniscient—quite the contrary. If power relationships have produced forms of investigations, of analysis, of models of knowledge, etc., it is precisely not because power was omniscient, but because it was blind. Because it was in a state of impasse. If it is true that so many power relationships have been developed, so many systems of control, so many forms of surveillance, it is precisely because power was always impotent.[23]

It has been precisely this blindness and impotence of power that allowed for the appearance of the multiple social movements of 1960s, 1970s, and beyond to press for the transformation of schools. What strategies and tactics, then, has power deployed to diminish the inconveniences and to counter the resistance of these movements in its efforts to restore schools to their traditional role? To answer this question, we must return to the theme of enclosure.

We see the ultimate strategy of today's counter-reformation movement in education reflected in the push toward the privatization and corporatization of schools. Private schools, of course, have always existed. Today's privatization movement, however, differs from conventional private schools. It aims to hand the traditional role of schooling over to private, for-profit corporations, such as the Edison Project. If successful, this transfer of power will create a new layer of enclosure.

As the dominant social paradigm, the market has always regarded democracy as one of the major inconveniences for the functioning of its power. The corporate privatization of schools will eliminate the inconvenience of democracy by removing the control of schools from the public/social sphere. Once this occurs, the public will lose whatever limited means it ever had for raising its voice and having its voice heard on matters concerning the purposes of education. There will no longer be any confusion over the purposes of education. The demands of the market (our A.I.) will, as they have traditionally had, determine those purposes. This is the overall strategy of the counter-reformation movement.

As for its tactics and how Foucault's ideas can help us understand them, current discourses and practices reflect the familiar Foucauldian themes of normalization, security, hierarchy, surveillance, and punishment. The normalization process began at the macro-level of policy shortly after Carter's PCNAE issued its report in 1980. Three years later, the Reagan administration's National Commission on Excellence in Education issued its report *A Nation At Risk* (NAR). This report triggered the normalization process by blaming the poor performance of schools on the reforms of the 1960s and 1970s—precisely the reforms effected under public pressure to tie the purposes of education to the demands of a functioning democracy, such as the demands for critical thinking and active participation. Furthermore, NAR cited the poor performance of schools, measured in terms of students' standardized test scores, as the principal cause behind America's economic decline in the global market. In doing so, this report made raising student scores on standardized tests a matter of national and, therefore, individual security.

Moreover, *A Nation At Risk* constituted the opening shot of an ongoing propaganda campaign aimed at normalizing the purposes of education—shaping the public mind to view schooling as a process created to increase one's economic capacities, as measured by standardized tests, to insure one's own economic security as well as the economic security of the nation. While NAR and an ensuing onslaught of other national and state reports worked to normalize this view at an intellectual level, restoring the schools to their traditional role would also require that it be normalized at a practical level. This has since been achieved through the *high-stakes testing* and *accountability* initiatives that began within individual states and, under the Bush II administration's *No Child Left Behind Act*, now have become the centerpiece of federal educational policy.

In combination, high-stakes testing and accountability situate students *and* teachers within an intensified enclosure based in part on the factory model of the school. Under this model, schools are responsible for producing a product—increased scores on standardized tests. The focus on test scores encloses the school curriculum from any inconveniences (i.e., anything that might interfere with the market utility of the forms of knowledge that students might encounter). The emphasis on testing creates a filter of sorts. Those forms of knowledge contained in the tests, controlled by state and now federal testing agencies, receive the overwhelming amount of attention, while those forms of knowledge not tested receive little, if any, attention. Not only does this filter inhibit the introduction of any ideas that might lead the coppertops (the students) to recognize their condition as slaves to the market, it has also had the effect of eliminating entire subjects from the curriculum—those subjects with the least economic utility. Some school districts, for example, have totally eliminated art and music from their schools' curriculum.

This emphasis on testing also creates an enclosure around teachers' instructional methods, also judged in terms of their economic utility—their utility toward increasing student test scores. Engaging students in learning activities aimed at cultivating independent thought or creative expression comes to be viewed as economically inefficient within the test score production process. Instructional strategies deemed most efficient intensify the disciplinary effects of schooling by requiring greater docility from students. In some schools, teachers are required to use texts and other materials that "script" their lessons, reducing their interactions with students to repetitive activities viewed as the most efficient means of "teaching to the test."

In the name of "accountability" these stultifying, albeit productive from the perspective of power, practices are enforced through patterns of hierarchical and normalizing judgment. Under *No Child Left Behind*, the federal government exerts pressure on state departments of education, who exert pressure on local school boards and superintendents, who exert pressure on building principals, who exert pressure on teachers, who exert pressure on students (and even their families) to increase standardized test scores. Those students, teachers, and schools judged to be failing become subject to punishment. Local school boards can terminate principals and teachers. Principals can deny students promotion or even graduation. The federal government can withhold funds from individual schools. Disgustingly, the schools servicing the poorest students with the fewest resources face the great risk of failing to meet *No Child Left Behind*'s outrageous requirement to have 100 percent of their students at or above grade level in reading by the end of third grade.

Even teacher preparation programs and other agencies responsible for the professional development of teachers have fallen under this umbrella of accountability. Soon their primary accrediting agency, the National Council for Accreditation of Teacher Education (NCATE), will begin assessing the quality of teacher education programs on the basis of the test scores registered by the K-12 students served by their graduates. Even though teacher education programs have no control over the professional cultures in which their graduates conduct their work, their practices cannot be left detached from the reinforcement of disciplinary power within schools. Potential teachers must only be trained in those methods that have been "scientifically proven" to raise achievement—the code word for higher test scores.

These current tactics have reached an important first stage in the larger enclosure movement to insulate schools from inconveniences emanating from the social through the eventual privatization and corporatization of schools. As late as 1993, I wrote that the archive of educational discourse was governed by one primary rule—what I termed the messianic principle of discursive inclusion. At the time, I believed that in order for your discourse to enter into the larger archive of educational discourse, you must present the school as a pastoral institution with the power to deliver the individual and/or society into some condition of secular salvation. This no longer applies. The first stage of the educational enclosure movement has placed radical new limits on what can and what cannot be said in the name of education. Whereas teachers feel compelled, if not coerced, to teach to the tests, discursive agents (researchers, policy analysts, etc.) must now *speak* to the test. Legitimate educational discourse must offer strategies and tactics for improving test scores, lest it suffer exclusion for being "irrelevant" or worse. (George W. Bush's Secretary of Education, Rod Paige, recently referred to the National Education Association—the largest teachers' union in the United States—as "a terrorist organization" because of its dissent against *No Child Left Behind*.)

The success of these tactics stems not from their ability to improve public schools, but from their ability to control educational discourse and, hence, educational practice. Not only have they enabled the state to restore schools to their traditional roles, in using high-stakes testing and accountability measures to keep students and teachers under constant surveillance, they have intensified the traditional role of the school. High-stakes testing focuses everyone's attention on increasing the market value or the use value of students (as human capital coppertops) as determined by their levels of achievement. At the same time, high-stakes testing exacts greater obedience from students as well as teachers.

Paradoxically, these tactics will ultimately ensure the failure of public schools. Under the *No Child Left Behind Act*, all students must be working at 100 percent proficiency. That includes children from extreme poverty and children with even the most profound disabilities. Historically, state planners have used third-grade reading scores to predict the number of prison cells they will need to construct over the next twenty years. Suddenly, it would seem, those planners have discovered a new faith in the remedial powers of schools. The programmed failure of schools currently underway will provide the rationalization, the political pretext for the final stage in the educational enclosure movement. No matter how "excessive" the "powers of political rationality" become, the ensuing privatization and corporatization of schools may never mirror the closed circuit of disciplinary power represented in the *Matrix* films. They will, however, continue to move schools closer in that direction.

Chapter 5

It Does Too Matter:
Michel Foucault, John Coltrane, and Dominant Positions

Tracey Nicholls
McGill University (Canada)

Michel Foucault is often credited with making space for new paths of critical inquiry (e.g., post-colonialism and queer theory) within the academy. Although his analyses of power typically offer little hope that individuals can extricate themselves from the relations that govern them, we might view the mere existence of these analyses as liberating. At the very least, they inform us of the processes of knowledge-production and social control that constrain what can be said, how it must be presented in order to qualify as knowledge, and how it will be heard. It may therefore seem odd to emphasize repressive elements within Foucault's writing, given his positioning as a resistant figure. However, this is precisely what interests me in this chapter—the extent to which a body of writings that have stimulated diversity within academic theorizing nonetheless retain traces of theoretical commitments that have been used to close down resistance and diversity. Given all that he has had to say about the structuring power of discourse, it is not surprising that a residue of formalism exists in Foucault. In an interview with Gérard Raulet, he talks about formalism as a theoretical current characterizing much of the politico-aesthetic thought of the twentieth century, including structuralism.[1] In conversation with Pierre Boulez, Foucault identifies the question of "form" as the frame within which theoretical inquiries into music have been conducted in the twentieth century.[2] Thus, it would be more surprising if Foucault had somehow managed to avoid having formalism filter into his theorizing.

The purpose of this chapter is to argue the problematic implications of formalism as a background assumption in Foucault's work, most evident in his 1979 essay "What Is an Author?" Based on my reading of this text, I want to demonstrate how Foucault's comments concerning the "death of the author" and his proposed elimination of its substitute, "the author-function," carry the residue of formalist aesthetic theory. The problem with this commitment, I shall argue, lies in formalism's capacity to function as a repressive social control mechanism within the art world, broadly construed.[3] I believe we can neutralize this "social control" function only by limiting the scope of our application of

Foucault's analysis. Furthermore, I believe we can achieve this limitation by introducing a distinction between types of artworks, a distinction grounded in cultural and aesthetic traditions and signalled in the purpose, or goal, of the artwork. I shall examine both the potentially repressive function of formalist aesthetic theory and the merits of my proposed distinction through contrasting two specific aesthetic projects which I see as exemplars: Marcel Duchamp's "ready-mades" and John Coltrane's improvisations. I contend that Duchamp's ready-mades arise from the same European aesthetic tradition that gave rise to formalist theory such that both theory and practice can, in this instance, be properly seen as organic developments internal to the tradition. Coltrane's improvisations, on the other hand, are grounded in a non-European ("Afrological")[4] tradition upon which formalism must be imposed, and is *in fact* imposed in a way that causes formalism to function as repression, rather than liberation, of possible meanings and aesthetic values, that is, causes formalism to function as a social control mechanism. To clarify, I believe that the question of whether formalism functions in a liberating or repressive way with respect to a particular artwork or artistic practice depends crucially on whether the work or practice under examination is internal to, or external to, the Eurocentric traditions which underpin formalism as an aesthetic theory.[5]

First, let me lay out my reading of the text. In the opening comments of "What Is an Author?" Foucault, quoting Beckett, poses the rhetorical question "What does it matter who is speaking?" as a starting point from which to acknowledge the "death of the author" in literary theory and draw our attention to current acceptance, in place of the author, of an "author-function."[6] This "author-function" puts the context and lived experience of the author/artist outside the bounds of our critical theorizing and substitutes an intertextuality that depends on a type-identification, using the author only as a "classificatory function."[7] But, Foucault argues, even this substitution of a posited function in place of an individual is insufficient; the power, whether of a culturally sanctioned function or of an actual person, to control the meanings we may derive from texts continues to exert its force. The author-function still permits us to restrictively group together texts whose relationships we wish to interrogate; for example, Shakespeare, qua "author-function," is the ideological figure through which we limit, exclude, and choose texts in order to close down the proliferation of meanings.[8] *True* freedom, that being the freedom to constitute meanings not sanctioned by a power structure acting upon us, would seem to be impossible until we move beyond the author-function and create a conceptual space in which we can interrogate textual meanings without reference to their moment of creation. This call for unlimited freedom to attribute meanings to artworks is what I understand Foucault to be endorsing in his comments about "the author" as an "ideological figure" who constrains "the proliferation of meaning."[9]

I believe that Foucault's endorsement of the demise of both authors and author-functions implicitly commits him to formalism based on the following textual claims. The overview of current theorizing about writing with which he begins his essay describes an artistic practice that has, in his words, "freed itself from the theme of expression."[10] Writing is no longer the activity through which a single person's thoughts are made public/accessible to others, but is instead "an interplay of signs."[11] Similarly, his account of the critic's task, as it is currently understood, is "to analyze the work through its structure, its architecture, its intrinsic form, and the play of its internal relationships."[12] These ways of understanding the creation and criticism of artworks are formalist in that they present the work as something that can, and should, be analyzed in isolation from its "creator" and on the basis of elements contained within the work itself. Formalism tells us that each of us should be able to stand before a sculpture, poem, or musical performance and, knowing nothing of the person who brought forth the work, imbue it with meanings and values derivable from the elements and relationships of elements which are "there" in the work. Foucault's formalist commitments arguably also appear at the end of the essay, where he predicts the disappearance of the author-function and the possibility that works will instead be subjected to questions about their "modes of existence"—how they can be used, circulated, and appropriated.[13] This strongly suggests an approach to works that treats them as discrete entities, theorizable only at the level of features contained within the work, and the extent to which those features differ from or resemble features found in other works. Where his comments about "modes of existence" diverge from the earlier observations about creation and criticism—thus making them *arguably* formalist rather than *clearly* formalist— is in the endorsement of appropriative possibilities, taking elements of a work and using them in other works. This is clearly a sort of intertextuality and, since intertextuality seems to be referencing the context of works (the relation of a work to other works), some may argue that the notion of formalist, or non-contextual, intertextuality is itself incoherent. I must confess here that I personally find it difficult to imagine a rich analysis of connections between works that makes no reference to the creators or moments of creation of the works under comparison.

Given this reading of Foucault's essay, I now want to identify the point of disagreement I have with his view. I share Foucault's desire to celebrate and make possible the proliferation of artistic meanings. However, I question whether identification of an author/artist always leads us to an authoritative restriction of the meanings and values we might attribute.[14] Foucault assumes that any identification of an artistic work's creator acts to suppress the meanings attributable to the artwork. While he is right to take seriously the notion of "ownership" as one of the ways in which European-influenced cultures exert power over our ability to think new or subversive thoughts, it is not at all clear to me that "ownership" functions in exactly the same way (that is, repressively) in all cultural contexts. In order to bring out the force of this worry more clearly, I want to draw on examples from within the framework of avant-garde, or experimental, artworks.

We can choose between at least two possible understandings of the purpose, or telos, of an avant-garde work. First, we might see it as an attempt to interrogate our assumptions about the nature of artworks themselves—type (i) artworks, exemplified in my description of Marcel Duchamp's introduction of the "ready-made" work. Alternatively, we might see it as an attempt to interrogate the relationship to his or her culture that the artist experiences—type (ii) artworks, exemplified by Coltrane's improvisations. In offering this distinction, I want to make clear that I am not claiming that all artworks, or even all avant-garde artworks, can have only one or the other purpose. In at least some cases, formal experimentation with the nature of artworks can be a political act. In those cases, I think it is important to both acknowledge multiple purposes and seek a pluralist framework of analysis. This distinction, then, is not intended to constrain artists to an exclusive choice of purpose; rather, it is intended to challenge the theorizer to examine the appropriateness of his or her theoretical analysis, given what we (the audience) can reasonably identify as the point, or points, the work is trying to make. Foucault's proposed approach, an attribution of meanings unconstrained by references to a work's creator, can clearly assist us in the first case, where the artist is trying to get people to see art differently, but it offers little opportunity for discourse with the artist who is trying to get people to see their cultural traditions, and by extension themselves, differently. The problem I see with Foucault's failure to recognize these two distinct teloi for artworks, and the point which I shall be concerned to make in my discussion of Coltrane's improvisations, is that we cannot legitimately assume that we all share the same cultural-aesthetic traditions, and therefore, the same interpretations of meanings and values. While this diversity of interpretations has the capacity to liberate meanings and values in type (i) works, it also has the capacity to erase them in type (ii) works precisely because divorcing them from their moment of creation erases the relationship to culture that the artist is scrutinizing.

In order to show how the application of formalist theory can entail both a liberation and a repression of artistic practices, I want now to engage the two examples that I mentioned earlier. Let me begin with an account of the example that I see as well suited to both formalist analysis and Foucault's prescription of radically unconstrained meaning—attribution—that of Marcel Duchamp's "Fountain." In 1917, the Society of Independent Artists in New York organized an "open" exhibition, one that departed from the traditions of the day by dispensing with a jury who would screen out all "inappropriate" submissions and instead announcing that the exhibition, "The Big Show," would be open to all exhibitors who paid the initiation and annual membership fees.[15] One such exhibitor, a Richard Mutt of Philadelphia, duly paid the required fees and entered his work, a porcelain urinal entitled "Fountain." Although many versions of this story have been circulated and none of these versions has ever been accorded the status of being a "true account" of events, we know two things about Richard Mutt's "Fountain." We now know that Richard Mutt was really Marcel Duchamp, and we know that, despite having met the entrance requirements, "Fountain" was never exhibited in "The Big Show."[16]

Left unresolved, however, was the question of how "Fountain" should be understood. Was it a joke or a test?[17] Given the motto of the Independents (as the society was popularly known)—"no jury, no prizes"—and the governing principle of "The Big Show"—"the independence of the work itself" —it seems clear that the only basis on which exclusion of the work from the exhibition could possibly seem legitimate is if it were deemed a joke.[18] And yet, with the passage of time, it now seems much more plausible (to me, at least) to understand Duchamp's "ready-made" as a test, a deliberate attempt to explore the limiting case of what an artwork is. It is a pivotal moment in a narrative in which formalist theory connects nineteenth-century European calls for "art for art's sake" (*l'art pour l'art*) to the later emergence of twentieth-century modern art with its focus on technique over representation. Part of "art for art's sake" was the view that one did not paint subjects; one simply painted. This shift in artistic practice led to development of language (and theory) primarily concerned with arrangement of formal elements. One of the early formalist theories, Clive Bell's 1914 attempt to explain the aesthetic merits of Post-Impressionist painting, hypothesizes that any work deserving of the label "genuine artwork" is characterized by "significant form"—which he defines as "relations and combinations of line and colour."[19] In this context, we can view Duchamp's submission of a "ready-made" object as a challenge to Bell's theory. The urinal, if presented and judged as an art object, can clearly be discussed in terms of its relations and combinations of line and colour. It thus urges an even more radical reconceptualization of the nature of the artwork than formalist theories had anticipated; "Fountain" takes seriously the idea that representation, or "message," is not the essential criterion by which an artwork ought to be judged, and poses the further question of why creatability ought to be a necessary condition of artworks. If only formal elements matter, "found" objects would seem to have as legitimate a claim to being art as "made" objects.

Formalism's focus on the artwork as a self-justifying entity liberated artists of the nineteenth century in two ways. It removed from them the imperative to create works in the representationalist tradition, and it provided them with theoretical grounds for resistance against the established practice of jury-administered *salons*.[20] Both of these liberating effects can be seen to manifest themselves in the circumstances surrounding Duchamp's work; the urinal, as an artwork, is not clearly representing (symbolizing) anything "outside" itself and the very notion of an open exhibition was a clear act of resistance against the guild principle of juried *salons*. Later artists working in avant-garde/experimental streams of European-American aesthetic traditions can be understood as taking up the challenge of Duchamp's test. The "ready-made" proved that an artwork did not necessarily need to meet the criterion of creation. Found objects, appropriately presented, could also qualify as artworks. Some of these later artists did exactly what Foucault suggests can be done with works once the author-function is eliminated. They used, circulated, and appropriated the notion of the found, or ready-made, object, refining the notion to the point that, in conceptual art, the "work" is simply an idea that may (or may not) be documented by a photograph or brief write-up. Taken to these extremes, works challenging the nature of the artwork also challenge the relevance of formalist theory. If there is no tangible object, how do we even identify, let alone assess the aesthetic merits of, the work's formal elements?

This move toward intangibility in avant-garde works introduces an interesting parallelism with avant-garde music. If we understand musical works as performances (rather than scores),[21] we see that music, much like the conceptual works of artists like Vito Acconci and Robert Barry, is also non-corporeal and endures over time only through some kind of documentation (be it scoring/transcription or recording). The worry, then, is that formalist approaches, entailing consideration of the musical work in isolation, present the same pitfalls in theorizing, say, Coltrane's "free jazz" improvisations as they do in theorizing conceptual art. How do we theorize the aesthetic merits of an improvised piece that is never transcribed? How relevant can formalism be to these types of works? These are precisely the kind of questions that are ruled out by Eurocentric analyses of jazz. Improvisation is explained in this framework as "real-time composition" and tempts one to believe uncritically that the improviser practices of African-American jazz musicians can be subsumed within a compositional framework of carefully arranged formal elements. Indeed, this temptation has driven much of the mainstream jazz journalism and criticism of the 1950s and 1960s, notably the analyses to be found in the American jazz periodical *Down Beat*. A good example can be found in journalist Ira Gitler's profile "'Trane on the Track," originally published in *Down Beat* on October 16, 1958. Gitler poses his questions about Coltrane's then-current style in purely formal terms: the much-quoted description of Coltrane's multi-note playing as "sheets of sound."[22] In fact, he talks about Coltrane's work without ever questioning what goals or social context might motivate that work. This is problematic because Coltrane, although somewhat reserved when he was being interviewed, was very articulate about his artistic development, goals, and influences and took great pains to situate himself within jazz traditions.

Even when Coltrane articulates his artistic "code of conduct": "Keep listening . . . Live cleanly . . . Do right . . . You can improve as a player by improving as a person,"[23] and characterizes this improvement as a duty that the player owes himself, Gitler leaves unexamined the obvious questions about what "doing right" and "improving as a person" might mean and what connection they might have to the kind of music Coltrane is trying to bring forth. In the writings of a much more sympathetic and sensitive interviewer, historian and freelance reviewer Frank Kofsky, however, this connection between the person and the music is made explicit. So when Kofsky thinks to question Coltrane about whether his music is commenting on social and political issues, we see Coltrane affirming that he does make a conscious effort to do so. "When there's something we think could be better, we must make an effort to try and make it better."[24] In the context of the interview with Kofsky, it is quite clear that this "doing better," this relentless desire to improve, is a principle that Coltrane applies to all aspects of life. It explains both his commitment to personal artistic development and his recognition of the role that social commentary/activism plays within the jazz world. Evidence that Coltrane understands the goals of his artistic projects in the context of both his own body of work and the works produced by others is even clearer in his declaration that "I want to progress, but I don't want to go so far out that I can't see what others are doing."[25] This attention to what others are doing is often explained by reference to the "dialogicality" of jazz—the extent to which, as an artistic practice, jazz represents a conversation (dialogue) among jazz musicians. One of the goals of jazz, then, is to respond not just to the music created by others but also to the others themselves. This imperative of response is a central point in Henry Louis Gates Jr.'s development of a distinctly African-American literary theory: responding to and revising other contributions to the art (a practice that Gates labels "signifyin[g]") is an artistic practice that is aesthetically valuable in African-American cultural traditions, and recognition of this contextually-grounded "call and response" practice is lost when the work in question is assessed in isolation.[26] Both Coltrane's mastery of this practice and the non-European—or, suggests Kofsky, counter-European—direction of his music during the 1960s, leads Kofsky to describe Coltrane as "the clearest possible expression of the African American mentality in the second half of the twentieth century: the quintessential distillation, conceivably, of what it meant to be black in that time and place."[27] The failure of mainstream critics to see the relevance of the musician's personal situation to the musical work is explained by Kofsky as part of "a decades-long tale of white incomprehension or outright rejection of black musical art."[28]

In the socialist newspaper *The Militant*, Kofsky reviewer Sam Manuel notes (no doubt paraphrasing jazz great Archie Shepp) that black musicians may create the art, but wealthy white businessmen own the means of production and distribution.[29] This racial divide is significant in that both Manuel and Kofsky implicate racism in the motivation for a jazz journalism predicated upon formalist analysis. The group of critics exemplified by Gitler offer us a tendentious view of avant-garde jazz music, one which severs formal criteria and stylistic trends from their cultural context, because of what Kofsky identifies elsewhere, in his book *Black Nationalism and the Revolution in Music*, as a "curious dichotomy" in the thinking of many white Americans, circa the 1960s.[30] Those outside the jazz world apparently had few qualms about acknowledging jazz as a black cultural tradition, although they resisted acknowledging it as an art worthy of their respect.[31] An example of this strand of thought can be seen in German theorist Theodor Adorno's contention that jazz has no aesthetic merit because all of its allegedly "new and original" musical features, such as syncopation, are already to be found in Stravinsky's musical experimentations.[32] Those inside the jazz world (the critics, producers, etc. whom Kofsky labels the "semi-literati"), on the other hand, were quite insistent about jazz's artistic merits but, for the most part, vehemently denied that there was anything black about it.[33] They quite deliberately presented the music as "an American music, that everybody plays equally"[34]—in contradistinction to understanding it as an "African-American music." Formalism aided these attempts to erase the cultural traditions from which jazz is derived by giving the critics a language in which they could endorse its claim to being art without conceding its roots in African-American culture. Analysis conducted with an emphasis on the formal elements of the music lent credence to their position that jazz was a musical product of mainstream—that is, white—American culture.

So the point I made earlier in clarifying my disagreement with Foucault—that "ownership" does not function in exactly the same way in all cultural contexts—should now be clearer. In the jazz world, we see the music industry using formalism to repress artistic meanings and aesthetic values, as opposed to Foucault's worry about authors using their authority to repress meanings. Here formalism enables precisely the sort of social control that I think Foucault would (should) find the most objectionable. Formalism is used as a cover for socially institutionalized racism that, in my view, gives us strong prima facie grounds to reject its use in this context. A further reason to reject its application to jazz lies in its status as a nonorganic imposition upon a different cultural tradition: it misrepresents, or erases, the goals of the artistic practice, thus repressing meanings and values derivable from musical works developed within this tradition. The corrective measure that I think we need to employ in this case is the distinction I proposed earlier: a limitation of scope for Foucault's formalist-inspired call for proliferation of meanings. Where the work is referencing European and American traditions of artistic practice and the work's goal is clearly to question the nature of artworks themselves, formalism's repressive potential is arguably benign and it can clearly be a fruitful theoretical tool. Where the work is coming out of a tradition to which formalism is alien and the goal of the work is bound up in the context of the artist and his or her social relations, application of formalism needs to be carefully examined to ensure that it does not close off the very proliferation that Foucault and I both ardently desire. This worry is particularly acute within theorizing about jazz because, as Ajay Heble observes in his discussion of Fred Wei-han Ho in *Landing on the Wrong Note*, jazz is not just outside of the Eurocentric tradition; it is, in many instances and incarnations, *opposed to* that tradition.[35]

Thus, in closing, I would like to say, in response to Foucault and Beckett, that in at least some cases, yes, it does too matter who is speaking.

Part III

Psychiatry

Chapter 6

Foucault and Psychiatric Power after *Madness and Civilization*

Mario Colucci
University of Trieste (Italy)

Pouvoir psychiatrique, Michel Foucault's course at the Collège de France in 1973-74, provides a key to understanding one of the most crucial periods in his intellectual journey. We could characterize this period as Foucault's "leap into practice," that moment when he committed himself to number of political movements in the wake of 1968 to contest the power of normalizing and disciplinary institutions. It should not surprise us that issues surrounding psychiatric practices and their accompanying legal apparatus provided the catalyst for Foucault's political engagement. We might even view his activism as an outgrowth of his publication of *Histoire de la folie* (*Madness and Civilization: A History of Insanity in the Age of Reason*). His inquiries into the history of psychiatry (power, knowledge, institutions, statements) ran forcefully through all his work. With the publication of *Pouvoir psychiatrique*, Foucault added—if he would forgive us the Darwinian allusion—the missing link in the chain of evolution of this thinking.

The basic tenets of *Pouvoir psychiatrique* had already existed, it is true, and had been widely circulated in Italy. Indeed, Foucault had proposed these himself (in a revised version) to Franco Basaglia in a collective publication that had a major impact in the 1970s.[1]

In the process of developing and delivering this course, however, Foucault entered into one of the most productive phases of his career. Ironically, it was also a phase in which he questioned himself and his own entanglements in the complex relations between theory and practice, between philosophical passion and political involvement. As we can deduce from his numerous interviews during these years, the questions about psychiatry clearly led to Foucault's turn toward militancy.[2]

Independently of this "new" interest in political practice and resistance to power, the law was already looming on Foucault's intellectual horizon and led during these years to his overt militancy with the creation of the *Groupe d'Information sur les Prisons* (GIP). We should remember, of course, that Foucault's commitment to activism took place alongside other struggles revolving around the same or similar issues. We could point, for example, to the anti-psychiatry movements that were emerging in Italy with Basaglia (who neverthe-less refused the label of "anti-psychiatry"),[3] in England with Laing and Cooper, in the United States with Szasz, and to some extent in France. They always served as central points of reference, seeming to remind Foucault of the extent to which the traditional role of the intellectual was outdated when limited to teach-ing and writing, and how it was necessary to move in the direction of political practice. After 1968, Foucault devoted much of his intellectual energy to devel-oping his relations with the psychiatric protest movements. It was also through these relationships, however, that he began to doubt the effectiveness of his in-tellectual experience, eventuating in his premonition of an urgent need to change his approach to political practice. While many within the anti-psychiatry move-ment used *Histoire de la folie* as historical justification for the political actions born of their own ideas and initiatives, the course on psychiatric power provided Foucault with an opportunity to rethink its message and its implications for po-litical struggles.

Foucault's Project

Despite the centrality of *Histoire de la folie* in Foucault's œuvre, it contains surprisingly little of the overall significance that Foucault's ideas brought to the political debate on the disciplinary functioning of psychiatry. On the one hand, as Foucault himself insisted, his history was essentially not a history of psychia-try but of madness itself.[4] In the 1961 preface (omitted from subsequent edi-tions), he rejected any reference to the idea of psychiatric "truth," calling instead for a language capable of reconstructing the experience of madness at the mo-ment that it separated itself from the language of reasoning.[5] This should not imply that Foucault sought such a language in order to describe an original, primitive, pure form of madness. He understood that writing the history of madness meant studying the whole historical nexus (notions, institutions, legal and policing measures, scientific concepts) that held the primitive state of madness captive.[6] Concurrently, he concluded *Histoire de la folie* with an analysis of representations; that is, the image that people had of madness in the Classical Age.[7] Twelve years later, in devoting his entire 1973-74 course to the theme of psychiatric power, Foucault returned to that discussion, while at the same time changing the object of his analysis. No longer focusing on questions of the representations of the mentalities and perceptions of madness, Foucault shifted to an analysis of the apparatus of psychiatric power itself—how it functioned as an authority that, itself, produced statements (*énoncés*) and discourse and, consequently, representations of madness. In other words, he reversed the principle of his research, focusing on psychiatry and contiguous fields such as psychology, psychoanalysis, pedagogy, criminology, and so on.

On the other hand, Foucault also altered the temporal axis of his inquiry. In the *Histoire de la folie*, he focused on the Classical Age (more precisely from 1657, with the creation of the General Hospital and the beginning of the *grand renfermement* [great internment] of the poor in France, up to 1794, when Pinel freed the inmates chained up at Bicêtre) that marked a passage between two eras and two mentalities. In *Le pouvoir psychiatrique*, however, he directed his attention to the nineteenth and twentieth centuries, indeed to the contemporary era. While his new focus centered most particularly on the contemporary situation, earlier reactions to madness, (e.g., those found in the religious communities of the Middle Ages and the treatment of George III), lost none of their relevance for Foucault's analysis, assisting him in tracing the affinities between past and present systems of psychiatric power.[8]

Following the publication of *Histoire de la folie*, Foucault had to frequently defend himself from the severe and often mischievous critics who accused him of being a *psychiatricide* intent on destroying everything psychiatry stood for, and of having reduced mental illness to no more than a cultural phenomenon.[9] Initially, failing to understand why contemporary psychiatrists would feel threatened by his book, he responded by saying that he was not talking about the present but only of the perception of madness in the Classical Age. In the 1970s, however, Foucault stopped being cautious and chose to speak openly about the contemporary context. This constituted a crucial change that demonstrates the full significance of the course at the Collège de France on psychiatric power.

The Anti-Psychiatry Projects

The initial public reaction to *Histoire de la folie* was rough, since the book proved to be difficult to read.[10] For the first few years, the book sold poorly and Foucault doubted the validity of his own language.[11] He ended up, completely unexpectedly, authorizing its publication in a shorter paperback edition. Unfortunately, it was this abbreviated paperback edition that was translated in 1965 as *Madness and Civilization* and began circulating within the emerging English-speaking circles of the anti-psychiatry movement. But it was also this version that provided the catalyst for his success. In France, the work was initially adopted in academic circles, being read as a doctoral thesis, an academic work on a philosophical subject, a theoretical project on how to conceive of a discourse on madness, which had nothing to do with psychiatry, psychology. or institutional practices. So, particularly at the beginning, the book gained attention in academic rather than clinical circles, in line with the epistemological research of the time. It was only later, in 1968, that it came to be seen as the *porte-parole* of anti-psychiatry and severely attacked by the French psychiatric establishment.

Its reception in England was very different. Once circulated, the book was well received and "used" in the community of psychiatrists and psychoanalysts in which Ronald Laing and David Cooper, among others, were developing their opposition to classical psychiatry. This opened up new, alternative practices, such as the running of Pavilion 21, which had already begun in 1962 in a London psychiatric hospital, or creating household communities, protected housing outside the asylums, among them Kingsley Hall, where Mary Barnes had lived. English anti-psychiatry rejected traditional science, accusing it of having violent consequences on the treatment of madness within a more generalized and repressive ideology exercised by the society, the family, and other institutions. English anti-psychiatry also defended the idea that schizophrenia was a creative and purifying journey, requiring protection from medicalization in order to bloom as a sublime experience.

For Laing, Cooper, Esterson, and all who identified with this movement, Foucault's book became an extraordinary tool providing support for experiments still at the embryonic stage. The text was attributed, not without some exaggeration, a political value that clearly it did not have when it first appeared. Foucault was even quoted for claims he had never intended to make. But he understood that this was inevitable, attributing it to the uncontrollable destiny of any book and to the imprecise definition of what constitutes an author.[12] Reading a work does not just consist of criticizing it, but it may also generate unconditional and sometimes excessive infatuation, resulting in interpretations that may completely distort the author's intentions. It is neither possible nor legitimate to stop any such proliferation; the text must stand as it is without the author exercising his tyranny and prescribing his law.[13]

But in a 1971 interview, Foucault tells us that this historical work in the book was in the process of generating a practical outcome, of which he was somewhat envious.[14] This is proof of his rapport with anti-psychiatry—changing so fast and becoming so controversial, at one moment characterized by Foucault adopting a certain distance, then associating with the new movement, always underpinned, in any case, by his subtle curiosity if not by his very strong fascination verging on jealousy.[15] Foucault felt himself being short-circuited by the anti-psychiatry struggles, as if his ideas had been a theoretical detonator causing the practices to explode, producing an unanticipated political effect, one that he had not been able to foresee, and which made him into a front-line protagonist in the struggle. His militant involvement emerged some years later, at the beginning of the 1970s, with the problem of prisons. It all happened as if Foucault, in this interview, was staggering under the blow and, because of these new practices, was forced to reflect upon his theoretical interest in madness.

But there remained a number of basic perplexities. He did not at all, for instance, share the central thesis of anti-psychiatry—the idea of a repressive power that crushes the so-called freedom of madness. Certainly, this was a fascinating image and one that had its disciples, but it failed to take into account the complexities of the specific functioning of psychiatric power. Those complexities became the focus of Foucault's 1973 course—*Pouvoir psychiatrique*.[16]

The position of anyone who says he is opposing the strategies of psychiatric power, if he is only contesting the violence contained within that power, is suspect and, to say the least, naïve. The image of a struggle which would provide freedom from the injustices of repressive authority clearly ends up coming too close to reproducing the hagiographic image that, strangely, psychiatry has revived as its founding myth: Pinel's unchaining of the insane. As if one could change the dynamics of the functioning of this power simply by eliminating what has remained of coercion and brutality. Seen in its microphysics, with its micro-political ramifications, power is always violent, but at the same time, rational.[17]

In the *Histoire de la folie*, Foucault had already used notions such as *violence* and *institution*, but, in the context of psychiatric power, these no longer seemed adequate.[18] Most of the anti-psychiatry and psychological analyses that had preceded his book continued to thrive and showed no sign of being abandoned. Foucault "reproached" anti-psychiatry, therefore, for wanting to continue asking the question of the history of psychiatry exclusively through these notions, in an "institutionalist"[19] perspective, focusing on the institution as a place in which violence was practiced. There was no doubting the horror of the violence, certainly. But this was not, in Foucault's eyes, the principal problem. In bringing the brutality of psychiatric power and the suppression of individual rights to the forefront, one ends up masking the real historical question about psychiatry: the relationship between psychiatric practice and the discourse on truth.[20]

"As for the hysterics, these famous and dear hysterics"

We should not attribute Foucault's interest in anti-psychiatry movements to the manner in which they posed the question of psychiatric power. This power is affected by a particular ideology, a particular Freudo-Marxism that chose as its battle-horse the concepts of "ideology" and "repression," reflecting a purely legal conception of power, founded on sovereignty and interdiction, on *right* defeating *violence*. But this conception is completely inadequate when elucidating the complex links created between the force of domination and the potential for revolt, between flexible control and disguised subordination, between directing consciousness and the constitution of the self.

This leads us to a crucial scene at the conclusion of Foucault's course on psychiatric power concerning the issue of the subtle relationship between Charcot and his hysterics, of the dissimulation of truth and the sudden explosion of truth. Sexuality is at the core of this perverse relationship, first misunderstood and minimized, then recognized in hushed tones, finally exorcised and ridiculed. At a fashionable reception, Charcot confided ironically to a colleague that there was indeed a link between hysteria and sexuality.[21] Freud, who was there at the same time, was astonished—almost paralyzed. He asked himself: If he knows that, why doesn't he come out and say it?[22] Charcot would forget about this link between sexuality and hysteria—before returning to it some years later when he developed his theory of the sexual etiology of neuroses.

These "famous and dear hysterics"[23] are, as Foucault calls them, anti-psychiatry's real militants,[24] for they were the first capable of opening up a space to escape from the truth imposed in the psychiatric hospitals. For this reason, they represent the defense against the diagnosis of *dementia*, against a classification of madness understood in terms of lost capacities as a feebleness of the mind. They stand against madness reduced to a reality imposed by psychiatric power—a sick person without symptoms, without crises, without violence, totally subjugated to the discipline of the asylum, not only for the docility of their behavior but equally for the absence of any specific pathological manifestations. It was a matter of being just the "poor madman," nothing more than that! All his reality is there, in the asylum that was constructed for him, and where he would live out his destiny. The hysterics opposed the psychiatric abuse of power by exaggerating all their symptoms and by exhibiting, with an unheard-of magnificence, the spectacle of their sickness. For Foucault, this was not a sign of disease, but a phenomenon of struggle.[25]

The answer of the mad to psychiatric power was to simulate madness within madness.[26] By doing this, they created a frontline of resistance to psychiatric power. These were its first militants. It was the most insidious way the mad could ask psychiatric power—that sought to impose its own reality—the question about truth.[27] Could we then conceive of a history of psychiatry revolving around the mad, instead of around the psychiatrist and his knowledge? Of course, this would be difficult if it were to start with hysterics. Their front of resistance, after all, relied on offering up the body—and it is precisely through the body that they unconsciously gave medicine the opportunity for self-renewal. In their efforts to escape the power of the asylum, with its diagnostic abuse of dementia and the excessive medicalization of madness, they ended up by hypermedicalizing their own condition, which, as Charcot had admitted, was less a matter of illness than a question of sexuality.

If the history of anti-psychiatry began when Charcot produced the hysterical crises that he described[28] eighty years before Laing, Cooper, and Basaglia, one can say that these beginnings were ambiguous. First, there was the ambiguity of Charcot, the master of madness who, in attempting to make madness submit to the definitive and uncontested power of psychiatry, ended up compromising this same power by provoking the suspicion of contagion and artifice. Second, there was the ambiguity of the hysterics themselves who, in trying to elude this power, provided it with the possibility of regeneration in other forms. This is why Freud was not an innocent observer of this scene. Foucault fully understood, at a time when psychoanalysis was triumphant, that it was not solely a question of transforming and adopting the powers of the medical figure.[29] Psychoanalysis did not just take up and exploit this role. On the contrary, it allowed psychiatry to reconstruct itself as medical truth by orienting its research toward a new object of study: sexuality. This, for Foucault, was our "great misfortune."[30]

Freud's *good genie, bad genie* managed to get us to submit to the "austere monarchy of sex" and made us believe that "our 'liberation' is in the balance."[31] Believing that we can be liberated is nothing but a pure illusion. You don't free yourself of psychiatry by fighting against the violence, the institution, or the moral doctrine. Saying "yes" to sex does not mean saying "no" to power. Liberation is a long and difficult process of struggle against the pathologization of daily life, against the dissemination of a medical truth controlling all discourse. What disturbs Foucault the most in psychiatry is the extension of the category of the illness beyond the walls of the institutional asylum.[32] So the struggle is not just against the psychiatric institution itself, but also in recognizing its tentacles throughout the fabric of our society, the dissemination of what Foucault called "the *Psy* function, in other words the function that is psychiatric, psychopatho-logical, psycho-sociological, psycho-criminological, psychoanalytic, etc. . . ." all related to discourse, the institution, and the psychological individual.[33]

The Inmates in Gorizia

It is likely that the position taken by Basaglia, and more generally the position of the Italian movement of institutional psychiatry, provided Foucault with new elements for reflection. Basaglia never tired of reminding those who did not share his battle that identifying the enemy against which one can fight (the social system, capitalism, etc.), in fact, interferes with the real motive of the struggle.[34] Action required a precise focus within one's own sphere of competence and daily practice.[35]

In other words, as early as the 1970s, at Gorizia and then at Trieste, Basaglia recognized a contradiction between the negation and the exercise of institutional power. The new psychiatric professionals coming out of the student uprisings leaned too frequently and too strongly toward the negation of that power. They failed to consider that the psychiatric institutions in which they carried out their work functioned as established organizations of power and ideology. They could not simply disregard the general level of social acceptance enjoyed by those institutions. Closeting oneself behind their negation to avoid any compromise in the daily running of the total institution would not suffice. One could not simply advocate the general freedom of madness without addressing the everyday rules of the functioning of the psychiatric machine. This issue became a point of discord for both Basaglia and Foucault with English anti-psychiatry, based as it was on the principles of liberation. They rejected that movement's vague and sterilely anti-scientific attempt to escape the institutional contradiction. That contradiction should have been at the center of the dialectic, all the more so because English anti-psychiatry did not, in the end, manage to significantly influence either the specific practices or the general policies of psychiatry.

The Italian position cannot, therefore, be neatly packaged with other anti-psychiatry experiments. It is not by accident that, when he was asked whether the experience created with GIP could extend to psychiatric hospitals in France, Foucault answered that he was continually preoccupied with the psychiatrization of everyday life. He added that the struggle of patients against the institutional asylum would be much harder to advance as a collective and political refusal of the system. He doubted that the so-called diseased, subjugated to segregation in the asylum, could protest their exclusion insofar as they are judged to be "mentally ill."[36] Psychiatric patients clearly do not have the same options as the prison inmates of the GIP, and their struggle appears more difficult. Foucault recognized, however, that Basaglia had tried experiments of this kind in Italy.[37] This interview dates from 1971, as said, and it is quite possible that Foucault had read Basaglia's *L'institution en négation*, which had just been translated into French. We can hardly doubt that he had understood the difference between the experiments of Basaglia and the others (Laing, Cooper, Szasz, the French experiences, etc.). He understood that the purpose of the Gorizia meetings was not therapeutic but political.[38]

The Gorizia meetings were organized to protest and contest, and to ensure that the discourse produced would be transferred from the psychiatrist to the interned. Therapy starts from the moment that the interned have an opportunity to express themselves, particularly those who oppose such internment, since one has to give them back the possibility of still expressing the aggression which is their only resource against institutional annihilation.[39] Here we see a complete reversal of the clinic and of the role that the social organization attributes to the doctor: to count on aggression, on the "strength of madness," which has historically been the target of the repressive intervention of psychiatry.[40] Such aggression intends not to suffocate that strength, but to enable the interned to rediscover their subjectivity in acts of resistance to scientific rationalization. Siding with the aggression of the interned represents the only way to break with the authoritarian and paternalistic rapports of institutionalization,[41] the only way to achieve an egalitarian rapport.[42]

The Infamous Men

In January 1976, when he began his course "Society must be defended" ("Il faut défendre la société") Foucault returned to the anti-psychiatry struggles to demonstrate the novelty and strength of "local" critical discourse in contradistinction to so-called exact science or, for that matter, such all-embracing theories as Marxism or psychoanalysis. The anti-psychiatry struggles were the prototype of an insurrection of subjugated knowledge, which made concrete action of resistance to disciplinary power possible.[43]

Foucault then discovered a surprising effect: the individual who opposes and resists power is just the principal effect of this same power or, at least, the opportunity which allows power to assert and perpetuate itself. Yet, if power really operates as a procedure in the construction of subjects, if the rapports of power can only exist in the service of multiple points of resistance,[44] can there be anything beyond what power says and does? When Foucault talks about "centers of resistance" ("foyers de résistance") at least up until La volonté de savoir, he does not really explain if and how these are constituted, beyond being in contact with power.[45] This issue caused the greatest consternation for Foucault throughout the latter years of his life. It also explains his decision to radically modify the Histoire de la sexualité project after the publication of the first volume.[46] This was the discovery of subjectivization as a process of resisting all objectivizations and going beyond the subject considered as a substance, an identity, or a person, and toward the production of a means of existing.

It was in light of this that Foucault introduced a possible new figure in the resistance to power. We can understand this new figure through the fragmented histories of minor and widely dispersed insurrections.[47] This is the history of lost lives, sometimes of long-forgotten individual acts, of fragments of facts from the past, of reports so brief and exemplary that they seem to belong less to life than to literature. "The Life of Infamous Men" (*"La vie des hommes infâmes"*), a short work of the mid-1970s, bears the signs of this. It appeared as the result of Foucault's long exploration in the internment archives of the *Hôpital Général* and of the Bastille. Beginning with the production of *Histoire de la folie*, this investigation would lead to an anthology of the *lettres de cachet*.[48] These are short but stunning and disturbing histories. Take the story of Mathurin Milan, who was assigned to the Charenton hospital on 31 August 1707 and whose madness consisted of hiding from his family to lead an obscure life in the countryside.[49] Or that of Jean-Antoine Touzard who was confined at the Château de Bicêtre on 21 April 1701 after being found guilty of committing sodomy and being an atheist.[50]

But where do all these infamous lives come from? For Foucault, these men are only on record because of a few "terrible words" thrown at them to disgrace them.[51] Is this another case of the delineation of power, of the incapacity of going beyond it, of going beyond struggling against one's own strength? No. This time there is something more. Foucault was writing here in the first person, even more explicitly than he had ever done before, writing of his "terror," of the "vibration" he felt in making contact with these words, words that had resurfaced precipitously after centuries of silence and within which a man's destiny has been decided.[52] It is Foucault himself who is there, directly confronting these stories and visibly disturbed.[53] It is strangely shocking that he was so affected, he who should have become accustomed to encounters with atrocities through the *lettres de cachet*, the police reports, the royal orders. Years after the *Histoire de la folie*, his encounter with the lives etched in the archives shakes him again.[54]

Why did these stories, which belong neither to history nor to literature, have such a disturbing effect on Foucault? Why did he exhume these secular accounts, while he could simply have continued establishing the micro-history of anti-psychiatry struggles and described the insurrections of his own times? [55]

Foucault understood before anyone else that the old forces of resistance to power are no longer able to explain changes taking place. The infamous man, in his abjection and his extravagance, is perhaps the new figure that Foucault would put in a genealogy of possible resistances. After the hysteric, who offered her body up to Charcot, after the inmate of Gorizia who resisted by the insurrection through his voice, there is now the infamous man, without either body or voice, and his "purely verbal existence"—*"pure existence verbale."*[56] He exists solely in the few words which power has uttered to crush him. His existence rests enclosed in its sarcophagus of phrases to which no appeal is possible, which can neither talk to us nor touch us, yet which still haunts us with the abysmal discourse with which he has been embalmed. His protest constitutes neither a symptom nor an act of revolt. It signifies neither an act of seduction nor of aggression. It is a life that lives on in what it possesses in its darkest and deafest recesses: coagulated blood in the extinguished heart of the discourse, the ultimate level of resistance, an anonymous resistance, fortuitous and silent, situated beyond the conflict with power. Anonymous because these lives are faceless,[57] fortuitous because their presence is the result of chance,[58] and silent because their resistance, consisting of those few words that have survived, is paradoxically mute. Their actions do not have a voice. And it is precisely in the opposition between a tacit and obscure presence and the light of sovereignty and of discipline that we can recognize the extreme example of resistance: to divest oneself silently of power's control.

Paradoxically, it is this infamy, at the same time both tragic and comic, that Foucault wanted to protect. This is perhaps why "The Life of Infamous Men" is "a beautiful comic master-piece" as Gilles Deleuze suggested.[59] It resonates not only with the distress that one would expect from encountering these harrowing lives, but also the laughter—the kind provoked by the impossible desire of wanting to belong to one of these existences, by the temptation to disappear in order to reappear in a way that is entirely unpredictable or, perhaps, never to reappear. Herein lies Foucault's extreme subjectivation, the existential aesthetic of his last years, his secret form of resistance within the folds of power, his defense of an ethical autonomy. It represents an abstemious style, a lucid and measured choice of words, an attentive and ironic regard, and finally the search for a silent freedom—that way of always losing himself, as Deleuze described it so well.[60]

Chapter 7

From Psychiatry to Bio-Politics
or the Birth of the Bio-Security State

Pierangelo Di Vittorio
University of Bari (Italy)

The currently voguish use of the term "bio-politics" stems from important theoretical advances such as those of Giorgio Agamben and Toni Negri. [1] For these authors, Foucault's death cut short his efforts to complete his theoretical project on power, generating the need for a philosophical supplement to bring that project to its conclusion. Attempts at generating such a supplement have become commonplace among those taking up the challenge of returning "philosophically" to Foucault. While we may lament the absence of some decisive element within Foucault's own efforts to elaborate a satisfactorily complete statement on the concept of bio-politics, we must also ask ourselves if our post-Foucauldian attempts to conceptualize bio-politics do not threaten to diminish, if not negate, his critical attitude by encapsulating it within philosophy. We should recognize the danger of treating his work as wholly philosophical, for while we may sometimes witness his critique operating within the bounds of philosophy, we also encounter many instances when it operates beyond philosophy.[2] There is a definite distinction between philosophy and criticism, between philosophy and the philosophical *ethos*. In fact, this latter is a double attitude, at once both critical and experimental.

It is clear that one of Foucault's most strongly-held and long-lasting concerns was to delimit the "theoretical" in general, to combat the tyranny of truth and all forms of theoretical avant-gardism. Toward the mid-1970s, looking back on his work at the Collège de France, Foucault came to recognize that all this research, which looked fragmentary and discontinuous, reflected the traits of the larger historical period in which it appeared. A number of extraordinarily effective and diverse offensives marked this era, directed against the institutional practices of psychiatry, against the judicial and penal apparatus, and against moral philosophy or the traditional sexual hierarchy.[3] Foucault had contributed to these struggles with his scholarly historical analyses, as well as with his militancy with the *Groupe d'Information sur les Prisons* GIP. This period witnessed a profound moment of openness in which the range of things open to critique and resistance (institutions, practices, and discourse) seemed limitless. Yet, alongside this astonishing openness, one discovered also the inhibiting effect of totalitarian and all-encompassing theories.[4] Foucault's diagnosis was that the critique had an essentially "local" character. On the other hand, efforts to incorporate Foucault's ideas into some totalizing theory (e.g., Marxism, Freudo-marxism, anarchism, Maoism, psychoanalysis, etc.) threw a brake on the critique itself as well as the fundamental struggles.[5] Foucault not only refused to provide a continuous and solid grounding for these dispersed genealogies, but he continued forcefully in his wide-ranging analysis of the different mechanisms of power by tackling the theoretical question "What is power?" He denounced its inhibiting effects on the emergence of criticism at the local level, in the absence of which it is probably impossible to open up a strategic space; that is, to transform truth and rights into political stakes. From this perspective, it appears completely illegitimate to envisage or assume that Foucault would have wanted to make the notion of bio-politics the theoretical summit of his research. On the contrary, we could say that if he did hold a "theory of power," it was limited to asserting the uselessness and strategic inappropriateness of theorizing about this.

So, beyond any judgment about legitimacy, the question then arises about the possible uses of the set of tools developed by Foucault. What space, which possibilities, were opened up by Foucault? We can use the notion of bio-politics either as a theoretical/exploratory tool, reflecting the reality of a unitary totality of meanings, or as a sort of critical echo of current struggles, an echo that allows us to acquire a perception of the present. In this sense, we should use the notion of bio-politics to make a "topographical survey" of ongoing struggles,[6] criticism being precisely a suspended event, like a footbridge between the historian's critical knowledge and the critique currently being produced by popular struggles and the knowledge being acquired through these struggles. As for the possible uses of the term bio-politics, the case of Italy may seem a bit bizarre, but not completely without interest. If, indeed, bio-politics plays an unquestionable role in the economy of important philosophical works that aim to go beyond Foucault in seeking a more complete theorization,[7] the concept of bio-politics is almost absent in the thinking of the psychiatrists linked to the anti-institutional movement around Franco Basaglia.[8] In the 1960s and 1970s, this movement, thanks in part to support provided by *Madness and Civilization*,[9] gave rise to a radical critique of the psychiatric system which culminated in the abolition of psychiatric hospitals. This is why we might have expected this local critique, which arose under the banner of the struggle against the asylum, to have been pursued in the more "advanced" field of bio-politics. Basaglia had, moreover, begun to analyze this new dimension of psychiatry in the mid-1960s, somewhat earlier than Foucault.[10] Foucault himself, following his initial "naive" genealogies (*Madness and Civilization* and *The Birth of the Clinic*) and his "diversion" following *The Order of Things* and *The Archaeology of Knowledge*, returned to genealogy only after May 1968.[11] We see this return both in his courses at the Collège de France and in *Discipline and Punish*.

The courses at the Collège de France confirm Foucault's renewed interest in the question of psychiatry. His analyses of medico-legal expertise, which were featured during his Monday lectures, constituted a common thread running from his first course entitled *La volonté de savoir* (1970-71) continuing through to *Pouvoir psychiatrique* (1973-74)[12] and *Les anormaux* (1974-75),[13] ending finally with *Il faut défendre la société* (1975-76).[14] This continuity shows that psychiatry, more particularly the analysis of the evolution of medico-legal expertise and the notion of the dangerous individual, had become the terrain in which Foucault began to outline the technology of power that would later become designated as bio-politics. But the critical and specific use of the term *bio-politics*, which nearly became accepted in Italy, never actually occurred. On the contrary, the theoretical and all-encompassing use of the term, which had not been foreseen, has today become widespread if not excessive.

We can propose a hypothesis to account for the lack of appeal that bio-politics has had for Italian psychiatrists. As already mentioned, Basaglia had begun to tackle bio-political psychiatry in the mid-1960s, particularly after his visiting professorship at the *Community Mental Health Center* of the Maimonides Hospital in Brooklyn, New York. The organization of psychiatry under "community mental health centers" (CMHCs) in the United States prompted Basaglia to engage in a series of reflections on the traditional asylum. He noted that the CMHCs, by adopting an apparatus of prevention, were becoming capable of classifying, pathologizing, and institutionalizing a much larger segment of the population, with fluid boundaries (the so-called marginals, deviants, poorly adapted, etc.), in such a way that prevention served to broaden the confines of mental illness rather than narrow its scope. This sociopolitical function of the CMHCs is revealed by the presence in the team of new actors, such as social workers and social advocates. Basaglia concluded that these new organizations were succeeding in creating a far more subtle techno-social network in which the boundary between the norm and deviance was becoming increasingly unclear.[15] Later, Basaglia would say that the medical model had beaten out the penitentiary model. The new bio-political psychiatry services (the psychiatry not of "mental illness" but of "mental health") emphasized the medical aspect of psychiatry and, through a diversified and multidisciplinary approach, made possible a more diffused form of control. It also expanded the number of people to be treated.[16]

By the time the Italian Parliament adopted Psychiatric Reform Law 180 in 1978, Basaglia had already recognized the direction "modernization" was taking, having intensely studied the reforms adopted in England, France, and the United States. In his own evaluation of Law 180,[17] he recognized that this reform had obviously legitimized the crisis of the disciplinary apparatus that had previously been centered on the asylum. The victory over the old system, however, would eventuate in the same medicalization of psychiatry that he'd witnessed in the U.S. system of CMHCs. Law 180 provided judicial consecration to bio-political psychiatry by focusing on the problem of public health and on the risks of pathology threatening the social body.

While this medicalization of psychiatry and the accompanying emergence of bio-political institutions generated little sustained critical analysis in Italy, Foucault's work offers us a useful starting place from which to initiate such a critique of our contemporary psychiatric discourses and practices. Foucault, of course, identified what he would later call bio-politics in developing his analysis of psychiatric power. More precisely, Foucault "discovered" bio-politics in his analysis of the generalization of psychiatric power and in initially considering this dispersion in primarily quantitative terms as an extension and proliferation of disciplinary mechanisms outside the apparatus of the asylum. Subsequently, he recognized these new power apparatuses, which no longer concern just individual people but whole populations, had begun adopting a specific quality that differentiated them from disciplinary technologies. From this differentiation, Foucault concluded that these technologies required an analysis couched in terms of bio-politics.

Foucault originally presented the analysis of the generalization of psychiatric power in his lesson of 16 January 1974,[18] though it became the centerpiece of the course in the following year: Les anormaux. In this course, Foucault examined the evolution of psychiatric expertise in the nineteenth century. He described, on the one hand, the historic pathologization of crime and the birth of a power/knowledge which invested the generalized domain of anomalies, and, on the other hand, the problematization of childhood as the historical precondition for the generalization of psychiatric power/knowledge.[19] Foucault began to use the terms bio-power and bio-politics in the following year, 1976.[20] The generalization of psychiatric power directly related to the medicalization of psychiatric power. Psychiatric power had undergone, in fact, two profoundly different processes of medicalization, even though these were, from a historical perspective, interrelated and superimposed on each other. The first process originated in the asylum with the coronation of psychiatric power as medical knowledge, and reached completion with the emergence of the neurological body, notably with Charcot, whose project, however, failed when the hysterics confronted him with their sexual bodies.[21] The sexualized body would, in turn, be invested by psychoanalysis and bio-political medicalization, each constituting a form of "depsychiatrization."[22] The second process was precisely that by which psychiatry medicalized itself as bio-political power/knowledge, that is, as a branch of public prevention and hygiene. The crisis of psychiatry as a medical specialty operating in specialized institutions of the alienated, falls between these two processes, as do the major reforms of the psychiatric system in the twentieth century (the National Health System in England, sector policies in France, Community Mental Health Centers in the United States, and Law 180 in Italy).

We cannot consider these reforms simply in terms of bio-political modernization, since they also reflected the intent to reaffirm the specificity of psychiatry relative to medical objectivism. In this sense, what was proposed was often not an abolition (which only happened in Italy), but rather a modernization of the psychiatric institution. So there was a dual process of modernizing psychiatry. The French experience is striking because the eclectic interests of the reformers envisaged the sector as an instrument for renewing the psychiatric apparatus, while retaining its specificity relative to medicine.[23] The end result was to obscure the motivating force played by another form of modernization that was strictly bio-political and was characterized by a new psychological culture obscuring the boundaries between the normal and the pathological, allowing for the treatment of all aspects of a person's existence.[24] In other words, the "myth" of sector psychiatry, as it emerged in France, consisted in its claim of managing the extra-hospital aspect that then had to function within the context of the specific apparatuses of a bio-political medicine—an all-inclusive management of pathological risks.[25]

Following his stay in the United States, Basaglia developed a highly lucid analysis of this issue, describing the institution of Community Mental Health Centers as the clearest demonstration of the reformed asylum. In bio-political terms, the modernization of disciplinary psychiatry and modernized psychiatry can coexist without any real difficulty. Moreover, such stratification and articulation of different technologies (disciplinary and bio-political) represent the most dangerous consequences of a complex and contradictory modernization of the psychiatric system. Recognizing the ambivalence of this modernization requires critical tools and the elaboration of strategies capable of confronting this phenomenon. To start with, we have to shed any simplistic or univocal attitude we might have. Crusading against the disciplinary specter brings with it the risk of materializing the bio-political phantom; and vice versa, attacking the bio-political specter risks reviving permanently the disciplinary phantom. In Italy, the modernization of psychiatry went further in its criticism of the disciplinary apparatus, focusing on the asylum. The radical nature of this critique should have led French psychiatrists long ago to distrust the therapeutic attitude. This attitude, of their own volition, is based on the same apparatus and, consequently, the same excesses of power.[26] But by putting so such energy into this anti-disciplinary process, reformed Italian psychiatry has failed to recognize that the new "mental health" policy is bio-political as well. It fails to understand how the "good" mental health policy—the one that addresses the question of health in the framework of the human, social, and political emancipation of the patients—can easily become the best alibi for a "bad" mental health policy—the one that involves control and social normalization through an apparatus of generalized prevention of pathology risks (screening, psychological and biogenetic expertise) and the massive prescription of psycholeptic drugs. From this perspective, rather than dismissing summarily the French reformers' approach to the issue, by looking for a new individual therapeutic relationship with patients, as just a dissimulation technique of the disciplinary apparatus, could provide Italian psychiatrists today with a model to analyze their own bio-political way of treating people.

It is appropriate here to consider why psychiatry played such a strategic historical role in the way bio-politics became so effective. It is true that psychiatry includes a very large number of other domains, (e.g., biology, medicine, eugenics, demography, ecology, and urban planning).[27] If we ground our future thinking in a Foucauldian analysis, however, we could ask if there is any domain that is "more bio-political" than the others. Does there exist an apparatus that, at the point of intersection between different levels of power, has more historical and technological "weight" and is therefore the most appropriate object for the critique of the political rationality that guides the functioning of bio-political technologies? Any serious effort to answer these questions must consider, at least, the following four sets of issues.

1. *The professionalization of doctors.* Since the eighteenth century, according to Foucault, doctors have seen their power increase from the time that they started to fill additional functions beyond those that were strictly therapeutic. This increase in medical power was related to the emergence of a bio-politcal apparatus for the government of the population. The professionalization of doctors was most evident in the context of public health. At the very time that a technical apparatus was required to manage the social body, medicine took on the function of public hygiene and, thus, became a fundamental authority for social control. The need for public hygiene justified and called for a certain number of positive medical interventions at the social and urban levels— authoritarian interventions concerning what were considered to be the principal sources of disease (prisons, ports, hospitals) and which needed urgent medicalization measures. It also called for a variety of pedagogical interventions aimed at instructing the population about hygiene regulations, as well as scientific interventions to study the state of the population's health. In this way, doctors became rooted in the highest levels of government, conducting government surveys and an increasing number of administrative functions. From this point onward, one sees the development of "medico-administrative" knowledge that had specific effects on the society. The interpenetration of the political and the medical through their work in the domain of public hygiene increased doctors' power. The doctor became the advisor and expert on the art of government by maintaining the social "body" in a permanent state of health.[28]

2. *The pathologization of crime.* Foucault explains the pathologization of crime in *Discipline and Punish.* Toward the end of the eighteenth century, the *"discipline blocus,"* the closed institution, firmly rooted in the scheme of exclusion (of which the model of the Middle Ages was the exclusion of lepers), began to be replaced by the "disciplinary mechanism" (the historical model of which was precisely the inclusion of the plague-stricken). This proliferation of disciplinary mechanisms led to a regime of generalized surveillance and prepared the ground for the mechanisms of bio-politics.[29] By 1975, however, Foucault had not yet discerned that normalizing power's generalization across society results from more than a diffusion of individualizing disciplines. It results also from the effect of the emergence of totalizing bio-powers. Centered on the normalized body, these totalizing bio-powers aim at regulating the biological processes of a population (fertility, mortality, health status, morbidity, life-expectancy, etc.). In 1975 *Surveiller et punir* focused on the past, and Foucault was still looking in the direction of the disciplines. During that same year, in his courses given at the Collège de France (*Les anormaux*), he was developing his analysis of the generalization of psychiatric power. This would project him directly into the field of bio-politics. In *Il faut défendre la société* (1976) and in *La volonté de savoir* (1976), Foucault would clarify the distinction between disciplinary power and bio-power, and he envisaged the normalization of society in terms of the articulation of disciplinary and bio-political mechanisms, at the center of which could

be found medicine and sexuality superimposed on and intersecting the two technologies.

As for psychiatry, if one reads *Les anormaux* in the light of the 1976 texts which immediately followed it, one can say that the grafting of one set of apparatuses on another, the bio-political on the disciplinary, occurred through the intermediary of a very precise historical and technical process. During the nineteenth century, we see the reciprocal exclusion of medical and judicial discourse (where there was madness there could be no crime, and vice versa) succumb to the medico-legal continuum. One could be judged guilty and interned in the asylum as diseased. This practice of dual qualification—medical and legal—predominated in the area of medico-legal expertise which was forging a new space of theoretical and institutional intervention focusing on the notion of "perversion."[30] This notion, which emerged in the second half of the nineteenth century, made it possible to develop an infantilizing terminology in psychiatric discourse, defining the individual as arrogant, lazy, stubborn, etc. Far from explaining criminal acts "scientifically," this vocabulary tended to construct a kind of psychologico-moral double. Through this mirror-effect—all the more grotesque because it claimed to explain scientifically "who" the criminal was—psychiatric expertise attempted to show that the individual resembles his own crime before committing it. This resemblance is nothing less than the attribution of perversion to the individual, and such reasoning meant that the medical discourse could function within judicial power, and, at the same time, the judicial discourse could function within a medical framework. The ambiguous and epistemologically unfounded phenomenon of perversion, which made it possible to speak both the medical discourse and the legal discourse, was grounded in the invention of a completely fictional object: pathological criminality.[31]

3. *The generalization of social danger as pathological risk.* Psychiatry is a disciplinary apparatus that, at a given moment, became medicalized through the intermediary of neurology:[32] Charcot's work at Salpêtrière consisted of producing a symptomatology of madness, that of hysterics—a perfect reflection of the norms of epilepsy and recognized as an organic disease.[33] But medicalized psychiatry also institutionalized itself as a bio-political apparatus of control and of the improvement of the health of a population, as a specialized branch of public hygiene, and as a particular means of protecting society against all the dangers associated with disease. It was at this point that we became aware of a breakdown of the field of symptomatology. Henceforth, a conduct could be identified as a symptom of mental illness. As such, conduct was to be medicalized through the intermediary of neurology. Conduct was no longer—as it had been for the alienists—"*le petit fragment de délire*" that it revealed, but the deviation of such conduct from the social norms.[34] Psychiatry thus opened itself up to all the possible disorders of conduct, finding itself overwhelmed by a plethora of behaviors which, up to then, had only been assigned a moral, disciplinary or legal status. Consequently, we would have a "true medical science" (anchored to medicine through neurology) to apply to all forms of conduct. This, in turn, would allow for at least two things. (1) Psychiatry would introduce the norm or the rule of conduct understood as the informal law; and (2) psychiatry, in the form of medi-

cal knowledge, would introduce a distinction between the normal and the pathological. Psychiatry therefore presented itself as a medico-political apparatus that
invested diffuse fields of deviations from norms of conduct, and these deviations
were then interpreted as pathological manifestations relative to normal functioning.

In following Foucault's analysis as developed in *Les anormaux*, medico-
legal expertise (along with the medicalization of the family, the psychiatric
problematization of childhood, the affirmation of a psychiatry that functions
primarily as social defense)[35] could represent one of the decisive turning points
in the emergence of a state of generalized prevention that is, in the end, the contradictory result of the stratification of different historical and technical forms of
power (sovereign power, disciplinary power, and governmentality). In fact, psychiatric expertise had the particularity of being the articulation point between
medicine and law, without being homogenous with either the former or the latter. Psychiatric expertise came from elsewhere. It did not seek to separate the
guilty from the innocent, the sick from the healthy. Rather, it addressed itself to
the normals/abnormals in attempting to establish the gradations between the
two.[36] Psychiatric expertise belongs neither to the mechanisms of legal power
nor to those of medical power; rather it belongs to the mechanisms of the power
of normalization which function between the poles of the disciplinary norm and
the bio-political norm, and which find their articulation in everyday sexuality.
The history of the pathologization of crime made this normalizing character of
psychiatric expertise increasingly clear. Yet this does not mean that the system
of coupling that became possible as a result of this (medicine and law, madness
and crime, disease and dangerousness, medicine and public health) would tend
to dissolve. On the contrary, medico-legal expertise created a psychiatry that
became more and more medicalized and criminologized.[37] Psychiatry, therefore,
would become medico-legal, not just in a few exceptional cases, but in its everyday activities. Psychiatry always finds itself halfway between describing social norms and rules, and conducting medical analysis of anomalies—serving,
essentially, as the science and technique of the abnormals. In brief, the meeting
between crime and madness had become the rule, leaving psychiatry to deal
with even the most minor forms of crime and mental illness, petty forms of de-
linquency, and almost imperceptible anomalies of behavior.[38] Herein lies the
state of generalized prevention, having become a permanent hunt for "abnormal-
ity as risk-factor."

4. *Bio-security racism as a factor in functionalizing the antinomies of power.*
Psychiatry is the terrain on which two ideas have become historically superimposed and organized: that of the dangerousness of mental illness—the subject of
exception that is absolutely beyond the norm—and that of pathologico-
normative risk—a factor that cannot be calculated in statistical or probabilistic
terms but which applies to the population as a whole, to the normalized man,
situated anywhere on the continuum between the normal and the abnormal. In
other words, psychiatry as a bio-political and social-defensive apparatus has
carved its place in the articulation between its status as a science of absolute
danger and its status as a science of generalized risk. This transition from the

science of human monsters to the science and technique of the normal/abnormal was not achieved through a process of exclusion, but by grafting and including. In the same way, psychiatry's disciplinary dimension has not been negated, but has become incorporated with the emergence of bio-political psychiatry.

In the wake of Foucault, Judith Butler thinks of power in terms of an "anachronism" rather than of a chronological consequence.[39] But here anachronism is the rule, not the exception. One can even assert that modern power only functions through anachronism: anachronism of sovereignty in the disciplines, anachronism of discipline in the bio-powers, anachronism of sovereignty in bio-politics and governmentality.

Psychiatry in some ways crosses over this paradoxical heaviness of modern power. It plays the role of a mass grave, articulating the articulations. Psychiatry creates, at several levels, a continuum—containing both heterogeneity and antagonism—that finally enables power to "run the system." In fact, psychiatry has contributed to creating the whole tissue of bio-security on which the state and governmental bio-policies have been able to establish themselves, both below and above the sovereign State. This tissue, of which psychiatry could be in some ways the eponym, is itself stratified, complex, and problematic—a sort of living archive of modern power in all its reaches. Examining this psychiatric tissue allows us to begin to answer a crucial question: How can we account for the coexistence of the excesses of normalization and the excesses of sovereignty that seem to increasingly characterize current policies?

The problem is that the power of sovereignty, as much in its mantle of absolute monarchy as in its opposite form of public rights, constitutes an outer limit for the powers of normalization that these powers can neither cross nor eliminate. On the other hand, they can functionalize this limit, re-absorbing it as a sort of antinomic condition of the exercise of power. And it is precisely this functional recovery of sovereignty that allows the power of normalization to function, while, at the same time, allowing sovereignty to outlive its own demise.

Foucault's assertion that neo-racism is the offspring of psychiatry merits special attention. Especially if one realizes that, in the name of the same bio-security requirement, neoliberal governments are not just able to declare war and exercise the function of death, but also suspend rights, to establish a whole area of extralegal, if not frankly illegal, governmentality, and, concurrently, legally acceptable derogations of constitutionality.[40] In *Precarious Life*, Judith Butler has proposed a very interesting analysis of the problems posed by the "indefinite detentions" at Guantanamo Bay of prisoners taken on suspicion of terrorism during the Afghanistan war. From her analysis, we can conclude that state sovereignty lives on anachronistically within the governmentality that radically erodes it. Furthermore, in the name of preventing danger, the agents of governmentality (government employees, bureaucrats, technocrats, managers—all without any political or legal legitimacy) colonize the space occupied by the state and the judiciary and manage sovereignty's excesses, tendentiously shorn of all legal-political constraints. The paradoxical functioning of mutual reinforcement between sovereignty and governmentality enables us to explain the "suspension of rights" in the case of the indefinite detention of the Guantanamo prisoners. On the one hand, this suspension, this "lawlessness," allows for the exercise of governmentality as extralegal or even illegal power; but at the same time the exercise of governmentality makes possible the supra-functioning of the state's power of sovereignty, rendering absolute a certain number of sovereign decisions with respect to the legal-political sphere in the name of a bio-security authority. These sovereign conditions include imprisonment without trial, determining who merits access to a trial, deciding guilt or innocence, whether or not to apply the death penalty or to make war, etc.

The challenge of the bio-security state is directly related to the possibility of resisting this excessive production of power which occurs as a result of the convergence of the double thrusts of normalization and legalization, which envelop each other as in a vortex. This whole game of add-ons and extras, which makes resistance to power increasingly complex and problematic, also brings out the multiple fracture-lines where the bio-security state is becoming weaker and undermined.[41] Is it too much to ask that the psychiatric genealogy of the bio-security state could make available a small part of its historical weight to this contemporary battle?

Part IV

Health Care

Chapter 8

Genetic Responsibility and Neo-Liberal Governmentality:
Medical Diagnosis as Moral Technology

Thomas Lemke
Institut für Sozialforschung (Germany)

From the mid-1970s on, the concept of governmentality plays a crucial role in Michel Foucault's theoretical work. Foucault defines government in a very broad sense as conduct or, more precisely, as "the conduct of conduct." It refers to all endeavors that guide and direct the government of others, but it also includes forms of subjectivation: the government of the self.[1] The analytics of governmentality links political strategies to the subject's capacity to govern itself and the mobilization of truth to the production of particular moral subject positions. Following Foucault, I am interested in the roles that genetic knowledge and genetic technologies are coming to play in the government of individuals and populations, how medical practices and diagnostic tools function as political technologies on the one hand and as moral technologies on the other hand.[2]

I will concentrate on a strategic element in this emerging phenomenon of "genetic government"—the discourse of *genetic responsibility*. My thesis is that the discourse of genetic responsibility relies on the scientific and technological progress in genetics since the 1970s, but its efficacy as a political and moral technology hinges on the success of neo-liberal programs and transformations that increasingly individualize and privatize the responsibility for social risks. By presenting material from popular medical advice books in which genetic information plays a crucial role, I try to show the rise of new obligations and the displacement of rights that are brought about by referring to a "genetic responsibility."

Archeology: A Short History of Genetic Responsibility

What is covered by the term "genetic responsibility?" An internet Google search conducted in December 2004 produced more than 429 "hits" for the phrase "genetic responsibility."[3] Because many references appear more than once, the number of actual listings is much smaller. Nevertheless, the phrase appears in an increasing variety of contexts, including conference reports, advertisements for movies, extracts from lifestyle magazines, and advice manuals written by medical doctors. Across this diversity of sources, we find that "genetic responsibility" carries two different meanings. On the one hand, it refers to a scientific complex of causality or competence. On the other hand, it is linked to a moral complex of culpability or duty. Genetic responsibility could mean that genes are the cause for a condition, an illness, or a certain characteristic, (e.g. genes are responsible for cancer or sexual orientation). Genetic responsibility, however, could also mean that individuals should deal with genetic information in a certain way; namely, they should deal with that information in accordance with moral values and social norms.

A conference report available through the internet serves as an example of the latter meaning. The text sums up the results of a meeting on "genetics in the workplace" that took place in the year 2000 in Colorado.[4] According to Richard Sharp, an ethicist at the *National Institute for Environmental Health Sciences,* the problem of "genetic responsibility" will arise from the increasing knowledge of genetic risks. "Once we know that an individual is genetically susceptible to certain disorders or diseases, is there a responsibility for that person to try to stay as healthy as possible? Are individuals obligated to not take a job that might put them at risk of getting sick? What obligation do employers have to protect their genetically vulnerable workers?"

We find the causal meaning of "genetic responsibility" illustrated by a webpage provided by the *Science Generation,*[5] an agency established by the European Commission to foster debates on the life sciences. Its objective is to create information networks and discussion platforms surrounding the question of the impact of the biosciences on society. Genetics plays a major role in this debate. In addressing the issue of "Genetics and polemics," *Science Generation* warns that the concept of a genetic determinism does not pay due respect to the complexity of the biological and social reality, since it neglects the role of environmental factors.

> Responsibility is shared 50-50: it is true that we are "made" by our genes, to a certain extent, but they are not the only factor in play. Without our environment, education, social contacts, we would probably not be what we are. . . . Genes responsible for susceptibility to certain diseases are no more than signs of a relative risk. Attempts to reduce disorders as complex as mental disease, or behavior such as alcoholism to genetic predisposition could lead to serious abuses and to people assimilating patients with their diseases, to the exclusion of other alternatives. Fortunately, the idea of the "bad gene" is rapidly losing support, whether the hardcore advocates of exclusive genetic responsibility like it or not![6]

These two semantic components of the discourse of genetic responsibility—the scientific and the moral one—are not simply defined by an additive relationship; the discourse of genetic responsibility is characterized by a specific tension that is generated by the combination of the two aspects. Repeatedly we hear it said that genomic research is threatening traditional concepts of personal responsibility and individual autonomy.[7] Contemporary biology, with its search for genetic determinants linked to a multitude of traits and modes of behavior, seems to subvert the substantial basis for responsible action—the possibility of individual decision making and choice. When genes are our biological fate, what place remains for personal responsibility? I do not think that this fear of genetic determinism is justified. What we observe today is not the reduction of individual responsibility by reference to genetic dispositions and inborn traits. The affirmation of genetic factors does not result in a position that negates or forecloses the responsibility of the subject. Quite on the contrary, the new genetic knowledge is the central point of reference to expand moral duties; it engenders new modes and fields of responsible action.

The discourse of genetic responsibility expanded over the past thirty years. While genetic responsibility in the 1970s exclusively addressed issues of reproductive behavior, referring to the care for "healthy" children and the concern for transmitting "disease genes,"[8] today two additional dimensions of responsibility have emerged. Obligations to communicate and control genetic risks complement the moral duty for risk prevention. Beyond the problem of transmitting "bad genes" to the next generations, we also find an anxiety about their possible effects for already living persons. Should not relatives be warned of genetic risks in order to realize options for prevention or therapy? If there are no such options available, should they not know about genetic risks, in order to seek genetic counseling or testing options to make "responsible" decisions concerning their future?

The second direction in which the discourse of genetic risk has expanded since the 1970s does not concern the relation to others, but the health behavior of the person himself or herself. Genetic responsibility in this case expresses itself as a demand for genetic diagnosis technologies and prevention procedures. As a consequence, only knowledge about the individual genetic risks allows for a responsible life. By presenting many diseases as genetic in origin, a "risk competent" or "rational" health behavior demands not only the acknowledgement of general risk factors like alcohol, smoking, or lack of exercise; it also necessitates a specialized knowledge based on an individual genetic risk profile.[9]

Genealogy: Medical Advice Literature as a Moral Terrain

To present some empirical evidence for the idea that the discourse of genetic responsibility expanded over the last thirty years, I will very briefly analyze three books by Aubrey Milunsky, who has been writing popular medical advice books on the prevention of genetic diseases and the use of prenatal diagnosis since the 1970s. My interest in this material stems from the fact that medical advice books and manuals have become a prominent genre for popularizing liberal models of governance. Paradoxically, these "guides" both presuppose and play a role in bringing about the existence of the responsible subject. The texts address individuals who are financially and intellectually capable of buying and reading this kind of literature, and who are ready to accept biomedical knowledge as an important authority for everyday decision-making processes and life-style options.[10]

Milunsky is a professor of human genetics at the Boston University School of Medicine. Since the beginning of the 1980s, he has directed the Center of Human Genetics. He also serves on the editorial boards of several prestigious medical journals, and has published many articles on the medical and legal aspects of genetic technology. Milunsky's medical advice manuals are highly relevant for a genealogy of genetic responsibility, since his books cover a period from the mid-1970s to the beginning of the new millennium. These texts and the medical authority of their author thus provide a very good indicator for studying the transformations and shifts in the genetic responsibility discourse.

Milunsky published his first advice book in 1977 under the title *Know Your Genes*. The text found a large audience, prompting its translation into several languages, including German.[11] In 1989, Milunsky augmented and reedited the book, changing the title to *Choices, Not Chances: An Essential Guide to Your Heredity and Health*. Another twelve years later in 2001, he reworked and added to that material, leading to the publication of *Your Genetic Destiny: Know Your Genes, Secure Your Health, and Save Your Life*. In the following analysis, I examine the modifications that Milunsky made across the twenty-five-year history of these various editions, exploring how his notion of genetic responsibility changes along the way.

Know Your Genes starts with a frightening message: Already in this early book published in 1977, Milunsky sketches an image of multiple dangers produced by genetic factors that will be repeated in the subsequent editions. The author warns us that genetic risks are even more dangerous than ordinary health risks, since they are invisible and may affect seemingly healthy people who carry dispositions for many diseases unknowingly. According to Milunsky, hereditary diseases that could be effectively prevented endanger 10 percent of the U.S. population. Milunsky for the first time formulates a theme that runs consistently throughout of the subsequent incarnations of his book, presenting the problem of a genetic responsibility as a precarious relationship between rights and duties, medical knowledge, and moral constraints that follow from this knowledge.

Choices, Not Chances, published in 1989,[12] begins with an invitation to the reader to contemplate his or her family history. "Have there been children with birth defects or mental retardation? Stillbirths? Infant deaths? Miscarriages? Does anyone have cancer, heart disease, diabetes, or mental illness?"[13] This is probably true for most readers, since there have certainly been miscarriages, cases of cancer, or heart disease in nearly every single family. However, Milunsky directly relates these incidents to genetic factors, and he wants to make clear why it is so essential to know about one's genetic risks. "Every fact of your health is regulated, modulated, or otherwise influenced by your genes. You are a carrier of about twenty harmful genes—as is each of us."[14] In the past twelve years, the number of the so-called harmful genes seems to have increased enormously. According to Milunsky in 1977, individuals carried four to eight harmful genes; the estimation today is twenty. Though the danger seems to be rising, the author repeats—often in the same words—the lesson he gave us in his previous book. The diagnosis of genetic risks does not imply fate. Rather, scientific and medical progress allows us to know more about the genetic origins of diseases. Hence, it becomes paramount for us to use this knowledge for practical purposes:

> Indeed, if you are planning to have a child, it is possible to understand, without extensive knowledge of biology or genetics, what your risks are in a given situation, what tests are available, and what options exist. I believe that you have a right to know this information and a responsibility to seek out the facts (at least for your children's sake), and that you should retain the freedom to exercise your options.[15]

Milunsky notes that there are more than 4000 diseases identified that are based in a single genetic mutation. For him, all of these diseases are preventable. Furthermore, it is not nature that is responsible for them, but the parents' ignorance. They simply didn't request genetic testing. Milunsky positions himself in the role of an enlightenment author who writes against the scientific ignorance and moral incompetence of society. All of us, in his view, must recognize that, since each disease depends on genetic factors, we must bear the burden of responsibility for knowing about our own personal genetic risks. Once we gain this knowledge, we must further meet its accompanying moral obligations.

> Morally, there is no family, and no person planning to have a child, who can ignore the new genetic discoveries and techniques for preventing genetic disease. . . . We have a right and, indeed, an obligation to know about our particular genes and to consider the options available that increase our chances of having healthy children. . . . Willy-nilly, we are involved in our genes. In a way, we are our genes.[16]

What are the differences and the parallels when we compare this book to the previous one? Like *Know Your Genes*, the 1989 book focuses on the problem of reproduction. Milunsky addresses his readers as potential parents. However, in *Choices, Not Chances*, he adds a new dimension of responsibility that refers to the communication of genetic risk information:

> Parents simply must understand their responsibility to tell. Equally important is the need for couples who have a defective child to inform their siblings, uncles, aunts, and cousins who are still in their childbearing years. . . . Avoidable births of severely mentally retarded children to near relatives, because of failure to inform about a chromosome defect, are unacceptable and irresponsible. *Families that share and tell, care.* (emphasis in original version)[17]

Milunsky regards the acknowledgment to transmit genetic information to relatives as an important indicator for a well-ordered and functioning family life, as a test for responsible thinking and caring for each other, as a symbol of superior moral quality.

Nevertheless, even if there is a new dimension of genetic responsibility emerging, Milunsky limits the discussion of genetic risks to the context of reproductive decision-making in each of the first two editions of his book. In *Know Your Genes*, there is only a single chapter that discusses the relevance of genetics for age, cancer and diabetes, intelligence and learning processes while the book concentrates on the question of transmitting genetic risks to the following generation and the opportunities of prenatal testing. In *Choice, Not Chances*, published twelve years later, the focus remains on birth defects, new reproductive technologies, prenatal care, and testing devices, but Milunsky devotes more space to the discussion of the hereditability of cancer or diabetes. He also offers more advice concerning the treatment of genetic diseases by drugs or nutrition.

Your Genetic Destiny,[18] published in 2001, differs in two respects from the previous books. Firstly, the focus of the argument shifts from genetic risks for succeeding generations to their medical relevance for the personal health of the reader. Still, we find the problem of a transmission of "bad" genes broadly discussed, and we see a renewed moral imperative to communicate genetic risks to family members, but the accent changes significantly. He introduces us to the idea of a genetic responsibility for one's own health. "This book," he proclaims, "is dedicated to informing you accurately of what you absolutely must know about your genes in order to recognize life-threatening and health-limiting factors and to exercise lifesaving and health-preserving options."[19]

Secondly, the main part of *Your Genetic Destiny* does not deal with rare hereditary diseases. The book focuses instead on the discussion of genetic factors that regulate or influence diseases such as obesity, cancer, schizophrenia, depression, Alzheimer's disease, diabetes, high blood pressure and coronary heart diseases. Milunsky describes genetic factors that might be involved in the development or severity of these diseases and informs readers of available genetic testing procedures. However, the author no longer stresses subjective rights but appeals directly to the interests of the individual in his or her health. The right to health asserts an imperative to seek as much information as possible about genetic risks:

> Know your family history, be cognizant of your ethnic origin, determine your genetic susceptibilities, opt for necessary gene tests, take preventive actions, establish appropriate surveillance, and seek preemptive treatment where applicable. In this way, you can exercise control over your genetic destiny, secure your health, and—in more ways than you yet realize—save your life."[20]

Let me conclude at this point the analysis of the modifications and extensions of responsible action presented in Milunsky's medical advice books to address a more troubling problem. The discourse of genetic responsibility is not limited to ethical considerations or medical guides; it already entered the legal sphere and tends to substitute the recourse to rights by establishing imperatives of duty toward oneself and others. The two new dimensions of genetic responsibility that I tried to discern—the duty to communicate genetic risks to others and the obligation to control one's own genetic risks—are about to undermine guaranteed rights and the freedom of choice concerning genetic tests. Let me very briefly point out two problems. Firstly, several cases in the United States, where high courts ruled that doctors are obliged to warn children of a patient that may be at risk genetically for acquiring the disease of their parent, illustrate a creeping tendency to establish a duty to warn family members about genetic risks. This legal obligation may contrast with the protection of privacy and the confidentiality of the doctor-patient relationship. Moreover, the imperative to warn others could erode their right for non-knowledge.[21]

Secondly, new forms of discrimination, exclusion, and paternalism might arise in a social and political conjuncture in which genetic information is getting increasingly irresistible.[22] In this climate, it will probably be judged irresponsible not to make use of genetic technologies and diagnostic devices. Paradoxically, the main point of reference for responsible action might not include the individual's will or the principle of self-determination, but, on the contrary, the personal decision could be challenged on the basis of the person's lack of "responsibility" or an excess of dependency.[23]

Problematization:
Genetic Knowledge and Neo-Liberal Risk Management

In the 1970s, the domain of genetic responsibility was limited to reproductive behavior that should be controlled in order to minimize disease and disability in the next generation. Today, it also refers to the control and communication of genetic risks. The discourse of genetic responsibility, however, is not only characterized by a quantitative expansion; we can also observe a qualitative transformation that brings us back to the two semantic components of the discourse of genetic responsibility—causality and culpability. With respect to the complex of causality we can observe a line of development that starts with a concept of a rather strict and rigid genetic determinism that is finally transformed into a more open and less determinant concept of genetic causation. Gene-environment interactions—complex causal models and systemic explanations—now receive more scientific attention in genomic research and molecular biology.[24] While the deterministic concept was used to explain a rather limited number of conditions, today genetic factors are supposed to be involved in many different diseases and characteristics. At the same time, the meaning of "genetic" did change. Rather than being viewed in terms of objective fate, today genes are increasingly seen to represent subjective potential and risks. Genes are about to constitute a somehow privileged field of intervention. Genetic knowledge provides the basis for an increasing number of diagnostic, corrective, or modulating interventions.[25] While in the context of prenatal diagnosis, abnormal testing results continue to present selective abortion as the only alternative to a problematic birth. The expansion of genetic tests for already-born individuals, however, enables us to move beyond the "either-or" decision—"for-or-against" the unborn life—with a series of procedures that cannot be subsumed under a binary logic. These cover such different strategies as taking drugs, control of life style, choice of partner, reproduction decisions, etc. In a word, not only is the model of causal explanation getting more complex, but also the possibilities of intervention on the basis of genetic knowledge.[26]

Secondly, we can observe a transformation in the mechanisms of responsibilization. One condition of existence for the discourse of genetic responsibility is the crisis of the Keynesian state and the successful implementation of neo-liberal policies from the mid-1970s on. As the "active management of responsible choice in risk taking is at the core of neo-liberal governance,"[27] the massive financial support and public acceptance of human genetic research could be conceived as part of a comprehensive political transformation that is increasingly individualizing and privatizing the responsibility for social risks. Not only in the field of health, but also in employment policies, crime prevention, or old-age insurance, individuals are expected to conduct a forward-looking approach to risk management. The retreat of the state goes hand in hand with an appeal to personal responsibility, self-care, and the promotion of self-regulatory competencies among individual and collective subjects. Within this more global political conjuncture, the idea of a personal responsibility for health takes shape. From the mid-1970s, we have observed an increasing individualization of conditions for disease. The scientific and medical interest shifts from environmental dangers like air or water pollution, radiation, or toxic substances and social conditions like poverty, stress, or exploitation to individual life styles that are held responsible for most diseases.[28] In the beginning, the accent in this health promotion and health education literature is put on smoking, alcohol, lack of exercise, or poor nutrition. Later, genetic factors also appear on this list. From this perspective, disease results from wrong choices or "bad" genes. The less the individuals can influence and change their objective conditions of life, the more they are confronted with the idea of an imaginary control of diseases by a rational government of health risks including genetic risks. "This shift in responsibility from society to the individual aligns with our current political climate, which increasingly blames individuals rather than social conditions for human problems. Thus genetics could become part of an ideological shift away from environmental and social analyses of problems, fostering the decline of public responsibility for human misfortune and misery."[29]

Conclusion

Genome analysis and genetic diagnostics do not rely on a deterministic relationship between genes and diseases but generate a "reflexive" relationship of individual risk profile and social requirements. The reference to personal responsibility and self-determination in the biosciences only makes sense if the individual is more than a victim or prisoner of her or his genetic material. The discourse of genetic responsibility frames individuals not as passive recipients of medical advice, but as active seekers of information and consumers of genetic testing devices and health care services.[30] If there were indeed a direct relationship between genotype and phenotype in the sense of genetic determinism, then it would be far harder to uphold the appeal to individual autonomy. By contrast, the construction of risk individuals, risk couples, risk pregnancies, etc. makes it easier to moralize on deviant behavior and to assign guilt and responsibility.[31]

The concept of information is crucial in this context since, at the same time, it serves as the "code of life" and as the "key to freedom." If we conceive the body as a genetic program, then disease points to a communication problem. In this light, the emergence of an illness indicates a functional disturbance that can be avoided to the extent that sufficient risk management is undertaken. Genetic enlightenment (as the deciphering of the "dark" code), therefore, also entails a precise notion of "Mündigkeit" (maturity), which is linked to "informed decisions" based on the knowledge of one's own genetic risks. From this perspective, the use of genetic diagnosis is not up to individual freedom or personal choice. We might see a time when it will be more and more problematic to opt against genetic information and the transmission of this knowledge, when a refusal of this knowledge will constitute objective evidence of one's moral incompetence or irrational behavior.

Paradoxically, it is exactly the invitation to engage in self-determination and the imperative of a "genetic responsibility" that renders individuals increasingly dependent on medico-scientific authorities and their expertise. The right to health takes on the form of duty to procure information. Only those who act responsibly will draw the correct (i.e. risk-minimizing and forward-oriented) conclusions from this range of information: "The healthy person is, in effect, symbolic of the ideal neo-liberal citizen, autonomous, active and responsible and the person who deviates from this ideal state is, at best, lacking in value and, at worst, morally culpable."[32] Put differently, the contemporary discourse of genetic responsibility has nothing to do with an increasing knowledge that engenders new duties and obligations, but it is embedded in the more global—neoliberal—discourse of responsibility that shapes our society today.

Chapter 9

The Problem with High-Maintenance Bodies or the Politics of Care

Monique Lanoix
Concordia University (Canada)

Media reports on health care tend to focus on the high costs of the health care system, privileging the economic aspects of this social service. We seldom hear about the quality of the services offered, except for the long waiting lists for these services. In Canada, long-term care institutions provide a type of service situated within the larger health care system. Typically, these institutions permanently house older individuals who have lost a significant amount of autonomy.

Long-term care has not attracted the attention of the media until recently. In the past year, reports of elder abuse have garnered a fair amount of media and, therefore, public attention. This changes the landscape of media reporting from one that is purely economic to one that focuses on the type of care given to individuals, albeit care that has gone wrong. Nevertheless, this change and the type of reporting it incurs are noteworthy and in need of critical examination.

The purpose of this chapter is to examine the reports of abuse in long-term care facilities, as well as to try to understand this abuse using Foucault's understanding of bio-power along with Agamben's use of Primo Levi's concept of the "gray zone." This approach enables me to develop a unique focus on the dispensation of care in an institutional setting. This different angle will elucidate the theoretical aspects of caregiving, and will also show how the practices of care are fragile and at risk in such institutional settings. Ultimately, even if I do not believe that Agamben's version of the "gray zone" is one that can characterize long-term care, it may prove useful in helping us decipher the power relations and the objectification involved in caring for compromised adults in such institutions. I hope to show that long-term care institutions need to be divorced from an understanding of care as a commodity to be dispensed in precise ways under the tight regime of a medicalized discourse. This market understanding of care relates to a wider understanding of vital needs as something detached from the individual herself. Needs are not necessarily reducible to possessions which can be acquired and disposed of under a market system; such an understanding is intimately tied to a concept of the individual as one who is isolated and atomistic. This criticism of the individual is one that is long standing in political and social theory; a clear understanding of "care" can help us toward resolving this issue.

The chapter will proceed as follows. I will first introduce institutionalization and its salient features. Next, I will examine the practices of care within an institutional setting and the implications of these care practices on the subjects of care, including the care receivers as well as the caregivers. Finally, I will discuss the media's portrayals of abuse of institutionalized individuals and the ramifications of those portrayals.

Institutions

As previously noted, long-term care or chronic care institutions permanently house adult individuals who have lost a significant amount of autonomy. This loss of autonomy may stem from physical impairments, but it can also result from cognitive impairments. These cognitive impairments typically result from some form of dementia, stroke, or other degenerative neurological disease.[1] Not all residents of these facilities have cognitive impairments, but they all require the maximum amount of "care," which is set at two and one-half hours of nursing care a day for the Québec health care system.

Such institutions are, in a sense, designated sites of care. That is, the residents housed within such facilities are there permanently and must have most, if not all, of their needs attended to. They must be "cared for" in the most literal sense.

Theoretical discussions on these types of institutions have centred around what I would term "meta-theoretical" problems. That is, they focus on the public or state funding of such facilities and the principles that could justify allocating those funds. Of prime importance in these discussions are the rights, if any, of unproductive individuals to flourish. Broadly speaking, these questions of justice are cast as questions of justice between generations, since the individuals who live in such facilities are typically seniors.[2]

These discussions offer little theoretical analysis of the practices within such facilities. Practical discussions, we might believe, rest with administrators, but these administrative discussions limit the scope of "practical" matter to vulgar utilitarian issues such as how to best give care to a large number of individuals in the most cost-efficient way.[3] Meanwhile, we find a dearth of theoretical work on the assumptions and concepts that ground the concrete practices of "care" within such facilities.[4]

If discussion of care practices is lacking in long-term care, some feminist theorists have given priority to "care" as a theoretical concept of political importance. Noteworthy examples incude the work of Eva Feder Kittay and Joan Tronto, who examine meticulously the various aspects of care. Tronto's work, in particular, holds tremendous value for its careful and multilayered conceptual analysis. Kittay's writings examine care in the case of persons who are dependent and not traditionally understood as productive members of society.[5]

In the practical field of health care, we do find literature on nursing and care, although these writings tend to privilege nursing and acute care.[6] Recent policy moves toward shorter hospital stays, however, has meant that caregiving has become more important in the home. This shift of caring to the private realm has put caregiving in the public eye. Consequently, this additional concern for families has stimulated the appearance of increasing numbers of writings that have begun addressing this new reality.[7]

These analyses of care are crucial to a better understanding of care as a theoretical concept with important practical considerations. The practices of care and caregiving as an ongoing practice need to be elucidated. Yet, the discussions dealing with ongoing care mostly center on caregiving in the home or in a private setting. There is a need to understand care as it is given in institutional settings, as this yields particular insights into the nature of care as it is actually practiced in those settings. When care becomes paid work, the caregiver is mandated by a third party, namely the institution, and is constrained by schedules, fixed timelines, and policies. The caregiving relation is no longer familial; it becomes legislated by economic and administrative considerations. To consider care as paid work is crucial in order to understand care, how it fits into the greater scheme of health care and, finally, whether it can and should be part of a greater political framework.

Technologies of Care

A person becomes a candidate for a long-term care facility when she can no longer perform the daily tasks of living without considerable help. In order to determine this, the needs of the individual are assessed and evaluated by professionals using a set of accepted standards.[8] Once it is established that the individual needs the maximum amount of help to accomplish all or most of the basic daily tasks, she will be placed in a long-term care facility.

Once in long-term care, the individual is considered a resident of the particular facility. The language is important here. The term client is usually reserved for persons who need assistance or care for a short period of time. For example, persons who need physiotherapy are called clients; persons in acute care are also called clients. They are seen as purchasing services that will enable them to become "productive" again.

However, in long-term care, the individual is considered a resident of the establishment; the pertinent literature will refer to her as such.[9] Residents are thus labelled as individuals who will be living in a "*milieu de vie substitut.*" The French expression used in Québec conveys well the meaning of long-term care; it is a "home" that substitutes for the real thing. Individuals in long-term care acquire a new identity: they are residents, not disabled individuals. This point is crucial and necessary in order to make the practices in long-term care cogent. Let me explain.

Because a long-term care institution functions as a health care facility, the individuals living under its auspices fall under the medical model of disability.

According to this model, a person who is disabled is a person who is sick and deficient in some way; the disability resides entirely in the person herself. This model has been subject to much criticism by many disability activists, who have developed and championed the social model of disability. This model understands disability as an interaction between the person and her environment. Nevertheless, the medical model remains unchallenged within long-term care institutions, in part because these institutions fall under the control of the health care system.[10]

Since long-term care is a substitute living space, the social model of disability does not apply here. Put differently, since the residents are in a facility that is outside "normal" society, it is difficult for them to be integrated within the greater social order. They are not officially cast aside, it is simply more difficult for them to be part of society. In this sense, they become more isolated and the social model of disability is not really applicable in their situation.

Long-term care institutions are privileged locations where society is excluded.[11] Such institutions constitute "medically constructed" spaces that group individuals together according to their level of "need," as opposed to their cultural identity, for example.[12]

The needs of residents are evaluated according to a medicalized discourse that relies on a set of scientific practices to identify and define the physical and medical needs of the residents according to an established hierarchy that determines both the importance of these needs and the appropriate response to them. Since needs are the noteworthy feature of the residents, they are the criteria by which the residents can be easily identified. For example, the person in Room 4 will be known as a "feeder" and the one in Room 10 as a wanderer who needs to kept under surveillance.[13]

The bio-politics at work here place an emphasis on understanding individuals through their needs. Furthermore, the practices of care will be subject to strict controls, because these practices must respect the established hierarchy of needs. Quite obviously, bio-politics not only order the needs of the residents, they also enclose them in an identity that easily reduces their subjectivity to their needs.

As Foucault has shown, the notion of government is "understood in the broad sense of techniques and procedures for directing human behavior."[14] The techniques of governmentality have been studied in the case of disabled individuals.[15] In "Breaking the Boundaries of the Broken Body,"[16] Shildrick and Price look at the disciplinary practices in which disabled persons must be engaged to qualify for disability allowances and help under the Disability Living Allowance in the United Kingdom. The person must report on the intimate details of her particular needs in order to qualify for benefits. Therefore, the confessional aspect and the disciplinary aspect combine to produce a subject who willingly puts herself through this self-scrutiny.

These analyses focus on individuals outside a formal institutional setting. Certainly, the technologies at work on individuals outside institutions will also be at work on individuals inside such facilities. However, another layer of governmentality accrues when individuals reside in an institutional setting. The manner in which society views institutions and the individuals residing in them and how the funding and the services are given to these facilities are all subject to a regimentation and ordering which devolves from a regime that understands that care and those who need large amounts of care are tangential to society. In other words, institutions themselves are subject to a discourse that sees such facilities as outside mainstream society. Thus any funding or any services which these facilities require are not considered primordial to society but, rather, incidental. We see this attitude reflected in the type of media reporting that focuses on the aging population. Usually, these reports invoke the cost to society of this future aging population, as if this future aging population is not part of society. The cost of unproductive individuals is always portrayed as a burden.

How the practices of care are viewed by the residents and the caregivers also stems from this government of care. The discourse into which the practices of care are situated requires that care be viewed primarily as instrumental. Disability theorists have written about the instrumental value of care, since this care can allow them to participate in society. This move is, in part, to destigmatize disabled persons who may require assistance to perform some tasks. Care is simply something they need to enhance their participation in society; it is much like needing a car in order to get to the office quickly.

Viewing care in this manner has merit, as it puts the emphasis on a person's participation in society. Nevertheless, this reductionist move can be problematic as it does not challenge the negative connotation of requiring care. Neither does it propose a deeper understanding of care. In this reductionist view, care remains the product of a medicalized discourse that defines it as something punctual, much like taking a pill to get rid of a headache. It does not question the deeper assumptions regarding what it means to require care, and it does nothing to further an understanding of care as a nonmedicalized practice that could be incorporated into daily life. Care and its dispensation remain carefully controlled by a state apparatus.

Disability activists correctly point out that we all need assistance in some way. We may be dependent on water from the tap, or a taxi to take us somewhere quickly, for example. The level of care or assistance we need may vary, and where we draw the line to call someone more dependent than another can be quite arbitrary.[17] The solution to understanding care critically, however, must avoid treating it instrumentally.

If the person requiring care is an individual who is an active member of society, the negative effects of viewing care in this reductionist way can be mitigated by the fact that the person requiring care is an agent, a citizen, and a "productive" member of society. Nonetheless, the person always has to surmount the assumption that she is "dependent" in some ways.

The resident in long-term care is not such a "powerful" agent; in fact, his or her agency can be quite limited or nonexistent.[18] Moreover, in long-term care, the care is instrumental to survival and is regulated as a medical practice; that is, care is given out as a medical procedure. The intervention given is punctual and regulated by efficiency and time constraints. For example, caregivers must conduct rounds at specific times. At these times, all the residents will be changed or repositioned. Thus, the orderlies will go into a room, perform their tasks, and promptly leave.

The government of care practices under the prevalent medical model thus limits the caring practice to one that is punctual and constrained by strict procedures. Not only is the subject of care identified with her needs and primarily her needs, the practitioners of care can only act in specific ways. Their practices are regulated by efficiency concerns; care is then commodified in specific ways. This, in turn, will constrain the caregivers and position them as agents who deliver a service with little or no need to interact with the care receiver.

It is difficult to explain why care practices have not received more scrutiny. In part, it stems from the fact that chronic institutionalization has tended to be a subject not worthy of theoretical attention. This was certainly the case for institutionalization in general, until the seminal work of Foucault.[19] Perhaps I can venture a few hypotheses on this. Given that the population within such centers is mostly one that cannot voice its discontent, given that such centers are costly and that, furthermore, they are seen as a dead end for most residents who are no longer contributing members of society, discussion about the practices of care within such centers has not elicited much interest amongst theorists.

This changes, however, when cases of abuse make their way to the forefront of the media. Irritated and disgusted citizens may take note that such centers can be problematic, and their ire can be even be more exacerbated if they think that perhaps their dear old grandmother could the object of such seemingly cruel treatment and abuse.

It is important to see how this abuse is portrayed in the media as it yields useful insights into existing care practices as well as the expectations which we, as a society, have of these caring facilities. I will now turn to events that made headlines in the last year.

Mediatized Abuse

A famous case of abuse in Montréal was brought forward in November 2003 by the two sisters of a disabled woman who was living in a long-term care facility, *Centre hospitalier de soins de longue durée (CHSLD) Charles-Borromée*. The orderlies harassed the woman in question by making inappropriate jokes, telling her obvious lies, and calling her names. The abuse was verbal and was caught on cassette tape; this tape was broadcast on the national news in Canada. In the months following this public case, a canadian television network produced several specials on elder abuse; these reports incorporated taped video footage of physical abuse of elderly individuals residing in assisted-living facilities.[20]

It is important to see how the abuse is portrayed in order to understand the various elements at play. The media's portrayal is as follows: the nasty caregiver is seen as an all-powerful individual who takes out her frustrations on her poor helpless charge. I am not contesting that abuse happens; however, the way in which this abuse is cast makes these seemingly cruel orderlies into inherently abusive individuals who are just waiting to do evil to some helpless person. What is shown is the one-sidedness of abuse that resides entirely in the evil orderly. There is no attempt to convey the atmosphere in which this type of abuse is likely to occur, nor is there any effort to understand or question institutional practices.

The discourse of abuse is one that gets attention in the immediate present; it is the type of reporting that can give the reader or viewer something to get emotional about. The scene is fairly straightforward. The resident is helpless, a pitiful individual whom the viewer can feel sorry for without identifying too closely with the person herself. Moreover, if the case can be easily resolved, then the viewer can feel good that a "happy" resolution is attainable. All the elements are present: a helpless victim, a quickly identifiable villain, a fast punishment that does not shake the foundations of the established order.

In this case, once the proper individuals have been chastised, the problem can be soon forgotten. By situating the abuse in the individual worker, the problem is one that seems quickly resolved. There is no attempt to question the ideology of the care practices promulgated within such facilities. It is taken for granted that such facilities are set up to deliver what they promise—total care.

One important point to be revealed here is that such places, either the long-term care institution or the assisted living facility, are never seen as problematic. The room in the video footage is the privileged location of abuse, but the abuse comes only from the worker who enters the room. The room is unquestionably understood as the site of care, regardless of the situation in which the worker may be immersed. In addition, the media representation sets up an "us against them" scenario where workers are pitted against the care receivers. This takes place within a zone, the room of the abused individual, which is assumed to be unproblematic and, therefore, never discussed.

I want to focus on the room, since it is the scene of the "crime." As such it is simply given as the backdrop for abuse. Yet, it is where the abuse takes place. This room is under the control of an institution mandated to promulgate care. How is it that such a site can become into a zone of abuse? Why is this site the "privileged" place of hurt and not care? What has gone wrong? The media report would locate the wrong in the worker only. I do not question that abuse has taken place; however, I believe that to focus solely on the worker is to misunderstand what is taking place in the room.

I borrow this move from disability activists and theorists who privilege the social model of disability. For these writers, the disability does not come from the individual herself but from the interaction of the person with her environment. If Jane cannot go to work, it is not because she cannot walk, it is because a ramp is not available to her. The social space is where the problem arises. Here, I propose to look at the room as the setting for abuse. I want to examine why abuse happens in this location—what circumstances may be conducive to the reprehensible behavior that occurs there.

In order to elucidate what is going on in these cases of abuse, I will turn to Giorgio Agamben's work. He has written extensively on the concept of "bare life" and he has also made use of Primo Levi's notion of the "gray zone." He traces "bare life" from its inception in Aristotle's work. Agamben then takes Foucault's idea of bio-politics and expands on it: it is the politicization of "bare life."[21]

From Primo Levi, Agamben takes the concept of the grey zone and develops it as an ambiguous zone within which "bare life" can be acted upon with impunity, even eradicated. These two notions are intertwined in Agamben's work. I want to examine, first, Agamben's use of the "gray zone"; it is also important to understand why Levi introduced this concept. The two authors do not use it for the same purpose; Agamben deviates from Primo Levi's original purpose in order to insert this idea of a "gray zone" into his theory of sovereign power over "bare life." This is a crucial point to understand and to examine critically. Finally, I want to consider whether our understanding of care practices within long-term care can benefit from these conceptualizations.

Agamben discusses Primo Levi's description of a soccer match at Auschwitz in *Remnants of Auschwitz*:

> This match might strike someone as a brief pause of humanity in the middle of an infinite horror. I, like the witnesses, instead view this match, this moment of normalcy, as the true horror of the camp. For we can perhaps think that the massacres are over—even if here and there they are repeated, not so far away from us. But that match is never over; it continues as if uninterrupted. It is the perfect and eternal cipher of the "gray zone," which knows no time and is in every place.[22]

The match took place between the *Sonderkommandos* and the SS. A game so ordinary, yet under such extreme circumstances.

It is important to situate Primo Levi's discussion of this "gray zone." For Primo Levi, the discussion centers on the *Sonderkommandos*; he is trying to understand those who may have collaborated with the Nazis, those who did not, and those who survived in the camps. All these men and women were intertwined within a complex system that is not easily decipherable. As he makes clear, it is difficult to lay blame on these "collaborators" because they were also the intended victims of the Nazis. These "collaborators" were both executioners and victims. Obviously, things were not black and white; Levi's point is that under such extreme circumstances one cannot judge easily. The *Sonderkommandos* were picked by the Nazis; their agency could not be clearly demarcated. The "gray zone" is just that, an ambiguous zone where one cannot judge easily.

Agamben uses this soccer match, this ultimate "gray zone," as a metaphor for the ambiguity of ordinary circumstances—to show us how we are never far from a zone where radical evil can occur under seemingly ordinary circumstances. There always lurks the potential for evil. This zone of ambiguity is where victim and executioner can mix; where radical evil can become benign. "A gray, incessant alchemy in which good and evil and, along with them, all the metals of traditional ethics reach their point of fusion."[23] However, in his discussion, Agamben enlarges the idea of the grey zone to one that can exist everywhere, at any time. If we take Agamben's concept of the grey zone, any area can potentially develop into this zone of moral unclarity and, eventually, evil. It is important to understand that, for Agamben, this is an inherent feature of society. It is necessarily so because "western politics first constitutes itself through an exclusion (which is simultaneously an inclusion) of bare life."[24]

Claudia Card, in *The Atrocity Paradigm,* explores the idea of a grey zone where evil can occur and where it may be difficult for agents to distinguish right from wrong. She uses the term "grey area" to point to that zone of ambiguity, but, at the same time, she is careful to state that the Holocaust is a particular form of evil which should not be appropriated lightly. As she states:

> Like Levi, I understand gray zones more specifically to result from choices that are neither gratuitously nor wilfully evil but that nevertheless implicate choosers who are themselves victims in perpetrating evils against others who are also themselves victims, paradigmatically victims of the same evils as the choosers.[25]

Card's use of the concept is precise; she is exploring extreme situations where ethical decisions are not straightforward. Unlike Agamben, she does not tie this concept with sovereign or political power. Her concern is ethical. For this reason, her use of the grey zone may be more appropriate than Agamben's for my purposes. Nevertheless, I want to explore all the facets of this possible appropriation of the grey zone.

The concept of a grey zone is one which is quite powerful. If we look at the media portrayals, long-term care can indeed be seen as an ambiguous zone. It is tempting to view this site as an instantiation of a grey zone. Located within this system of care are individuals who have very little or no agency and who depend on others for their survival. In the media reporting, the orderly or caregiver has all the agency; the resident has none. Both are situated in a room or a zone where evil acts can occur, where seemingly benign individuals commit acts of cruelty. Here we are in the presence of possibly oppressed workers who, in turn, abuse their charges.

If the idea of the grey zone does draw our attention to this rigorous politicization of certain bodies, I claim that this is too facile a step. Not only does it overdramatize long-term care, it also misses some crucial points. Although I believe that we must be careful not to assimilate too readily the paradigm of the grey zone with other ambiguous states in modern society, my point of concern here is not with this appropriation, but with the effects such an appropriation entails. To make such a leap would eschew the critical assessment of the practices of care that encompass both care receiver and caregiver.[26] We cannot forget that such practices are necessary for the survival of the care receivers; this distinguishes long-term care from other ambiguous zones. Nevertheless, the ideology and the discourse which immerse these care practices must not escape our critical attention.

If we immerse ourselves in Agamben's framework, we can, nonetheless, extract some interesting insights. It could be argued that what compels such seemingly ordinary individuals to commit abuse is the fact that they are situated within a system which over-politicizes "bare life."[27] To continue with

Agamben's terminology, this "bare life" is the raw existence of individuals who have no political agency, no place in political society. A person can become predominantly "bare life" because of an illness or accident, Agamben refers to persons in deep comas, for example, because of a criminal act or even a political decree. Such individuals have been excluded, yet remain within the system; for Agamben, they are examples of the "included exclusion."

In many ways, the individuals in long-term care have been excluded. They are living in a special place. Their agency is quite limited, since they have to continually battle the bureaucratic regime of the institution in which they are placed.[28] In this sense, we have a parallel development with the camps where bare life is regimented to the point that extermination falls within the power of the ones who have political power. This extermination is no longer seen as murder within such a scheme, according to Agamben.

In long-term care institutions, we now enter a zone in which abuse may appear simply as just one more step in the regimenting of life. In such a zone, where life is so regulated, it becomes difficult to distinguish where "power over" becomes an act of blatant cruelty. The point Agamben helps us make here is that this cruelty was bound to happen in a system that consistently devalues "bare life" and continually tries to regulate it.

The important point here is not that abuse is excusable, but that caring in an institutional setting needs to be considered very carefully as it involves an ongoing interaction between two individuals of very different capacities and agency. It is a regulated space, where power is thought to be determined and controlled in very specific ways. However, as the cases of abuse have shown, this power often fails to protect the vulnerable persons who need help. Moreover, as I have suggested, the power structures which regulate the relation between caregiver and care receiver may actually be conducive to abuse. That does not excuse inappropriate or criminal behavior, but it does show that a system which does not value those who need care as whole persons irreducible to their needs will be fraught with problems.

When Care is Work

The discourse of institutions does two things. It places the recipient of care into a role which she cannot contest—as a set of needs. When framed in this way, it is easy to see this person only as a task to be done. Institutionalization also ensures that such a role is permanent. Thus, a dubious role is assigned to her, and it is permanent.

Here the notion of "bare life" is relevant. The care receiver becomes a body upon which care is practiced. She may have some autonomy, legally she has the power to refuse a treatment; however, she is solidly enshrined within a regime of care that is difficult to contest. In addition, her body is set within a medical discourse which encompasses all her existence. She is unescapably "bare life" and only that.

This is obviously problematic for the care receiver, and it is also problematic for the caregiver since this reduces her multifaceted task of caregiving to one that is easily commodified. In this type of caregiving, the power relations are not punctual; they are ongoing and immerse the care receiver completely. It is not only that the caregivers are the powerful agents in the care relation, but it is also the sense in which their attention is given to their charges. The care relationship is always unidirectional, toward the needy individual. It distorts care as it makes it into practice that is given out regardless of how it is received. The recipient of care is passive. Thus, care can only function in one way; it can never be multidirectional within the discourse of care which is set up in long-term care institutions. It necessarily shapes the recipient of care as a passive bundle of needs.

An important point about these considerations of care is that, ideally, care is a practice that enables. It allows the person cared for to flourish, which, in fact, defines the purpose of care. This is true whether care is considered in the private realm or the public one. Moreover, care is a practice that binds individuals.

Persons who need a great deal of assistance risk being isolated. Caring practices, even if they viewed as instrumental, must aiim to break up this isolation, as disability activists have shown. If we look at the care practices in long-term care, we can see that these caring practices isolate. In the first place, they must take place within an institution that groups together individuals according to their level of need. The care practices also imply that care is parceled in specific ways within a tight regime which medicalizes and commodifies it.

Not only do care practices force the residents into a subjectivity that identifies them strictly with their needs; the caregivers are also regulated as to the manner in which they give care. The implications of this are that long-term care facilities must group together individuals who require similar levels of care. The manner on which the residents will be dealt with are regulated quite specifically. Therefore, both care receiver and caregiver are seen in one dimension and ultimately are isolated from each other and from themselves by this practice.

Conclusion

In an institutional setting, the person requiring vast amounts of care will be seen as a set of needs. These needs are easily quantified, arranged, and satisfied within a regime that understands needs as commodities kept under strict economic control. Needs should never be too costly. This, in turn, presents the institutionalized person as a "task to be done" and not a "person to be attended to." "Caring for," in this sense, becomes a job to be done. The systematic quantification and regulation of needs implies that the "caring for" can be done in a systematic, detached manner where the "cared for" is no longer a person. "Bare life" is acted upon by a political system; such ""bare life" ' is completely alienated. The state can effectively deny "caring about" bare life, as it equates it with troublesome persons/bodies which it chooses to located in specific institutions.

The biomedical regimenting of "bare life" further exemplifies how the state privileges a specific reductionist ontology of the individual. It encourages the commodification of the care given to the institutionalized person's body in specific ways. This, in turn, accommodates the alienation of that person's being. This alienation is not only at the personal level and the level of care recipient /caregiver relationship. It also occurs at the societal level. Institutionalized persons are outside political society both figuratively and actually.

"Bare life" is multidimensional; institutionalization tends to make it one-dimensional. By this, I mean that "bare life" is life in its many facets: it cannot be reduced to a mere set of needs. There are vital needs as well as drives; which ones are primary, which ones should and can be satisfied within a regime of care, and which ones fall outside such an understanding is a complex problem that is not addressed by the discourse of needs satisfaction in long-term care.

The current institutional discourse of care requires a reductionist ontology. The care receiver"s dignity is always assaulted within such a system. The institutional care practices are the mediation between care receiver and caregiver; therefore, cases of abuse should not surprise us given the way in which care has become a rigid practice to be given to individuals who are devalued.

Furthermore, the way in which we understand this type of instrumental care is symptomatic of the way in which we conceptualize the needs of citizens: commodities which can be delivered efficiently within the tight regime of a professional discourse. This discourse is meant to encompass all relevant needs, and the ones which cannot be addressed are assumed to be outside the realm of consideration or simply irrelevant.

What are the implications for greater society? In our current understanding, health care needs are separate needs that can be easily satisfied within a capitalist framework of dispensing x over time period y. The political citizen remains disembodied; the current practices of care further eliminate any hope of rethinking the citizen in ways in which she would be understood as an embodied and sometimes needy person. "Bare life" plays no role except to be the subject of regulation and alienation, further enhancing the state's control of its subjects as docile bodies. Such docile bodies will be acceptable if, and only if, they are maintenance-free.

Part V

The French Context

Chapter 10

Subverting Social Order:
Foucault and Derrida on the Role of the Intellectual

Christian Lavagno
University of Osnabrück (Germany)

In the 1970s, a controversy on the status of the intellectual emerged in France that continues today. This controversy revolves around the issue of which questions intellectuals are entitled to raise. According to their critics, intellectuals are outdated figures who have lost all of their value and should be dismissed immediately. Their defenders, on the other hand, maintain that they still play an important role in society and should therefore be conceded the same privileged status as in the era from Zola to Sartre. Among the radical critics is Lyotard; the most prominent defender is Bourdieu.

Bourdieu falls back on the old model of a republic of scholars and artists obliged only to reason and truth. He develops his argument by referring to the contrast of autonomy vs. heteronomy, assuming that in many sectors of society the life of individuals is determined heteronymously by economic and political powers. In his view, only art, literature, and science succeeded in maintaining a certain independence. Thus, artists, writers, and scientists have become experts in autonomy, so to speak, and this is why they are cut out for public engagement. When taking a stand on present-day social debates, thereby investing the "cultural capital" they accumulated in one of the autonomous spheres, they can insist on supporting the interests, not of a particular social group, but of the community as a whole. Due to their specific relationship to autonomy, they are predestined to appeal to the higher targets of society. By this very act they become intellectuals, that is, "the advocates of the universal."[1]

In a way, one would not expect the sociologist Bourdieu to refer to the autonomy of the intellectual sphere, since it is sociology that denies the independence of any subsystem of society. In fact, Bourdieu does not naively assume the absolute autonomy of the *république des Lettres*. He is aware of the fact that writers are dependent on the book market, that a scientific career requires more than the discovery of truth, and so on. What he claims, however, is that the intellectual sphere contains a permanent struggle against heteronomy. Art, literature, and science have developed a number of techniques by which they preserve a degree of relative independence. Hence, intellectuals may intervene in the political field in a nonpolitical way, that is, without backing specific interests. What enables them to do so is, according to Bourdieu, the theoretical framework of "the unwritten laws of an ethical and scientific universalism."[2]

This is exactly the point where Lyotard applies the lever of his criticism. He starts with the assumption or, rather, the diagnosis that in the present time the great narratives *(grands récits)* that were characteristic of the philosophical discourse of modernity have become implausible. Above all Marxism, for a long time the theoretical foundation of left-wing engagement, has lost all of its credibility, beginning with Solzhenitsyn's disclosures about the Soviet camps and ending, in 1989, with the collapse of those regimes that mistook themselves for socialist. However, given that there is no longer a comprehensive theory, and that the fragmentation in discourse and reality has reached a degree where any kind of universalism is obsolete, it follows, according to Lyotard, that intellectuals have lost the basis of their engagement. When taking sides in a public controversy, for example in the Dreyfus Affair, they did so referring to general values and acting as if they were the speakers of the collective conscience. It has always been their task to rise above the diverging particular interests and to bring to memory the homogeneous common interest of society. Lyotard, however, maintains, "Now it is precisely this totalizing unity, this universality, that thought has lacked since at least the middle of the twentieth century."[3] If this is true, intellectuals may no longer appear to be the way they used to.

This does not mean, however, that Lyotard denies the possibility of any intellectual activity at all. On the contrary, he enumerates a number of activities that require highly developed intellectual faculties: (a) the management of cultural events and performances (which requires the ability of organization and can be measured by the relation between effort and result); (b) the creation of pieces of art in a broad sense, including music and literature; (c) public appearance as a *citoyen* making specific suggestions for a better organization of the community. What he does deny, though, is that any of these activities presupposes the reference to a universal subject such as "the intellectual." Thus, intellectuals are significantly different from artists, *les citoyens*, or persons responsible for cultural administration. Their necessity is in no way warranted by the fact that the community is in need of highly qualified persons with enormous intellectual capabilities. The crucial point remains that "the intellectual" refers to some entity of universal value, for example "man, humanity, the nation, the people, the proletariat, the creature, or some such entity."[4]

Therefore, whereas Bourdieu upholds the existence of a basic stock of general values to which intellectuals can refer, Lyotard insists that the universalism underlying that assumption holds no credibility. The opposition seems to be an aporetic one, because it is nothing but a new version of the old conflict between fundamentalism and relativism. On the other hand, it is remarkable that Bourdieu and Lyotard have a number of assumptions in common. Implicitly, they agree in presupposing the intellectual's claim to tell a truth that is located beyond everyday power struggles and that is not polluted by them. It is true that Lyotard challenges the validity of such a truth, but it is no less true that, within his refutation, he accepts the underlying model (i.e., the separation of power and truth). A second agreement resulting from the first one is that for both Bourdieu and Lyotard a certain transfer is characteristic of the intellectual. First, intellectuals win renown in the apolitical sphere of art, literature, and science, and then they give effect to the reputations they gained by employing it in the political field. Thus, despite the differences between them concerning the evaluation, Bourdieu and Lyotard have the same notion of the intellectual. They are standing on the same platform.

In order to restore movement to the petrified debate, we must abandon that platform and search for another theoretical foundation. I suggest doing so by turning to Foucault, who defines the relationship between power and truth in a different way and, therefore, arrives at a new concept of the intellectual.

Foucault successfully undermines the dichotomy of repressive power and liberating truth by demonstrating the complexity of the relations between power and truth. On the one hand, truth is in many cases an effect of power, since the preservation of power requires the production of truth. On the other hand, there is no devaluation of truth because the resistance against power takes place within the framework of power as well. Foucault rejects the simple model that naively assumes a clear distinction between two domains, a heteronymous one reigned by power, and an autonomous one reigned by truth. Instead, he shows that there are elements of power in *all* human relationships including the seemingly autonomous realm of art, literature, and science. "The important point, I think, is that truth is not independent from power. . . . Truth belongs to our world; it is produced in the world by a series of constraints. And truth owns some of the effects of power."[5] This is the primary consequence of Foucault's microphysics of power.

For intellectuals, these consequences prevent them from referencing any truth beyond power. In Foucault's view, traditional left-wing intellectuals stood for total liberation, that is, liberation *from* power (instead of liberation *within* power). They spoke on behalf of "the universality of justice and the equity of an ideal law."[6] For this reason, they may be called universal intellectuals. The problem is that, according to the microphysics of power, freedom can be obtained in specific power struggles only. Liberation does not depend on a global strategy based on a comprehensive theory of society, but on local resistances against specific forms of domination. Hence, no need emerges for anyone to situate themselves as an advocate of universal values.

This does not mean, however, that Foucault suggests erecting a tombstone for the intellectual, as Lyotard did. On the contrary, he believes society needs critical intellectuals. He insists, however, upon a different foundation for their engagement. Besides criticizing the universalism attached to traditional concepts of intellectuals, Foucault also criticizes the traditional intellectual's general incompetence. When famous novelists employ their reputations in political struggles, they may successfully attract media attention. In many cases, however, their utterances will sound like those of an amateur. For, as novelists, they are not directly involved in those struggles. Furthermore, they possess only a partial and mediated knowledge of what is at stake in them. Consequently, their statements will remain quite global and superficial.

For this reason, Foucault introduces the idea of a new kind of intellectual, the specific intellectual who only comments on fields of discussion in which she or he holds a recognized expertise. In many cases, specific intellectuals hold important positions in the field where the debate occurs, for example as scientists, physicians, judges, or social workers. Thereby, they witness firsthand the situation in which the truth of the controversy develops, and they may even take part in its production. They become intellectuals by reflecting on the social consequences of the practices and discourses in which they participate. When presented with a questionable task, they will not hesitate to publicly discuss their misgivings. Foucault holds up Oppenheimer as an example. Oppenheimer, of course, refused to take part in the development of the hydrogen bomb because he was aware of the danger it posed for mankind. For that refusal he was subjected to massive repression in the 1950s. In Foucault's view, it was the first time that an intellectual was persecuted, not because of his overall moral reputation, but because of his specific professional competence. (Both Socrates and Galileo, however, would qualify as an earlier examples.)

Therefore, whereas traditional intellectuals face a gap between the field where they acquire renown and the field in which they engage themselves politically, specific intellectuals take up a position only on problems on which they can comment competently because of their background knowledge. From Bourdieu's perspective, one could raise the objection that since specific intellectuals find themselves directly involved in the struggles, they lack the necessary degree of impartiality to hold credibility. In response, we could argue that the microphysics of power has proven the supposed neutrality and indifference to be a chimera.

However, Foucault did not stop at the microphysics of power. In the second half of the 1970s, he moved on to what he called the analysis of governmentality. This is an enlargement of his theory with important implications for his views on the role of the intellectual. The fundamentally new idea is that power preserves itself not only by producing truth, but also by producing subjectivity. Modern regimes of power *govern* individuals in a sophisticated manner. They do so by urging them to sketch an image of themselves and to feel bound to that image from then on. The danger herein is that a certain identity is forced upon the individuals to which they may remain chained until the end of their lives. On the other hand, the possibility opens up that the individuals are free to form themselves as ethical subjects.

What impact does this hold for the notion of the intellectual? We should first note that the concept of a specific intellectual still contains a number of traditional elements of thought. In the first place, she or he still acts as a spokesperson *(porte-parole)*, that is, being present in the media is an important criterion of her or his success. Secondly, by virtue of her or his competence one might think that she or he is in possession of the "right" theory, a theory, besides, that provides us with instructions for its application in practice as well. As I will try to show, Foucault abandons both elements when he develops the concept of governmentality (thus performing his personal turn to ethics). After accounting for the issue of subjectivity, he produces a new concept of the intellectual that goes beyond the concept of a specific intellectual.

We can identify *subjectivation*, understood as the process by which an individual is bound to a certain self-concept, functioning at once as both a technology of power and a source of freedom, as the essential though ambivalent consequence of Foucault's analysis of governmentality. This situates intellectuals as persons whose awareness of the latent possibilities within that process enables them to make conscious use of their potentials. They endeavor to govern themselves, as far as possible. For this reason, they reject the attempts of spokespeople to influence their ways of thinking and acting, and they make no attempt to become spokespersons themselves. Foucault explicitly demands, "It is necessary to do away with spokespersons,"[7] concluding that freedom depends not on standing on the "right" side but on being engaged personally. He ascribes the greatest significance not to doctrine, but to the ethos that provides the foundation of a specific engagement. Consequently, intellectuals, as imagined by Foucault at this stage of his work, do not tell others which way to go. Rather, through the correspondence between the conduct of their lives and their political engagement, they model behaviors that might encourage others to find their own ways, as well.

An ethos, however, cannot be deduced from a theory. It emerges as part of a decision concerning how one will live his or her life and how he or she will *act* in the world. Therefore, Foucault does not claim that there is an unbroken connection between the analytic of power and a specific political engagement. No theory can anticipate what has to be done in a specific historical situation. Free and responsible individuals must decide. Intellectuals, too, must make active and conscious use of their freedom, thereby constituting themselves as subjects. When giving their support to a specific cause, however, they must also remain vitally aware that the decision to lend that support stems from the prior decision concerning how they seek to conduct their daily lives.

In other words, intellectuals should ponder the claims they raise. Having long overestimated themselves, Foucault recommends that intellectuals should deflate the pretentiousness of their messianic habits. "I hold, " he claimed, "that the role of the intellectual today is not that of establishing laws or proposing solutions or prophesying."[8] Foucault himself interpreted his own intellectual work as an attempt to pave the way for an alteration of society, but he never claimed to be *the one* who knows how to solve social problems. On the contrary, he believed that solutions must be found by those directly involved. "It is all a social enterprise (*travail*). I would like to facilitate this work, with its special problems, by working inside the body of society; and I'd like personally to be able to participate in this enterprise without delegating the responsibility to any specialist, much less to myself."[9] Therefore, he never intended to tell a definitive truth. Rather, his works give expression to an experience that Foucault himself had and that he wants to render possible to his readers, too. *Madness and Civilization*, for example, is more than a history of psychiatric institutions from the seventeenth to the nineteenth century. The essential goal of the book is to show that modern society constituted itself by excluding certain people as "mentally ill"; it implies the idea that the notion of mental illness partly depends on contingencies and is therefore open to alteration. Thus, the book allows us to establish a new relationship to insanity, including the possibility of fundamentally redefining that term. This represents exactly what Foucault has in mind when speaking of experience. Each of his books is a "*livre-expérience*" instead of a "*livre-vérité*" or a "demonstration-book."[10] It is up to intellectuals to take part in that experience and to draw conclusions from it.

Obviously, the Foucauldian concept of experience implies a factor of unforeseeability. When beginning a book he never knew what the outcome would be, for he explicitly intended to be changed by the experience of writing it. Hence, we see a parallel in Jacques Derrida's notion of an event where the unforeseeable and uncontrollable are equally central. For this reason, I want to turn to Derrida now. As I will argue, Foucault and Derrida reflect upon the social role and the critical impact of thinking in a similar way.

In 1999, Derrida held a famous lecture entitled "The University Without Condition"[11] in which he presented his ideas concerning political engagement. Derrida never developed a detailed theory of power comparable to Foucault's. He does not even speak of the intellectual; instead, he deals with the university and, in particular, with the professor. Nevertheless, there is a connection to the ideas of Foucault deriving from the fact that Derrida makes use of the ambivalence of the word "professor." A professor is, on the one hand, a person whose job it is to teach at the university. On the other hand, a professor makes a public profession in the sense of giving a declaration of belief. Now, Derrida's fundamental idea is that the two dimensions of the word should no longer be torn apart. In his view, teaching at the university should also become an act of public confession. Thus, professors in the Derridean sense of the word do not satisfy themselves with presenting their ideas to an audience; rather, they intend to represent or "live" those ideas at the same time. Not only do they impart information concerning scientific issues, but they commit themselves to what they report on. Consequently, for Derrida, as well as for Foucault, their teaching constitutes a kind of *engagement*.

Derrida's idea is based on John L. Austin's distinction between *constative* and *performative* speech acts. In the traditional view, scientists are obliged to confine themselves to constatives, describing the state of affairs in objective statements. Their personal views and, in particular, their political opinions are not part of their scientific work. As we have seen, even Bourdieu and Lyotard accept the model of the purity of the scientific sphere. Derrida, on the contrary, holds that the discourse of a professor goes beyond the stating of facts. Properly understood, it always implies assuming responsibility since professors answer for what they teach. Thus, Derrida lays stress upon the performative aspect of theory. That is exactly the point where he meets with Foucault, since it is an ethos that guides the performance. Foucault and Derrida agree in that philosophy is true only to the extent that it infiltrates into our conduct of life.

At a certain stage of his thought, however, Derrida concluded that accounting for the performative dimension of science required him to go beyond Austin, as well. According to the famous definition given by Austin, a performative generates an event only by making appropriate persons say appropriate words under appropriate circumstances. A civil marriage, for example, demands to be performed by a registrar asking the right questions with a bride and groom giving the right answers. Now, the problem is that the performative *controls* the event in question. Everything is fixed in advance and must follow the prescribed procedure; as soon as there is a deviation, the event simply ceases to take place. For example, if the registrar turns out not to be authorized to perform a marriage ceremony, bride and groom remain unmarried for the time being. Thus, a performative act is based on a number of agreements and conventions, and it takes place within a horizon; there is nothing surprising about it. Derrida, on the other hand, holds that an event, in the strong sense, comes up suddenly and unexpectedly bursting any horizon. It can neither be controlled nor even foreseen. Therefore, it does not belong to the order of the performative (nor to the order of the constative). Derrida is aware of the fact that most of what happens in the world is not an event in this sense. He admits that his way of understanding the notion is an emphatic one and that, given his definition, events are very rare. Nevertheless, he insists that they may occur and that, consequently, philosophy is to set apart a notion for them.

Thus, there is an element of unforeseeability in both the Foucauldian concept of experience and the Derridean notion of an event. This signals an analogy indicative of substantial agreement, the fundamental differences between Foucault and Derrida notwithstanding. In both cases, that which matters cannot be regulated or even described beforehand. The only thing we can do is prepare a place for it to arrive. This, on the other hand, requires an open mind not influenced by prejudice. We can make an experience, or appreciate an event, only if we are ready to abandon all the views and beliefs we are accustomed to. Consequently, we might say that it is the intellectual to whom the respective reflections are addressed. It is true that Derrida, as mentioned, prefers speaking of the professor, and it is also true that, in his explanation of the concept of experience, Foucault never explicitly referred to the intellectual. But who else is likely to show the required open-mindedness? Obviously, what Foucault and Derrida have in mind is a mental disposition that is best dealt with by using the expression "intellectual."

Of course, we are talking about a new kind of intellectual, characterized, above all, by flexibility of mind. These new intellectuals remain poised to abandon the habitual path of thought at any time and to take into account that which previously seemed impossible to imagine. This is true even if the political impact of the new idea points to the necessity of social change. So, being an intellectual primarily means being willing to listen to new evidence. It no longer has to do with becoming a spokesperson who appeals to her or his set of envisioned universal values of mankind. Bourdieu's model is obsolete (namely, the idea of a transfer of the cultural capital accumulated in science and literature to the political sphere). On the contrary, the new intellectual is convinced that the force behind social change must arise from society itself. Consequently, instead of making efforts to obtain the leadership of a social movement, the new intellectuals oblige and content themselves to merely take part in it.

Chapter 11

Foucault and the "Hydra-Headed Monster":
The *Collège de Sociologie* and the Two *Acéphales*

Frank Pearce
Queen's University (Canada)

This chapter focuses on the important relationships between Michel Foucault (1926-84) and three significant and connected twentieth-century French thinkers: Michel Leiris (1901-90), Pierre Klossowski (1905-2001), and Georges Bataille (1897-1962). Foucault made significant use of the work of all three, but particularly the latter two, and a discussion of Foucault's relationship to this work constitutes the first part of the chapter. The work of a fourth connected thinker, Roger Caillois (1913-78), also receives some attention, but I do not treat Caillois' work in such depth. True, there was an indirect link between Caillois and Foucault in that they both had a relationship to Georges Dumézil. Also, Caillois had supported Foucault during his unsuccessful efforts to publish *Histoire de la folie à l'âge classique* with Gallimard, and then, during his successful attempt to publish *Les mots et les choses* with the same publisher—part of the latter text was published in Caillois' own journal, *Diogènes*.[1] Nevertheless, no evidence exists to suggest that Caillois' thought constituted a significant resource or reference point for Foucault. Finally, there is no discussion here, of the work of Maurice Blanchot (1907-2003), largely because he had no connection with the *Collège de Sociologie*—he did not meet Bataille until 1940—but also because of the limitations of space.

Leiris, Klossowski, Bataille, and Caillois were all steeped in classical mythology, read Friedrich Nietzsche appreciatively, were linked to Surrealism and were intrigued by the work of the Marquis de Sade. Michel Foucault shared these same interests. But, in the 1930s the four older thinkers were also all involved with the *Collège de Sociologie* that met in Paris between 1937 and 1939, the journal *Acéphale* (published between 1936 and 1939) and the secret society, Acéphale, which was active between 1936 and 1939. We find the only explicit indication of Foucault's awareness of these early endeavours in his essay "The Prose of Acteon,"[2] where he refers to Pierre Klossowski's lecture at the *Collège de Sociologie*: "The Marquis de Sade and the Revolution."

Yet, Foucault wrote the "Présentation" to the first volume of Bataille's collected works, which includes many of Bataille's early philosophical and social scientific writings, along with his writings in *Acéphale*, the note announcing the foundation of the *Collège de Sociologie* and its declaration on the International Crisis, as well as the article "The Sorcerer's Apprentice," published in the July 1938 "Collège de Sociologie," issue of *Nouvelle Revue Française*. Furthermore, there had long been a reek of scandal about the secret society, Acéphale, including rumours of human sacrifice. Patrick Walberg had written somewhat elliptically about it in 1944,[3] and in 1974 Roger Caillois reminisced about it.[4] Moreover, in 1979 Hollier's published the first French edition of his book, *The Collège de Sociologie*, a work that generated both critical acclaim as well as some controversy. It is hard to believe that Foucault was not aware of at least some of this, and it is a great shame that he did not draw upon this work in the last decade or so of his life, when, arguably, his work was compromised by liberalism. The development of his own work might well have been quite different had he engaged with more of the concepts explored and developed by these thinkers in the twenties and thirties.

Foucault and Leiris

Leiris was a dissident surrealist, an ethnographer and longtime man of the left. He authored poetry, novels, scholarly works on art and artists, many volumes of autobiography, and important empirical and theoretical books on ethnography; he served on the board of *Les Temps Modernes* and was active in anticolonial struggles. One of Leiris's interests was the writings of the somewhat eccentric author of poetry, plays, and novels, Raymond Roussel. Leiris's father managed Roussel's finances, so Leiris knew Roussel personally and started writing about his books in the 1930s.[5]

Now, it is in the context of also writing about Roussel that, in 1962, Foucault first makes explicit reference to Leiris.[6] In 1963 he praised Leiris's "admirable *Rules of the Game*"[7] (at the time, the first two volumes, of *Rules of the Game, Biffures* (1948) and *Fourbis* (1955) had been published) and, in the same year, in "Preface to Transgression" approvingly cites Leiris's *La littérature considerée comme une tauromachie* (1948).[8] In a later interview on André Breton, he showed even greater familiarity with the range of Leiris's works and the context of its production. "There is no doubt," Foucault said in that interview, "that the whole network connecting the works of Breton, Georges Bataille, Leiris, and Blanchot, and extending through the domains of ethnology, art history, the history of religions, linguistics, and psychoanalysis, are effacing the rubrics in which our culture classified itself, and revealing unforeseen kinships, proximities, and relations."[9] In "Theatrum Philosophicum," he suggested that some of Deleuze's ideas were well represented by the image of "fibrils and bifurcations (Leiris's marvelous series would be well suited to a Deleuzian analysis)"[10]—a clear reference to Leiris's *Fibrilles* (1966), the third volume of *Rules of the Game*. Finally, in an interview conducted in 1983, he again mentions Leiris positively but restricts his comments to saying that Leiris's "*Biffures* has a number of things reminiscent of Roussel."[11] He was thus familiar with a range of Leiris's writings but, as we will see, he read them in a somewhat partial manner.

Roussel was one of a number of French-speaking thinkers, of varying sophistication, intrigued by word games. Ferdinand de Saussure was fascinated by anagrams as well as, of course, developing arguments about diachronic change through chains of signifiers: "the diachronic identity of two words as different as calidum and chaud ("hot") means simply that one passed from the former to the latter though synchronic identities"[12] (i.e., *calidmus/calidu*; *calidu/caldu*; *caldu/cald* through to "*chaud*"). Then, Jean-Pierre Brisset, also valorized by Foucault,[13] played endlessly with homophones and paronyms:

> *Les dents, la bouche,*
> *Les dents, là, bouchent,*
> *Les dents la bouchent,*
> *L'aidant la bouche, etc. etc.*[14]

Roussel revealed posthumously that he had developed a range of writing machines, one of which was not too dissimilar in its use of wordplay to that of Brisset. According to Roussel's own account: "I chose two similar words. For example *billiards* and *pilliards* (looter). Then, I added to it words similar but taken in two different directions, and I obtained two different sentences thus. The two found sentences, it was a question of writing a tale which can start with the first and finish with the second."[15] For example, the sentence "*les lettres du blanc sur les bandes du vieux billard*" (the letters in white around the edges of the old billiard table can very easily be transformed into "*les lettres du blanc sur les bandes du vieux pillard*" ("the white men's letters about the old plunderer's gang"). Thus was born Roussel's short story *Parmi les noirs* and from it his novel, *Impressions d'Afrique*. This was only one of a vast array of techniques deployed by Roussel to rhetorically break down and reconstruct language, in other words, to explore "the tropological space" of language.

Foucault argues that certain kinds of tropes informed a number of the different levels of Roussel's writing at all its different levels. In identifying these, Foucault cites eighteenth-century grammarian Dumarsais: "The same words obviously had to be used in different ways. . . . Thus by necessity and by choice, words are often turned away from their original meaning to take on a new one which is more or less removed but that still maintains a connection."[16] One can, indeed, locate such tropes in the thematics of Roussel's works. There, one typically finds a "machine" that, in some often unspecified way, produces in circular time a repetitious nonidentity. Thus, in *Impressions d'Afrique,* Bedu, an engineer, a member of a profession (*métier*) which rises at dawn (*aube),* constructs on the shores of a river a paddle loom (*métier à l'aubes*). This is designed so that, in response to the chance movement of the water, it selects a preprogrammed image that, through a series of repetitious movements, weaves a coherent design. Over time, the loom weaves the image of the Flood and then that of the Ark. The image of the ark can be seen as a figure of the weaving machine (its opposite) and of Roussel's writing machine, representing the chance meetings of opposites within confined or demarcated spaces in a self-referential and self-enclosed linguistic game.

Foucault provides an interesting account of the relationship between the work of Roussel and that of Leiris. He writes:

> Michel Leiris, in the admirable *Rules of the Game*, uses the same tropological space for an experiment that's related and also opposite (the same game according to another set of rules): in the shifting of words which contaminate things—superimposing them into marvelous and monstrous figures—he tries to grasp the fleeting but inevitable truth about what has occurred. From so many things without any social standing, from so many fantastic civic records, he slowly accumulates his own identity, as if within the folds of words there slept, with nightmares never completely extinguished, an absolute memory. The same folds Roussel parts with a studied gesture to find the stifling hollowness, the inexorable absence of being, which he disposes of imperiously to create forms without parentage or species, Leiris experiences the fullness of this moment as an inexhaustible truth in which he can immerse himself without respite, the same expanse that Roussel's narratives cross as if on a tightrope above the void.[17]

Leiris's work, then, seems blighted by phenomenology, and Roussel's project was also doomed by its limits: "Roussel appears as he defined himself: the inventor of a language which only speaks about itself, a language absolutely simple in its duplicated being, a language about language, enclosed in its own sun in its sovereign and central flaw."[18]

Foucault often refers to this space of (almost) identity and (almost) repetition as a "neutral space," but it is also inhabited space. Inside Bedu's machine, there is "a complex meshing of the automatic with the willed, of chance with the finite, the blending of the found with the sought after" and this happens within an "oblong forever-closed black box . . . strangely resembling a coffin."[19] Thus, language is put into contact with what is radically exterior to it, namely, death. Yet, brilliant as is Foucault's discussion of Roussel and Leiris, his judgments are less than adequate. He seems to ignore Dumarsais's comment that it is "by necessity and by choice, words are often turned away from their original meaning." Roussel himself wrote: "one needs to know how to use it [the method]. For just as one can use rhymes to compose good or bad verses, so one can use this method to produce good or bad works."[20] Leiris recognizes these complications.

> Not only does the process employed by Roussel for the composition of his prose works have the immense interest of adding up to a deliberate promotion of language to the rank of creative agent, instead of contenting itself with using it as an agent of execution, but it seems that the subjugation to a specious and arbitrary law (obliging a concentration on the difficult resolution of a problem whose given facts are as independent as possible of each other) has as a consequence a distraction whose *liberating power appears much more efficacious than the abandon, pure and simple, implied by the use of a process like automatic writing*. Aiming at an almost total detachment from everything that is nature, feeling and humanity, and working laboriously over materials apparently so gratuitous that they were not suspect to him, Roussel arrived by this para-

doxical method at the creation of authentic myths, in which his affectivity is reflected in a more or less direct or symbolic way, as it is shown by the frequency of certain themes which constitute the leitmotivs of his work and of which the omnipotence of science, the close relation between microcosm and macrocosm, ecstasy, Eden, the treasure to be discovered or the riddle to be solved, artificial survival and post mortem states, masks and costumes, as well as many themes which could be interpreted as stemming from fetishism or sado-masochism, constitute examples (here enumerated without any attempt at a methodical inventory).[21]

While language and its tropes are seen as sites of play, what is selected is an effect of aleatory processes and individual or collective conscious and/or unconscious processes. It is, perhaps, not surprising that Leiris believed that Foucault rendered Roussel too philosophical.[22]

More generally, there is something tendentious in Foucault's argument that, in Roussel's writings, discourse was always so linguistically self-referential. As Alan Stoekl has shown, there is an aspect of the image of Noah's ark,

[I]ts status as a mythical-historical account of the (doubled) origin of humanity . . . [that] while internal and essential to the movements of Roussel's textual machine is . . . external to (or excluded from) the movement of Foucault's. . . . [T]he ark may . . . be seen as a kind of vast encyclopedia. . . . The kind of research with which we would associate such an encyclopedia . . . involves the possibility of a confrontation exterior to the play of language: . . . of natural, historical, economic and social phenomena.[23]

If Klossowski's judgement that Foucault's goal was "the liquidation of the principle of identity,"[24] is accurate, we can see how he differs from Leiris who, in this account, evidently provides a depriveleging but not a total negation of the self-conscious subject as the site of creativity. Indeed, as Seán Hand argues, Leiris's major project, *Les règles de jeu*, taken as a whole, can be seen as demonstrating that the subject is both "a constructed effect" of the kind of processes and relations that Foucault describes in *The Archaeology of Knowledge* as a "discursive formation," and also operates, in part, through the "dialectic of praxis" explored in Sartre's later work.[25] The question of the relationship between discursive practices and what is outside of it, including its conditions of existence, was a question that always interested Leiris, a point to which we will return.

Foucault and Klossowski

In a 1978 interview Foucault singled out Klossowski, Bataille, Blanchot, and Nietzsche as authors who had enabled him to deviate from his university training.[26] Klossowski was a translator, belle lettrist, philosopher, one-time Cistercian monk, novelist, and painter. Foucault was an avid reader of his work, came to know him personally in the early 1960s, and read in manuscript form his novel *Le Baphomet* (1965), which, in turn, Klossowski dedicated to Foucault.

From 1963 to the late 1970s, he frequently cited Klossowski and in 1964 he wrote an appreciative review of his translation of the *Aeneid* (1964) as well as an important article on his work, "The Prose of Acteaon."[27] In the latter, Foucault focuses on Klossowski's retelling of the myth of Actaeon and Diane (*Le bain de Diane,* Paris: Pauvert, 1956) in which the huntsman Actaeon, a grandson of Cadmus, violates the goddess Diana while she has taken human form. In retribution, she transforms him into a stag to be torn to pieces by his own hounds. He also draws on the novelistic trilogy, *Les lois d'hospitalité* (Paris: Gallimard, 1965), comprised of *Roberte Ce Soir* (1954), *The Revocation of the Edict of Nantes* (1959), *Le Souffleur* (1965), and the essays *Un si funeste désir* (Paris: Gallimard, 1963), as well as his lecture, "Sade and the Revolution."[28] Foucault ended his 1970 article "Theatrum Philosophicum," with a clear reference to *Le Baphomet,* for he mentions that Duns Scotus is "sporting an impressive moustache; it belongs to Nietzsche disguised as Klossowski."[29]

In *Diana at Her Bath,* the goddess Diana is successfully tempted by a demon to enjoy the experience of female humanity in its chastity, lasciviousness, and violability, but only vicariously, because, as the book makes clear, her embodiment is theophanic. She exists in human form only as a "simulacrum"—"a sign of an instantaneous state . . . not purporting to fix what it represents or says of an experience."[30] Here, Klossowski clearly roots his discussion and deployment of simulacra in religio-mythic contexts, doing so in order to show that what looks like her submission to sexual violence is no such thing, although it has all-too-real consequences for Acteon. She is, in fact, neither human nor even partially human. Here we find Klossowski's Gnosticism at play with probable references to myths involving Sophia, the female principle of wisdom. After all, Klossowski later declared his "affinities with the great heresiarchs of Gnosticism (Valentinus, Basildes, Carpocrates),"[31] and Klossowski was no doubt familiar with the writings of the Church Fathers, Iraneus and Tertullian, whose accounts seem not to be simple distortions of, at least some, Gnostic beliefs.[32]

In a discussion of the simulacrum, Foucault notes that while, usually, "the sign derives its meaning only from the interplay and the sovereignty of all other signs," that is synchronically, Klossowski has identified a sign, often found within the religious domain, with a completely different structure, "that says what it is though a profound appurtenance to the origin, through a consecration"; for example, for Christians, the connotations associated with "tree" will include "the cross" and "the tree of knowledge."[33] Reference here might be made to the multiple significations of the lone tree in the desolate stage setting of Samuel Beckett's *Waiting for Godot,* a play much admired by Foucault.[34]

Such a sign has the dual property of "designating no meaning but referring to a model . . . and of being tied to the history of a manifestation that is never completed"; it is a "simulacrum . . . a vain image (as opposed to reality), a representation of something (in which this thing designates and manifests itself, but withdraws and in a sense conceals itself), a false God that causes one to take one sign for another, a sign of the presence of a deity (and the converse possibility of taking the sign for its opposite), the simultaneous coming of the same and the other (originally, to simulate meant to come together)."[35] Foucault comments on the implications of *Diana at Her Bath*, "when divinity ceases to sparkle in the clearings and doubles itself in appearance where it succumbs while justifying itself, it leaves mythical space and enters the time of the theologians. The desirable trace of the gods is collected (is perhaps lost) in the tabernacle and the ambiguous game of signs."[36]

In the novels *Les lois de l'hospitalité*, "the two great configurations that make appearance alternate are hospitality and theater—two structures that face each other in reverse symmetry."[37] The novels are constructed from memoirs, diaries, plays, and "realist" narratives, and organized around the relationships, emotional and sexual, between a Professor of Scholastics, Octave, his wife Roberte, their nephew Antoine, guests, and sundry other male figures. Some at times, speak for the author, K, and, it is of distinct relevance that Klossowski's own wife and model for the drawings that illustrate the text was Denise Marie Roberte Morin-Sinclair. But there is even greater complexity: *Roberte ce soir* already exists within the text itself, since the latter recounts Roberte's decision to censor one of the episodes of the novel. But this first narrative also exists in the second that contests it from within through Roberte's diary, then in the third, when one sees the preparations for its theatrical performance, a performance that escapes into the very text of *Le souffleur*. Here Roberte, urged to animate Roberte with her identical presence, "doubles herself in an irreducibale hiatus," and so on. Thus, "as Klossowski's language recasts itself . . . the speaking subject scatters into voices that prompt one another, suggest one another, extinguish one another, replace one another—dispersing the act of writing and the writer into the distance of the simulacrum where it loses itself, breathes, and lives."[38] He points out that in the lecture "The Marquis de Sade and the Revolution," Klossowski multiples his "Simulacra Men."[39] As we shall see below, this judgement about the text reads it a very restricted way.

Foucault was to enthusiastically sum up Klossowski's work by saying that it captured "the experience of the double, of the exteriority of simulacra, of the theatrical and demented multiplication of the ego."[40] Although their personal relationship cooled after 1970, Foucault's continuing respect for Klossowski is indicated by the fact that in 1981 Foucault successfully nominated him for the *Grand Prix National des Lettres*.

But perhaps, at the same time as Foucault was praising Klossowski's deconstruction of the subject, he was also recognizing the possibility of historical recuperations. While Foucault wrote admiringly of Klossowski's "constellation" of "simulation, similitude, simultaneity, simulation, and dissimulation" (and this configuration bears a remarkable similarity to what in *The Order of Things*) he would identify the Renaissance episteme grounded in resemblances. Yet, Klossowski's work comprised part of the movement by which one could leave behind the contemporary episteme. A useful place to go here is one barely mentioned by Foucualt, Klossowksi's writings on Sade, particularly the edition of *Sade mon prochain* published in 1947.

Klossowski's position on Sade was complex. He believed that some of the latter's denial of God was based upon disappointment. If religion was an enterprise of mystification and human actions were solely motivated by self-interest, then generosity and self-sacrifice were illusions. Because of this, Sade would play the same game: "Others are pretending and masking themselves? Give us simulacra and masks."[41] Sade, however, wished to challenge God to manifest himself. After all, in *The 120 Days of Sodom*, the Duc de Blangis's harangue of the women "destined" for the men's pleasure included the following words:

> Would this all-powerful God permit a feeble creature like myself, who would, face to face with him, be as a mite in the eyes of an elephant, would he, I say, permit this feeble creature to insult him, to flout him, to defy him to challenge him, to offend him as I do, wantonly, at my own sweet will, at every instant of the day.[42]

However, Klossowski's "argument centers on the problematic of Sade's violent desire insofar as this desire structures the encounter between self and other,"[43] particularly the relationship between the libertine and his victim. For example, in an Augustinian interpretation, if the self unleashes its aggression to annihilate the other, doing so in order to do evil, then it affirms the existence of the same moral categories it seeks to negate. And it is possible to unify this position and others adopted by Sade by adapting the Kojèvean interpretation of the Hegelian dialectic.

Hegel, according to Kojève, believed that intrinsic to meaningful human action was the desire to negate some existing state of affairs in pursuit of desire. This desire can only become truly self-conscious if it is directed toward another desire, like itself, a human desire. But my desire can only be satisfied by negating this other desire, by substituting myself for the value desired by this desire, by removing the autonomy of the bearer of this desire, by forcing him to *recognize* that "I am," or I "represent" the value desired by him and "to recognize me as an autonomous value." But, each of the two beings is "ready to risk its life—and, consequently, to put the life of the other in danger—in order to be "recognized" by the other, to impose itself on the other as the supreme value; accordingly, their meeting can only be a fight to the death. If this fight does not lead to the death of both, it must lead to the victory of the braver and the defeat of the one who was not willing, when it came to it, to risk his life for the satisfaction of his desire for "recognition." Defeated, "he must give up his desire and satisfy the desire of the other," "recognizing" the other without being "recognized" by him, but recognizing him as Master and "recognizing" himself, and being "recognized" by others as the slave of this Master. The Master accepts this arrangement because it is pointless to kill his defeated adversary, better to overcome him "dialectically," to destroy only his autonomy, but to leave him life and consciousness, so that he can through his labour transform the material world to satisfy some, but only some, of the master's desires.

But this is an inherently unsatisfactory and unstable arrangement. The warlike master is being "recognized" by somebody he does not "recognize"; there is little possibility of his self-development. The slave, because he "recognizes" the master, comprehends autonomy, and, by his own work, the slave increasingly becomes the master of nature, transcending the given, producing a world—his world, (or potentially his world), transcending in himself what is given to him by the given.

> History must be the history of the interaction between Mastery and Slavery: the historical "dialectic" is the "dialectic" of Master and Slave: But the opposition of "thesis" and "antithesis" is meaningful only in the context of their reconciliation by "synthesis," if history (in the full sense of the world) necessarily has a final term, if man who becomes must culminate in man who has become, if Desire must end in satisfaction, if the science of man possess the quality of a definitively and universally valid truth—the interaction of Master and Slave must finally end in the "dialectical overcoming" of both of them.[44]

Klossowski adapts particular elements of Kojève's version of Hegel's work. Important to him is the dialectical movement of Sade's consciousness as he makes various attempts to liquidate moral categories (both the other and God), in a movement that passes through a number of dialectical phases where moral categories are both negated and maintained. We have already mentioned the first version of this—in promoting Evil for Evil's sake, moral categories are, in fact, conserved.[45] Second, there is then an almost Gnostic attempt to define God as an Evil creator God,[46] but he is seen as violating moral contracts from the beginning. Therefore, again, he is interpreted in relationship to moral categories. After all, Sade revealed a "frenzied aspiration to try out all the imaginable forms of pleasure, to become the subject capable of exhausting the totality of the possible" and these two attitudes could be read in terms of the Carpocratean Gnostic doctrine that "[c]rime is a tribute paid to life" and, thus, the soul should "deliver itself over to sin as soon as temptation presents itself, lest . . . it be . . . cast into a new body—until it has paid all its debts."[47] Sade demonstrated both a fascination with and a "hatred of the body."[48] Then, third, the notion of an evil God is rejected in favor of a conception of nature as a demonic destructive force. "Evil seems . . . the sole element in nature." Thus, these ideas work "within the sphere of moral categories."[49] Finally, nature may be conceived as a perpetual movement of creation and destruction, part of which is a universal, impersonal desire for destruction that founds human passions. However, "if man thinks he is satisfying himself by obeying them, in reality he is satisfying only an aspiration that goes beyond his individual self."[50] We will briefly return to Klossowski's interpretation later.[51]

Foucault and Bataille

Bataille was a novelist, poet, anti-surrealist art critic, philosopher, one-time seminarian, social theorist, and a man of the left. Foucault had first read Nietzsche "because of Bataille,"[52] and, since he seems to have started to read Nietzsche in 1953, he must have been reading Bataille from at least that same time. He published a number of essays in Bataille's journal,[53] and he wrote the introduction to the first volume of Bataille's collected works.[54]

Foucault had started to read Sade as early as 1946,[55] and he was particularly strongly influenced by the interpretations and developments of Sadean thought found in Bataille's writings of the 1950s. Now, in *Literature and Evil,* Bataille, while appreciative of much of Klossowski's writing on Sade, was nevertheless critical, from a Kojèvean perspective, of his attempt to apply dialectical categories to Sade's work. Klossowski's studies lack the rigour of Hegel's *The Phenomenology of Mind*, to which such dialectics bear a resemblance. Further, as Ian James points out, it is "not clear how one phase of this process," identified by Klossowski, "follows on from or supersedes" the previous one "by the operation of a mediating term (as a strictly Hegelian dialectic would demand)."[56]

For Bataille a main problem confronting Sade was that he, "who loved Evil, whose entire work was intended to make Evil desirable,"[57] could not find grounds to either condemn it or justify it. In the context of this failure, Sade shifted his focus, so that his main goal became "the clear consciousness of what can be obtained by 'release'—though release leads to the end of consciousness," that is, "the clear consciousness of suppression—of the difference between subject and object."[58] His lifelong occupation was the enumeration "to the point of exhaustion the possibilities of destroying human beings . . . of enjoying the thought of their death and suffering," and this, in turn, had as its only conceivable end the "desire of the executioner to be the victim of torture himself."[59] Bataille's life and work, too, can be seen as a continual engagement with the brute fact that, as individuals, we always live under the inescapable shadow of death, and this in part explains the importance to us of the sacred and particularly of sacrifice. "In order for man to reveal himself ultimately to himself he would have to die, but he would have to do it while living, watching himself ceasing to be. . . . In sacrifice the sacrificer identifies with the animal struck by death. Thus he dies while watching himself die, and, even, after a fashion, dies of his own volition, as one with the sacrificial arm."[60]

Now, "human life strives toward prodigality to the point of anguish, to the point where the anguish becomes unbearable. . . . A febrile unrest within us asks death to wreak its havoc at our expense."[61] Sex and death are intimately linked, for, while "sexual disorder discomposes the coherent forms which establish us, for ourselves and for others, as defined beings—it moves them into an infinity which is death"; when we experience "the anguish of death . . . the state . . . we enter is similar to that which precedes a sexual desire."[62] A sexual union is "a compromise, a half-way house between life and death;" but if the "communion" is ruptured then "the true violent nature of eroticism can be seen, whose translation, in practice corresponds with the notion of the sovereign man."[63] Such a man has freed his existence from subordination to necessity, and is willing to squander his resources in the utmost pursuit of what he desires. But, this pursuit should ideally involve an actively cruel indifference to others and the turning of a cruel energy against oneself—one's own inherited nature.

> Excess leads to the moment . . . when, what is felt through the senses is negligible and thought, the mental mechanism that rules pleasure, takes over the whole being. . . . Without this excess of denial pleasure is a furtive, contempti-

ble thing, powerless to keep its real place, the highest place, in an awareness
that is ten times as sensitive.[64]

This can be reached by a transgressive violence—"crime is the only thing that
counts and whether one is the victim or not; all that matters is that the crime
should reach the pinnacle of crime" and, thus, "the transcendence of the personal
being" is a "concomitant of crime and transgression."[65] Since carnal pleasure can
be accomplished as readily "by murder or torture, in the course of a debauch, or
by ruining a family or a country, or even just by stealing,"[66] transgression is central.

This was clearly true for Foucault too; the title of his major essay on
Bataille was "A Preface to Transgression." This was published in 1963 and its
major points of reference are the "novels" *Histoire de l'oeil* (1928), *Eponine*
(1949), *Madame Edwarda* (1937), *Bleu du ciel* (1957), *Guilty* (1961), and the
non-fiction works, *Literature and Evil* (1957/1973), *L'Expérience intérieure*
(1943), *Erotism* (1957/1962), and *Les larmes d'Eros* (1961). Bataille in *Erotism*[67] had explored the complex interrelationship between sensuality, mysti-
cism, and death, and Foucault drew on this work in his opening remarks.

> [T]he whole tradition of mysticism and spirituality . . . was incapable of divid-
> ing the continuous forms of desire, of rapture, of penetration, of ecstasy, of that
> outpouring which leaves us spent: all of these experiences seemed to lead,
> without interruption or limit, right to the heart of a divine love of which they
> were both the outpouring and the source returning upon itself. . . . From the
> moment that Sade delivered its first words and marked out, in a single dis-
> course, the boundaries of what suddenly became its kingdom, the language of
> sexuality has lifted us into the night where God is absent, and where all our ac-
> tions are addressed to this absence in a profanation that at once identifies it,
> dissipates it, exhausts it itself in it, and restores it to the empty purity of its
> transgression.[68]

But, of course, what Foucault references here is not just Sade, but Bataille's
interpretation and development of Sade. Bataille's works force us to recognize
that one reason to "kill God" is to render our existence immediate, and another is
to lose language and find "communication," restoring us "not to a limited and
positivistic world but to a world exposed by the experience of its limits, made
and unmade by the excesses which transgress it."[69] Foucault goes on to provide
his own original development of the concept of transgression.

> Transgression is an action that involves the limit, the narrow zone of a line
> where it displays the flash of its passage . . . [T]ransgression incessantly crosses
> and recrosses a line that closes up behind it in a wave of extremely short dura-
> tion, and thus it is made to return once more right to the horizon of the uncross-
> able. . . . [A] limit could not exist if it was absolutely uncrossable and recipro-
> cally, transgression would be pointless if it merely crossed a limit composed of
> illusions and shadows. . . . [T]heir relationship takes the form of a spiral that no
> simple infraction can exhaust. . . . Transgression is neither violence in a divided
> world (an ethical world) nor a victory over limits (in a dialectical or revolution-

ary world). Transgression contains nothing negative, but affirms limited being .
. . correspondingly, this affirmation contains nothing positive.[70]

By "dialectical," Foucault refers to the tradition running from Plato to Kant, and
by "revolutionary," that which runs from Hegel, through Marx, and then Kojève,
and, to complete the circle, back to Hegel. There is little doubt that Foucault
overemphasizes the separateness, as opposed to the relational differences between Bataille and Kojève's Hegel and Marx.

For Foucault, transgression is connected with a philosophy of non-positive
affirmation, a philosophy of contestation, and one that needs extreme forms of
language that go beyond the standard discourse of philosophy and the controlling function of the philosophical subject. Indeed, "in a language stripped of
dialectics" even the philosopher is aware that he "does not inhabit the whole of
his language." Here, Bataille is exemplary, for in such works as *Inner Experience,*

> language proceeds as if through a labyrinth, . . . proceeds to the limit and to this
> opening where being surges forth, but where it is already lost, completely over-
> flowing itself, emptied of itself to the point where it becomes an absolute
> void—an opening which is communication. . . . Essentially the product of fis-
> sures, abrupt descents, and broken contours, this misshapen craglike language
> describes a circle; it refers to itself and is folded back on a questioning of its
> limits.[71]

In the course of this article Foucault had occasion to also acknowledge the importance of the thought of Nietzsche, Klossowski, and Blanchot, and it seems
fitting to end this discussion of it with Foucault's reference to the work of another major thinker with whom we have been concerned.

> Perhaps this "difficulty with words" also defines the space given over to an ex-
> perience in which the speaking subject instead of expressing himself is ex-
> posed, goes to encounter his finitude, and, under each of his words, is brought
> back to the reality of his own death: that zone, in short, which transforms every
> work into a kind of "tauromachy" suggested by Michel Leiris, who was think-
> ing of his own actions as a writer but undoubtedly also of Bataille.[72]

There is little doubt that much more could be written about the explicit and
implicit importance of the works of these thinkers for Foucault's work, *Madness
and Civilization* and *The Order of Things* immediately come to mind. Foucault
himself, however, was to subsequently make judgments of the importance of
their work which were in part illuminating, but, particularly when negative, ob-
scured how much he benefited from his engagement with them and how much
more he could have derived from their work.

Foucault's Reassessment of French Literary Theory

In some of his later work Foucault became much more critical of Sade and Bataille. For example, in *History of Sexuality,* vol. 1, he writes: "to conceive the category of the sexual in terms of the law, death, blood, and sovereignty—whatever the references to Sade and Bataille, and however one might gauge their 'subversive' influence—is in the last analysis as a historical 'retroversion.'"[73] We can view these remarks and others as elements of a more general reassessment not only of Bataille but of the 1960s avant-garde literature as a whole. In a 1977 interview, Foucault said:

> The whole relentless theorization of writing which we saw in the 1960s was doubtless only a swan song. Through it the writer was fighting for the preservation of his political privilege; but the fact that it was precisely a matter of theory, that the needed scientific credentials, founded in linguistics, semiology, psychoanalysis, that this theory took the references from the direction of Saussure, of Chomsky, etc. and that it gave rise to such mediocre literary products, all this proves that the activity of the writer was no longer at the focus of things.[74]

In this same interview, he drew a contrast between the "universal" and the "specific" intellectual. Previously, the former "spoke and was acknowledged the right of speaking in the capacity of master of truth and justice" and this "intellectual through his moral, theoretical and political choice, aspires to be the bearer of this universality in its conscious, elaborated form."[75] Contemporaneously, it is the latter that is of most importance—a "person occupying a specific position—but whose specificity is linked in a society, like ours, to the general functioning of the apparatus of truth."[76]

There were two quite distinct possibilities of development from this analysis. One was to accept that the specific intellectual as a savant had a distinct sphere of competence and that their responsibility lay in acting ethically in the narrow confines of this institutional role. When they spoke about matters affecting society as a whole they either spoke from their specific expertise or they would speak as a concerned private citizen. This does not mean that there were not issues of general concern. For Foucault, in 1984, domination was "the hinge point of ethical concerns and the political struggle for respect of rights, of critical thought against abusive techniques of government and research in ethics. That seeks to ground individual freedom."[77]

However, late in his life Foucault continued to emphasize the importance of Nietzsche, Bataille, and Blanchot to his work, particularly because for them:

> experience has the function of wrenching the subject from itself, of seeing to it that the subject is no longer it, or that it is brought to its annihilation or its dissolution. This is a project of desubjectivation. The idea of a limit-experience that wrenches the subject from itself is what is important too in my reading of Nietzsche, Bataille, and Blanchot, and what explains the fact that however boring, however erudite my books may be, I've always conceived of them as direct

experiences aimed at pulling myself free of myself, at preventing me from being the same.[78]

But this statement can be drawn upon to think through other possibilities inherent in the position of the specific intellectual. It is necessary to recognize both
the potentially genuine but nevertheless necessarily restricted validity of the
knowledge of the specific intellectual, and to understand that the very forms of
this knowledge and indeed the basis of their authority to speak were an effect of
discursive formations with extra-discursive conditions of existence.[79] Professional boundaries create taboos. People within a profession usually only think to
raise a relatively a narrow range of questions about their activities, and they also
routinely deny the legitimacy of those outside the profession to question its activities. They also often claim the right to make decisions in areas where any
such decisions are clearly political and not simply technical—judgments involving outcomes scaled according to incommensurable value criteria.

   This means that such conditions of existence and such social practices may
have played a role in denying other interests, but new configurations of social
forces may well lead to "an insurrection of subjugated knowledges."[80] Such
change may be facilitated by using some of the expertise of specific intellectuals
in wider social movements, but this imbrication is likely to produce a disruption
in the boundaries "protecting" their profession and a profound displacement in
the form and content of their knowledge, not least because they may experience
a transformation of the extradiscursive conditions of their discourse. This happened to many chemical engineers and to their discourses in the context of the
oppositional social movement unleashed by the Bhopal Gas Tragedy.[81] What
produces social stasis and social movements and energizes them must be understood in terms of social collectivities, social relations, and how, in turn, these are
located within some wider system itself requires analysis. For some insight into
these questions it is worth turning to the early work of Bataille, Klossowski, and
Leiris, particularly that associated with the *Collège de Sociologie*.

The Hydra-Headed Sacred Monster

Bataille had first become familiar with Sade's work in 1926[82] and was already
writing about him in 1929. In the article "The Language of Flowers,"[83] he cites
the (apocryphal) story, that, locked up as a madman, Sade "had the most beautiful roses brought to him only to pluck off their petals and toss them in a ditch
filled with liquid manure."[84] Then, in the "The Lugubrious Game,"[85] he specu-
lates that when Sade was "screaming insanely" through the Bastille pipe designed for his own bodily wastes, "People of Paris, they are killing the prisoners," this was a repetition of an earlier incident. After he had "tortured with a
whip" a young woman, Rose Keller, "she tried to move, with her tears and en-
treaties, a man both so pleasing and so evil; and as she invoked everything in the
worlds that was saintly and touching, Sade, suddenly gone wild and hearing
nothing, let out horrifying and perfectly nauseating screams."[86] As is well

known, these articles were linked with the dispute between Bataille and Breton about the true significance of Sade's work.

At that time, Bataille's own position was most clearly articulated in his extraordinarily imaginative letter "The Use-Value of D.A.F. de Sade: An Open Letter to My current Comrades."[87] Sadism appears "positively . . . as an irruption of excremental forces (the excessive violation of modesty, positive algolagnic, the violent excretion of the sexual object coinciding with a powerful or tortured ejaculation, the libidinal interest in cadavers, vomiting, defecation . . . and . . . as a corresponding limitation, a narrow enslavement of everything that is opposed to this irruption . . . sad social necessity, human dignity, fatherland and family, as well as poetic sentiments." Here, Bataille renders Sade's work interesting, but whatever his affinity with parts of it, he also distorts it, turning it into a key source of his own heterology. Sade as a libertine lived a life of projects in an economy of accumulation of pleasure of possession, while Bataille was "debauched." True, they both obsessed with death but the "eroticism Bataille puts into play soils, spoils and wrecks . . . memory, self-indulgence, vows, the possibility of beauty or salvation, fidelity, education, morality, women, God . . . it's all the same."[88]

Soon afterward, Bataille extended some of these arguments in his article "The Notion of Expenditure," (published in 1933 in *La Critique Sociale*, the journal of the socialist group, the Democratic Circle). He argued here for a significant shift in the understanding of what constitituted fundamental human activities. The commitment to production and exchange and the setting aside of consumption to render these reproducible should be see as an analytically subordinate moment to a movement of expenditure oriented to wasteful loss and destruction. Contemporary "civilized" societies were seen to be reduced through the principle of utility to, on the one hand, the Bourgeois's privatized accumulation, sterility, and apathy, and, on the other, the possibility of "the *great night* when their beautiful phrases will be drowned out by death screams in riots" and the "workers' movement" will force the production of a "mode of expenditure as tragic and free as possible" and will introduce powerful "new sacred forms."[89]

In an important autobiographical note, Bataille writes that:

> The Democratic Circle went out of existence in 1934. Bataille personally took the initiative in 1935 to found a small political group . . . Counterattack. . . . Some meetings . . . took place with the last on January 21, 1936, dedicated to the death of Louis XVI. . . . Counterattack was dissolved, Bataille immediately resolved to form a "secret society," which, turning its back on politics, would pursue goals that would be solely religious (but anti-Christian, essentially Nietzschean). This society was formed. Its intentions are, in part, expressed in the journal, *Acéphale*. . . . The *Collège de Sociologie*, founded in March 1936, represented, as it were, the outside activity of this "secret society." . . . Of the secret society, properly so-called, it is difficult to talk, but certain of its members have apparently retained the impression of a "voyage out of the world." Temporary, surely, obviously unendurable; in September 1939, all of its members withdrew.[90]

These collective endeavors can each be seen as part of a *sacred hydra-headed monster*, which centered on the role of the sacred in the life of society, sub-collectivities and the life of individuals. Bataille, Klossowski, Caillois, and Leiris were key figures in all three of its component parts.

Between 1936 and 1939, Bataille, Klossowski, and the physicist Georges Ambrosino, edited and published the journal *Acéphale*. Its cover was the drawing by André Masson (1896-1987) of a headless man with a skull covering his genitals. Among the contributors were Bataille, Klossowski, Roger Caillois, Jules Monnerot, Jean Wahl, and Jean Rollin. The journal was notable for its Dionysian themes, its recuperation of the work of Nietzsche from its Fascist appropriations, and for its attempt to explore the radical forms of social order that Nietzsche's work might herald. In its second issue, Bataille wrote that the death of God opened the possibility of the "formation of a new structure, of an 'order' developing and raging across entire earth"; this could not be monocephalic, no matter how formally democratic such a political system might be, for, "the only society full of life and force, the only free society," was "the *bi-* or *poly- cephalic* society that gives the fundamental antagonisms of life a constant explosive outlet, but one limited to the richest forms," after all, "the very principle of the head is the reduction to unity, the *reduction* of the world to God."[91]

In the July 1937 issue of *Acéphale*, in a note signed by Ambrosino, Bataille, Klossowski, Caillois, Monnerot, and Pierre Libra, was the "Declaration Relating to the Foundation of a *Collège de Sociologie*." This included the following dramatic sentences:

> 1. It seems that there are obstacles of a particular nature opposed to the development of an understanding of the vital elements of society: The necessary contagious and activist character of the representations that this work brings to light seems responsible for this.

> 2. It follows that there is good reason for those who contemplate following investigations as far as possible in this direction, to develop a moral community, different in part from that ordinarily uniting scholars, and bound, precisely, to the virulent character of the realm studied and of the laws that little by little are revealed to govern it.

> 3. The precise object of the contemplated activity can take the name of Sacred Sociology, implying the study of all manifestations of social existence where the active presence of the sacred is clear. It intends to establish in this way the points of coincidence between the fundamental obsessive tendencies of individual psychology and the principal structures that govern social organization and are in command of its revolutions.[92]

In the event, Caillois, Bataille, and Leiris came to be responsible for the actual organization of the *Collège de Sociologie*. The *Collège* met between October 1937 and June 1939 and the reputations, connections, and networks—political, artistic, and academic—of its initiators and the promise of the "note" in *Acéphale* helped bring to its sessions an extraordinary collection of philosophers, social theorists, historians, and literary figures, including many from the surrealist movement. Among those lecturing were Bataille, Caillois, Leiris, Klossowski, and Alexander Kojève.

The Radical Durkheimianism of the Collegians

The major focus of the *Collège*'s activities was to be the study of "the problems of power, of the sacred, and of myths"; this required forms of inquiry which would embrace "a person's total activity" and would entail working in common with others, "seriously, selflessly, and with critical severity."[93] In order to understand manifestations of the sacred and to explain their attenuation or, indeed, their absence, there was a need to attend to historical and comparative anthropological materials and theories. In practice, this meant drawing on the work on the sacred as developed in the works of Emile Durkheim, Robert Hertz, Henri Hubert, and Marcel Mauss, and also aspects of the work of Nietzsche, Hegel, and Marx.

At the *Collège*, Bataille's interpretations of the Durkeimian tradition were sometimes rigorous, sometimes tendentious, sometimes inaccurate, but always imaginative. For example, speaking for many members of the *Collège*, in his presentation "Sacred Sociology and the relationships between 'Society,' 'Organism,' and 'Being'"[94] Bataille agreed with Durkheim that society was an emergent *sui generis* reality: "society . . . combining organisms, at the highest level, makes them into something other than their sum," and that, while these human "linear" organisms naively represent themselves to themselves as indivisible unities, they are transformed by their subjection to the "communifying movements" of society, which is a "compound being." Such movements create a feeling of being a "society," but this may be precarious, since "a single society can form several crowds at the same moment." Nevertheless, "there is a particular structure to which institutions, rites, and common representations contribute, which provides the deep support for collective identity."[95] An indication of the compound nature of societies is that while most contemporary societies are aggregates of other simpler societies, their reorganization can successfully create a new society on a higher structural scale. Furthermore, Durkheim's focus on how collective assemblies and related collected effervescences can transform collectivities and individuals and the relation between the "sacred" and the "profane" was take up—but given a distinctly radical interpretation—by the members of the *Collège*.

Durkheim argued that society is marked by a profound polarity between the sacred and profane, a distinction which, for him, was one between phenomena or categorizations that are homogeneous internally but heterogeneous each to the other. Bataille, in a reading which is in part a misreading and in part a critical re-evaluation of Durkheim's categories, had in an article, "The Psychological Structure of Fascism," represented this as a distinction between the heterogeneous and the homogenous.[96] And, as we have seen, the profane is associated with: homogenization; deferred gratification; analysis and calculation; planning and utility; the production and controlled consumption necessary for the reproduction and conservation of productive human life; individuals conforming to social roles experiencing themselves as separate self-sufficient subjects who possess and consume objects.[97] The sacred, on the other hand, is associated with heterogeneity, socially useless activity, unlimited expenditure, excremental collective impulses (orgiastic impulses)—sexual activity, defecation, urination, ritual cannibalism[98]—with extreme emotions, tabooed objects and their transgression—"corpses, menstrual blood or pariahs."[99] The sacred evokes feelings of both attraction and repulsion,[100] and is linked with violence and its violent containment—with the cruelty of sacrificing others[101] and with the subsumption of individuals within totalizing group processes when they fearlessly confront death and are willing to sacrifice themselves.[102] It is potentially dangerous and destabilizing. More generally, while in contemporary societies sacral processes have become more obscure and suppressed, less obviously religious, they are still present, as can be seen in the way that men are attracted to sacrificial ceremonies and festivals.[103] In fact, historically, the sacred has been generated by taboo-violating rituals, and sacrifices have been key elements in festivals which both regenerate the sacred and corral it. Bataille provides a model which presumes a much lower level of integration than does the model found in the dominant discourse in Durkheim and, subsequently, in *The Accursed Share* (1948) Bataille would analytically distinguish between two kinds of societies, of "consumption" and of "enterprise."[104]

For Caillois too, the sacred played a significant role. The sacred is a key element both in ordinary life and in the festivals found in "primitive" societies (and to a much attenuated degree in contemporary societies); it becomes of greater significance but also something different in such festivals. Ordinary life tends to be regular, busy, and safe; it is part of a "cosmos ruled by a universal order" in which "the only manifestations of the sacred are interdictions, against anything that could threaten cosmic regularity, or else, expiations, redress for anything that might have disturbed it."[105] Under these conditions, for individual human beings and for social institutions—both of which get used up and accumulate "poisonous wastes" which are "left behind by every act performed for the good of the community"—regeneration and purification are possible but involve "some pollution of the one who assumes responsibility for this regeneration," for what is unclean often "contains an active principle that can bring prosperity."[106] "Time is wearing and exhausting" and there is a need for social regeneration which is made possible by the "popular frenzy" of the festival. It releases an active sacred energy, reverses the normal course of time and the forms of social order, and is associated with widespread excesses and sacrileges, "debauches of consumption, of the mouth or sex" and also "debauches of expression involving words or deeds."[107] The festival provides *"access to the Great Time"* and through its holy venues *"access to the Great Space"*; it is *"Chaos rediscovered and shaped anew."*[108] The festival is "the paroxysm of society, which it simultaneously purifies and renews," and it may even change the established social order.[109] For example, if the King, "whose normal role consists in maintaining order, moderation and rules," dies or weakens, then the "strength and efficacious power" of these "are lost" and this opens an "interregnum of a reverse efficacious power; that is the principle of disorder and excess that generates the ferment from which a new, revived order will be born."[110] Caillois, commenting on how modern carnivals are but dying echoes of earlier festivals, gives, as an example, the joyful destruction of a cardboard representation of a "huge, comical, colorful, king" which no longer has any religious value because "[t]he moment the human victim is replaced by an effigy, the ritual tends to lose its value for expiation or fertility."[111]

Overall, the views of Bataille and Caillois, however dramatic they might seem, remain in accord with Durkheim's belief that all forms of social phenomena that keep recurring within societies of a particular species—whether the phenomena superficially seem conformist or deviant—are socially produced and either themselves functional for society as a whole or a necessary concomitant of something that is functional. Thus, for neither Durkheim, Caillois, nor Bataille is such activity asocial; it is profoundly but differently social. It is sociogonic, renewing and transforming cosmological social meanings and interpersonal and social relations.

There has already been occasion to refer to Klossowksi's lecture to the *Collège de Sociologie*, "The Marquis de Sade and Revolution." Its main interest for Foucault rested in Klossowski's multiplication of his "Simulacra Men." Ian James suggests that Klossowski simply situated the "relationship between libertine and victim within [the] Hegelian framework of the encounter between Master and slave." It certainly does this, but it does much more; it helps render intelligible the systems of relations, and their representations, that obtained in France under Feudalism, Absolutism, and the Revolution. In the period between ancient conditions of slavery and the Century of the Revolution, the Church had tried to ensure moral significance to each category of individuals by developing its system of "theocratic hierarchy" that was supposed to end "the ancient law of the jungle."

> Human beings created in God's image cannot exploit human beings. . . . The king, appointed by God, is his temporal servant; the lord, appointed by the king, is servant to the king; and every man who acknowledges that he is servant to his lord is the servant of God. The hierarchy assigns the lord military, judicial, and social functions entrusted to him by the king. For him these are obligations toward the king and toward the people, but exercise of these functions assures him to the right of gratitude and fealty from his vassal and servant. The servant, for his part, having put himself under the protection of his lord, to whom he renders homage and fealty, performs an act of faith in his God and his king. Hence, at the last level of the hierarchy, he fulfills his individual significance because he is participating in an edifice whose keystone is God.[112]

With the decline of Feudalism and the growth of Absolutism this order becomes subverted.

> As the king concentrates power more and more, while the lord abandons his functions one by one, the latter not only frees himself in relation to his obligations toward the king, but he still claims to maintain the rights and privileges ensuing from these. Then the lord only needs to develop an existence for its

own sake, making his privileges something he enjoys without accountability to God or anyone else, least of all to his servant—the lord only needs to put God's existence in doubt for the whole structure to totter. The fact of serving at the bottom of the social ladder loses all meaning in the eyes of the servant. And, finally, when the lord seems to want to maintain the structure of theocratic hierarchy for the sole purpose of guaranteeing an unwarranted existence, an existence that is the very negation of this hierarchy, an existence that consists of demonstrating that the fear of the Lord is the beginning of madness, then the law of the jungle comes back in full force. The conditions of the ancient relationship strong to weak, master to slave are reestablished.[113]

Thus, if there had originally been a social order which worked as a theocratic hierarchy, by the end of the eighteenth century it was, in practical terms, largely dead. The revolt of the libertine lords, exemplified above all by the Marquis de Sade, was both an effect of, and a further source of, the decline of this model, for he "no longer has undisputed authority in his own eyes (whereas he has kept his instincts for it) and there is nothing sacred about his will anymore."[114] This makes it virtually impossible for the system to sustain its legitimacy in the eyes of the "man at the bottom of the hierarchy whose closeness to God was in the act of serving and who has fallen into slavery," for, "now that God is dead at the top of the hierarchy," he "remains a servant with no lord to the extent that God lives in his conscience."[115] True, he may become an atheist like his master, but in either case his subordination is akin to slavery and leads to rebellion. The execution of King Louis XVI is "only the most extreme phase of the process whose first phase is the execution of God by the revolt of the great libertine lord. The execution of the king thus becomes the enactment of execution of God."[116] Any new order found after this act would be haunted by the absence of God, perhaps even by a feeling of abandonment by *Deus Absconditus*.

Klossowksi's discussion indicates that the articulation of the religious and other institutional forms differed substantially from era to era. Hence, during the long period when Catholic Christianity played a key role in social life, religious and sacral institutions must have been articulated differently at different times with other state apparatuses, and socioeconomic relations, and differing forms of governance. Nevertheless, this representation of the issue is problematic because it presumes both that this theocratic hierarchy had at some time been the actual and sole organizing principle of social life, and that alternative forms of organization were merely permutations of this originary principle, and, further, that oppositional values are all in one way or another directly derivable from a coherent functioning social order and a coherent ideological rationale. At any time, however, extant social relations and also specific institutions constitute individuals in a number of relational positions and they will also be traversed by a series of discourses. All of these may vary in the degree to which they are complementary or contradictory. Nevertheless, subjects tend to narrativize these to provide a sense of coherence. When individuals work at sustaining, developing, or modifying their social position, they will confront exigencies which require a focus on, and possibly a prioritization of, particular subject positions and discourses. Over time, this may produce standardized rituals and standardized ra-

tionales. These rituals cannot be read as fundamentally an expression of the ra-
tionales. Rituals are not only polysemic, but polyfunctional. For example, when
the Queen gave birth it was a ceremonial that took place in front of members of
the Court, and however many religious meanings were associated with this, it
also guaranteed the legitimacy of the child.[117]

Although in his book *Miroir de la tauromachie* (1938) Leiris made specific
reference to Mauss and Hertz, in his sole presentation at the *Collège de Sociologie*, "The Sacred in Everyday Life" his emphasis was micro and personal. He
was concerned with the "objects, places, or occasions" that awaken "that mixture of fear and attachment . . . that we take as the psychological sign of the sacred."[118] Much of his lecture was devoted to the symbolic meanings and associations of "objects, places or occasions" that he was familiar with in his own early
years. This was indeed a form of writing in which he was to engage all of his
life—from *Manhood* (1939) to the four volumes of *La Règle du Jeu* (1948-76)—
but as a style of engagement it seemed to have few resonances with the rest of
what was happening at the *Collège*. In fact, Leiris soon distanced himself from
the activities of the *Collège de Sociologie*, but he did so, in a sense, from another
place, as a professional ethnologist. In a letter to Bataille he suggested three major objections to the way the activities of the *Collège* had developed. It tended to
work "from badly defined ideas, comparisons taken from societies of profoundly
different natures," its "moral community" was in danger of becoming a mere
clique, and, finally, by overemphasizing the "sacred" there was a tendency to
subvert Mauss's idea of a "total social fact."[119] Caillois, too, became uneasy
about the extent to which this was being achieved and eventually he also with-
drew. Bataille, alone of the three, attended the last session.

One of the peculiarities of the *Collège de Sociologie* is that despite its desire
to operate in a way that was different from normal (social) scientific discourse,
the format of its actual meetings (i.e., lectures followed by a discussion) seems
to have been very traditional. It is true that one characteristic of the relationship
between the texts and the main speakers was that much of the time there was a
significant attenuation of the proprietorial practices associated with the "voice"
of specific authors. Bataille, for example, would read and re-present the thought
of Caillois demonstrating what Lévy dismissively describes as a surrealist "col-
lectivization of thought."[120] Yet there seemed little evidence of specific practices
appropriate to producing the sacred, or dealing with its "virulence," and hence,
thereby, understanding it better. A more thorough investigation of the matter
will reveal a more complex and nuanced situation.

In the final issue of the journal *Acéphale*, Bataille pointed out that "No one
thinks any longer that the reality of communal life—which is to say human existence—depends on sharing of nocturnal terrors and on the kind of ecstactic
spasms spread by death."[121] But the year before, he had founded the secret society, Acéphale. Only a little is known of Acéphale, but this includes knowledge
of its goals—"to change the torture that exists in the world into joy within us;
the Crucified into happy laughter; our old immense weakness into will to
power"[122]—which were clearly Nietzschean. Bataille, like Nietzsche, had little
interest in recruiting disciples and, unsurprisingly, Acéphale seems to have been

essentially "communifying" and egalitarian (although there were three levels of membership); there were some rules of conduct—for example, its members refused to shake hands with anti-Semites[123]—and some rituals, some culinary and one involving a pilgrimage to a tree struck by lightning in the forest of Saint-Nom-la-Bretèche. Others were only dreamt of, for example, in 1937 members of Acéphale planned to leave a skull soaked in brine, representing that of the King Louis XVI/Louis Capet, in the Place de la Concorde where he had been guillotined, and, at another time, they intended to leave rags, soaked in what appeared to be the blood of the Marquis de Sade, there; both rituals were to be witnessed by the eight armoured and acephalic figures that watch over the square.[124] Neither plan was ever realized. One ritual, planned but never realized, was a human sacrifice. They had no difficulty in finding a willing victim, but they could not find a sacrificer. Marina Galletti suggests that Michel Leiris, who had already contemplated suicide, may have been a potential victim,[125] and there is some evidence that Caillois was offered the role of sacrificer. Blanchot points out in *The Unavowable Community*,[126] that immediately after the sacrifice, the sacrificer was also expected to kill himself. Perhaps Caillois found this unappealing. There may have been another reason for the failure of the plan, for according to French sacrificial theory, each sacrifice involves not only a victim and a sacrificer (the person performing the sacrificial act) but also a sacrifier (the source of the desire for the sacrifice), and in this case each member of the group was a sacrifier, (each was a source of the sacrificial desire) and presumably each of them—through "contagion"—could have been both sacrificer and victim—"the desire of the executioner is to be a victim."[127] Under these circumstances, there might have been no record of Acéphale at all, and, for that matter, no further intellectual output of any kind produced by its members, the key members of the *Collège de Sociologie*.[128]

Foucault and the *Collège de Sociologie*

Foucault could well have benefited by this more sociological work that drew upon and went beyond both the Nietzschean and Durkheimian traditions. That is not to advocate human sacrifice and secret societies. In this context, the first can be ignored and there is little reason to imagine that a gay man living in France needed to be instructed about the importance of secrecy and the need to find elective communities. However, one might see Foucault's distinction between a society where political order is known through "a spectacular expression of potency, an 'expenditure,' exaggerated and coded in which power renewed its vigor"[129] and a society with "a parliamentary representative regime" and a "juridical form that guaranteed a system of rights that were egalitarian in principle" but "supported by all those systems of micro-power that are essentially non-egalitarian and asymmetrical that we call disciplines"[130] as a sociologization of Bataille's distinction between "societies of consumption" and "societies of enterprise." But this was just a beginning and a form of analysis abandoned by Foucault. He needed to develop a more complex understanding, to paraphrase the *Collège de Sociologie*, of the points of coincidence between human subjectivities and the principal structures that govern social organization and are in command of its reproduction and transformative movements. His later work organized around the axes of care of the self, and governmentality signally failed to do this.[131] An interdiscourse making use of some of the work of Foucault and much of that associated with the *Collège de Sociologie* has the potential to do just that.[132] It is perhaps important to end by realizing that Foucault's extraordinary output of books, articles, and particularly interviews might be seen as his way of living a life of expenditure without calculation of return.

Notes

Chapter 1

1. Michel Foucault, *Discipline and Punish: The Birth of the Prison*, 1st American ed., (New York: Pantheon, 1977); and "Governmentality," in *Power: Essential Works of Foucault 1954-1984*, vol. 3, ed. J. Faubion (New York: The New Press, 2000), 201-22.

2. See Hans Kelsen, "The Conception of the State and Social Psychology," *The International Journal of Psychoanalysis* 5 (1924): 1-38; or Hans Kelsen, "Der Begriff des Staates und die Sozialpsychologie," *Imago* 8 (1922): 97-141.

3. See, for instance, Ernst Cassirer, *The Myth of the State* (London: Oxford University Press, 1946).

4. Besides the works already referred to in note 1, see *The History of Sexuality*, vol. 1, *An Introduction* (New York: Random House, 1978); in French, *La volonté de savoir* (Paris: Gallimard, 1976).

5. Foucault, *The History of Sexuality*, 1: 88.

6. On his relationship to the thought of Herbert Marcuse, for instance, see Paul Breines, "Revisiting Marcuse with Foucault: *An Essay on Liberation* Meets *The History of Sexuality*," in *Marcuse: From the New Left to the Next Left*, ed. J. Bokina and T. J. Lukes (Lawrence: University Press of Kansas, 1994), 41-56.

7. I am a sort of "witness" to this in the sense that, in the 1970s, Massimo Pavarini and I wrote about the origins of imprisonment from a Marxist perspective (see Dario Melossi and Massimo Pavarini, *The Prison and the Factory: Origins of the Penitentiary System* [London: Macmillam, 1981]). What eventuated from these efforts was a story very similar to the one Foucault was trying to weave in those very years, much more similar to Foucault's than to Rusche and Kirchheimer's *Punishment and Social Structure*, for instance. David Garland, *Punishment and Modern Society* (Chicago: The University of Chicago Press, 1990).

8. Foucault, *Discipline and Punish*, 221.

9. It may be worthwhile to cite extensively from an answer Foucault gave in an interview in 1975, at about the same time that he was publishing *Discipline and Punish*:

> I often quote concepts, texts and phrases from Marx, but without feeling obliged to add the authenticating label of a footnote with a laudatory phrase to accompany the quotation. As long as one does that, one is regarded as someone who knows and reveres Marx, and will be suitably honored in the so-called

Marxist journals. But I quote Marx without saying so, without quotation marks, and because people are incapable of recognizing Marx's texts I am thought to be someone who doesn't quote Marx. When a physicist writes a work of physics, does he feel it necessary to quote Newton and Einstein? He uses them, but he doesn't need the quotation marks, the footnote and the eulogistic comment to prove how completely he is being fateful to the master's thought. And because other physicists know what Einstein did, what he discovered and proved, they can recognize him in what the physicist writes. It is impossible at the present time to write history without using a whole range of concepts directly or indirectly linked to Marx's thought and situating oneself within a horizon of thought which has been defined and described by Marx. One might even wonder what difference there could ultimately be between being a historian and being a Marxist."

Michel Foucault, "Prison Talk," in M. Foucault, *Power/Knowledge: Selected Interviews and Other Writings 1972-1977* (New York: Pantheon Books, 1980), 52-53.

10. Karl Marx, *Capital*, vol. 1 (New York: International Publishers, 1967 [orig. 1867]), 167-76.

11. Foucault, *Discipline and Punish*, 222.

12. See, among others by Michel Foucault, *Society Must Be Defended: Lectures at the Collège de France 1975-1976* (New York: Picador, 2003 [orig. 1975-1976]), the first two lectures.

13. Foucault, *Discipline and Punish*, 194.

14. Foucault, *The History of Sexuality*, 1: 159.

15. Emile Durkheim, *Montesquieu and Rousseau* (Ann Arbor: University of Michigan Press, 1960 [orig. 1901-1902]), 83.

16. Durkheim, *Montesquieu and Rousseau*, 133-34.

17. Emile Durkheim, *Professional Ethics and Civic Morals* (Glencoe, IL: Free Press, 1958 [orig. 1898-1900]), 49-51.

18. In such connection, one should furthermore mention the visionary insight of Tocqueville who, seventy years earlier, had already noted this striking characteristic of American democracy–and, we could now add, of democracy generally (see Alexis De Tocqueville, *Democracy in America*, vol. 1 (New York: Schocken, 1961 [orig. 1835]).

19. Foucault, "Governmentality," 220.

20. Arthur F. Bentley, *The Process of Government* (Cambridge: Harvard University Press, 1908), 263-264. Alessandro Passerin d'Entreves noted, about statements such as this one by Bentley, that "[t]he disruption of the notion of the State in modern political science is such a challenging and portentous event that it is surprising no detailed study should yet have been made to account for it and to explain it" Alessandro Passerin d'Entreves, *The Notion of the State* (Oxford: Clarendon Press, 1967), 60.

21. Richard Rorty, *Consequences of Pragmatism* (Minneapolis: University of Minnesota Press, 1983), xviii.

22. Also because, in the situation of the "cold war," all European societies, East and West, basically shared a status of "limited democracies" in which the type of socio-economic regime and the militancy in one international field could not be changed.

23. Georg Simmel, "The Metropolis and Mental Life," in G. Simmel, *The Sociology of Georg Simmel* (Glencoe, IL: Free Press, 1950 [orig. 1903]), 409-24; and Louis Wirth, "Urbanism as a Way of Life," *The American Journal of Sociology* 44 (1938): 1-24.

24. Wirth, "Urbanism," 23.

25. Jürgen Habermas, *The Theory of Communicative Action*, vol. 2 (Boston: Beacon Press, 1987 [orig. 1981]), 301-403.

26. Ford even created an aptly named "Department of Sociology," the function of which derived from Ford's conviction that such higher wages

entailed a standard of living to which some workers had to be trained. Under the direction of John R. Lee, the company's Sociology Department (as the Personnel Office was called) prodded workers toward the ideal of a single nuclear family living in a single family dwelling (with no boarders) tended by a non-working mother whose children attended school. Ford workers were expected to maintain bank accounts, to purchase the domestic products of technology, to learn to speak English if they did not already, and to pursue an American way of life based on the industrial virtues of sobriety, punctuality, and reliability. To automotive workers in Detroit in 1914, all this spelled the American dream of dignity and prosperity for all.

Michael S. Mahoney "Technology and the Democratic Ideal: the Search for a Middle Landscape," www.princeton.edu/~hos/h398/midland.html (6 February 2004).

27. Walter Lippmann, *Public Opinion* (New York: Macmillan, 1922).

28. George H. Mead, "The Genesis of the Self and Social Control," in G. H. Mead, *Selected Writings* (Indianapolis: Bobbs-Merrill, 1964 [orig. 1925]), 267-93.

29. Karl Marx, "On the Jewish Question," in K. Marx and F. Engels, *Collected Works*, vol. 3 (London: Lawrence & Wishart, 1975 [orig. 1844]), 146-74.

30. Marx, "On the Jewish Question."

31. Karl Marx, "Contribution to the Critique of Hegel's Philosophy of Law, Introduction," in K. Marx and F. Engels, *Collected Works*, vol. 3 (London: Lawrence & Wishart, 1975 [orig. 1844]), 182.

32. Max Horkheimer and Theodor W. Adorno, *Dialectic of Enlightenment* (New York: Herder & Herder, 1972 [orig. 1947]). See especially the notes on "A Theory of Crime," 225-29.

33. Also Marx's debt to Tocqueville remains to be seen.

34. Thomas L. Dumm, *Democracy and Punishment: Disciplinary Origins of the United States* (Madison: University of Wisconsin Press, 1987).

35. Dieter Grimm, "Does Europe Need a Constitution?" *European Law Journal* 1, (1995): 282-302.

36. Grimm, "Does Europe Need a Constitution?" 293-94.

37. Grimm, "Does Europe Need a Constitution?" 295.

38. As Jürgen Habermas seems to suggest in "On the Relation between the Nation, Rule of Law, and Democracy," in J. Habermas, *The Inclusion of the Other,* (Cambridge, MA: MIT Press, 1998 [orig. 1996]), 154.

39. Grimm, "Does Europe Need A Constitution?" 297.

40. According to a Flash Eurobarometer Poll, 55 percent of the EU citizens had not even heard of the Convention that in 2003 drafted the Project of a European

Constitutional Treaty, almost the equivalent of a European Constitutional Assembly! (See Neil Walker, "After the Constitutional Moment," (Materials from the Permanent Seminar of Political Theory and the Law by Prof. Gianluigi Palombella, Department of Legal and Social Studies, University of Parma, 2003).

41. Trying to shift the whole question toward a problem of "simple translation" will not help. Habermas, for instance, tries, surprisingly, to underplay the issue (see Jürgen Habermas, "Why Europe Needs a Constitution," *New Left Review* 11 (Sept.-Oct. 2001): 5-26). Neil Walker discusses it in the context of the "translation" from national to supranational constitutional frameworks. See Neil Walker, "Postnational Constitutionalism and the Problem of Translation," in *European Constitutionalism Beyond the State*, ed. J. H. H. Weiler and M. Wind (Cambridge: Cambridge University Press, 2003), 27-54. On the "cultural embeddedness" of language and particularly of social control language see Dario Melossi, "The Cultural Embeddedness of Social Control: Reflections on the Comparison of Italian and North-American Cultures Concerning Punishment," *Theoretical Criminology* 5 (2001): 403-24: and Dario Melossi "Translating Social Control: Reflections on the Comparison of Italian and North-American Cultures Concerning Social Control, with a Few Consequences for a 'Critical' Criminology," in S. Karstedt and K. D. Bussmann, Eds., *Social Dynamics of Crime and Control*, (Oxford: Hart, 2000), 143-56.

42. Hans-Joerg Trenz "Governing Beyond Public Legitimation? Some Reflections on the Role of the Public Sphere in the Intergovernmental Framework of European Immigration and Asylum Policies," in *Migrazioni, interazioni e conflitti nella costruzione di una democrazia europea*, ed. D.Melossi (Milano: Giuffrè, 2003), 751-76.

43. On this see also Habermas, "Why Europe Needs a Constitution," 21.

44. Marx, *Capital*, vol. 1, 713-41.

45. In the *European* of 28-31 January 1993, one could read the following letter written (in English) by a Filipino worker from Milan, Italy: "It is important for English to be understood and spoken throughout Europe. I am a Filipino and have studied English since I was eight. English has been the language of learning in schools and colleges in the Philippines for more than 50 years. I am now in Italy working as a domestic helper and find it very difficult to communicate with Europeans who do not speak English. I agree . . . that English is an enriching influence in Europe."

46. The proposal (then rejected) advanced at the time of the Maastricht treaty to sever the European citizenship from national citizenships, would have reflected such a historical social reality.

47. See Dario Melossi, "Symposium Issue on Migration, Punishment and Social Control in Europe," *Punishment and Society* 5, no. 4 (2003).

48. David Matza, *Becoming Deviant* (Englewood Cliffs, NJ: Prentice-Hall, 1969). On such themes, see also Giorgio Agamben, *Homo Sacer: Sovereign Power and Bare Life* (Stanford: Stanford University Press, 1998 [orig. 1995]).

49. To expand on this, see Dario Melossi, *The State of Social Control: A Sociological Study of Concepts of State and Social Control in the Making of Democracy* (Cambridge: Polity Press, 1990); and *Stato, devianza, controllo sociale: Teorie criminologiche e società tra Europa e Stati Uniti* (Milano: Bruno Mondadori Editore, 2002).

50. See Matza, *Becoming Deviant* and the revisited *Punishment and Social Structure* by Georg Rusche and Otto Kirchheimer (New Brunswick: Transaction, 2003 [orig. 1939]); Erving Goffman, *Asylums: Essays on the Social Situation of Mental Patients and Other Inmates* (Garden City, NY: Anchor Books, 1961); and Franco Basaglia, *L'istituzione negata* (Torino: Einaudi, 1969).

51. I would like to thank Alain Beaulieu and the other organizers of the Meeting "Michel Foucault and Social Control," and Giovanna Jatropelli, Director of the Italian Cultural Institute in Montreal–not only for having made possible this event, and my participation in it, but also, and especially, for their exquisite hospitality in Montreal.

Chapter 2

1. Michel Foucault, "Human Nature: Justice versus Power" (debate with N. Chomsky), in *Reflexive Water: The Basic Concerns of Mankind*, ed. F. Elders (London: Souvenir Press, 1974), 133-97.

2. This is precisely the dimension of law absent from Derrida's "Force of Law." For him law remains systematic and calculable, as opposed to the absolute alterity of an incalculable justice. To the extent he thinks the materiality of law, it appears as the force necessary to law which therefore stands in contrast to an unenforceable justice. Cf. Jacques Derrida, "Force of Law: The Mystical Foundation of Authority," in *Acts of Religion*, ed. G. Anidjar (New York and London: Routledge, 2002), 228-98.

3. Michel Foucault, "Human Nature," 184-85.

4. Benedictus de Spinoza, *Complete Works*, (Indianapolis: Hackett, 2002), 527.

5. Michel Foucault, *Discipline & Punish* (New York: Vintage Books, 1977), 25.

6. Giorgio Agamben, *Homo Sacer: Sovereign Power and Bare Life*, (Stanford, Stanford University Press, 1998), 5-6.

7. Thomas Lemke, "A Zone of Indistinction: A critique of Giorgio Agamben's Concept of Biopolitics," unpublished ms.

8. Antonio Negri, *Insurgencies: Constituent Power and the Modern State*, trans. Maurizia Boscaglia (Minneapolis: University of Minnesota Press, 1999), 8.

9. Walter Benjamin, "Theses on the Philosophy of History," in *Illuminations* (New York: Shocken, 1968), 257.

10. Benedict de Spinoza, *Tractatus Politicus* (Indianapolis: Hackett, 2001), Chapter 3 Section 2.

11. Vladimir I. Lenin, *The Proletarian Revolution, and the Renegade Kautsky* (Peking: Foreign Language Press, 1970), 16.

12. Foucault, *Discipline & Punish*, 218.

13. Foucault, *Discipline & Punish*, 221-22.

14. Foucault, *Discipline & Punish*, 222.

15. Foucault, *Discipline & Punish*, 222.

16. Foucault, *Discipline & Punish*, 222.

17. Foucault, *Discipline & Punish*, 222.

18. Foucault, *Discipline & Punish*, 222.

19. Pierre Macherey, "Towards a Natural History of Norms, " in *Michel Foucault, Philosopher*, ed. T. J. Armstrong (New York: Routledge, 1992), 176-91.

20. Foucault, *Discipline & Punish*, 27.

Chapter 3

1. Michel Foucault, *Discipline & Punish* (New York, Random House, 1977).

2. Michel Foucault, *Power: Essential Works of Foucault, 1954-1984*, vol. 3, ed. J. D. Faubion (New York: The New Press, 2000), 70.

3. Foucault, *Power*, 81.

4. Gilles Deleuze, *Negociations* (New York: Columbia University Press, 1995 [orig. 1990]), 178.

5. Georg F. Hegel, *Elements of the Philosophy of Right* (New York: Cambridge University Press, 1991 [orig. 1921]).

6. Foucault, *Power*, 79.

7. Michel Foucault, *Dits et écrits*, vol. 2 (Paris: Gallimard, 1994), 465.

8. Foucault, *Power*, 71.

9. Foucault, *Power*, 65-66.

10. Taken from Michel Foucault, "Right of Death and Power over Life," in *The Foucault Reader*, ed. P. Rabinow (New York: Pantheon Books, 1984), 263.

11. Foucault, "Right of Death and Power over Life," 264-65.

12. Foucault, *Power*, 57.

13. Michel Foucault, "The Punitive Society," in *Ethics, Subjectivity and Truth*, ed. P. Rabinow (New York: The New Press, 1997), 23-38.

14. Foucault, *Power*, 85. See also *Discipline & Punish*, 200 ff.

15. Foucault, *Discipline & Punish*, 228.

16. Foucault, *Dits et écrits*, vol. 2, 596.

17. Foucault, *Dits et écrits*, vol. 2, 601 and 748; see also *Dits et écrits*, vol. 4, 195.

18. Foucault, *Dits et écrits*, vol. 2, 470 and 718; see also *Dits et écrits*, vol. 3, 93.

19. Foucault, *Dits et écrits*, vol. 2, 417; see also *Dits et écrits*, vol. 3, 76, 225, and 228.

20. Michel Foucault, *Histoire de la sexualité*, vol. 1, *La volonté de savoir* (Paris: Gallimard, 1976), 192 ff.

21. Foucault, *Dits et écrits*, vol. 2, 390.

22. Foucault, *Dits et écrits*, vol. 2, 610.

23. Foucault, *Dits et écrits*, vol. 3, 21, 25.

24. Foucault, *Dits et écrits*, vol. 3, 233.

25. Michel Foucault, "Michel Foucault à Goutelas: la redéfinition du 'judiciable' intervention at a seminar of the Syndicat de la magistrature at Goutelas on 19 May," *Justice: Syndicat de la magistrature* 115 (June 1987): 36-39.

26. Foucault, *Dits et écrits*, vol. 2, 662.

27. Foucault, *Discipline & Punish*, 211.

28. Foucault, *Power*, 343.

29. Foucault, *Power*, 342-45.

30. Foucault, *Discipline & Punish*, 304.

31. A Foucaldian analysis of the logic that leads to the privatization of national States and to the reinforcement of the international institutions remains to be made.

32. Foucault, *Discipline & Punish*, 207.

33. Michel Foucault, *Naissance de la biopolitique: Cours au Collège de France, 1978-1979* (Paris: Gallimard/Seuil, 2004), 79. (our translation)

34. Foucault, *Power*, 58.

35. Foucault, *Discipline & Punish*, 210.

36. Foucault, *Dits et écrits*, vol. 3, 386.

37. Foucault, *Dits et écrits*, vol. 3, 670.

38. Michel Foucault, taken from "Human Nature: Justice versus Power" (debate with N. Chomsky), in *Foucault and his Interlocutors*, ed. A. I. Davidson (Chicago: University of Chicago Press, 1997), 130.

39. Michel Foucault in *Technologies of the Self: A Seminar with Michel Foucault*, ed. L. H. Martin, H. Gutman and P. H. Hutton, (Amherst: University of Massachusetts Press, 1988 [orig. 1983]), 18.

40. Foucault, *Dits et écrits*, vol. 4, 171, 374, 451, 727.

41. General title of Foucault's last courses given at the Collège de France (1982-1984).

42. Foucault explains his conception of "oubli" (forgetfulness, oblivion) in *Dits et écrits*, vol. 4, 723.

43. Foucault, *Technologies of the Self*, 38. See also Foucault, *Dits et écrits*, vol. 4, 364; Michel Foucault, *Herméneutique du sujet* (Paris: Gallimard/Seuil, 2001), 438, 483-84; Michel Foucault, *Histoire de la sexualité*, vol. 24, *L'usage des plaisirs*, (Paris: Gallimard, 1984), 40.

44. Foucault, *Herméneutique du sujet*, 227-28.

45. Foucault, *Dits et écrits*, vol. 4, 403.

46. Foucault, *Herméneutique du sujet*, 114. See also *History of Sexuality*, vol. 3, *The Care of the Self* (New York: Random House, 1986 [orig. 1984]), 69-95.

47. Foucault, *Herméneutique du sujet*, 169.

48. Foucault, *Technologies of the Self*, 153.

49. Michel Foucault, *Il faut défendre la société* (Paris: Gallimard/Seuil, 1997), 35. In "Confronting Governments: Human Rights" (*Power*, 474-75) Foucault speaks about a "right of intervention in international politics"; in *Dits et écrits*, vol. 4, 311-14, he also refers to a "new relational right" made of "mobile norms." See also Jean-Claude Monod, *Foucault. La police des conduites* (Paris: Michalon, 1997), 88-97.

50. Michel Foucault in *Foucault Live* (Interviews, 1961-1984), ed. S. Lotringer (New York: Semiotext(e), 1996), 389.

51. The audio versions of those courses can be found at the Foucault-Archive in Paris (IMEC-Institut mémoires de l'édition contemporaine), documents C-68 and C-69. See also the lectures given by Michel Foucault at Berkeley in 1983, "Discourse and Truth: The Problematization of Parrhesia" available at www.foucault.info. This text is reproduced in *Fearless Speech*, ed. Joseph Pearson (New York: Semiotext(e), 2001).

52. Taken from the 1983-84 lectures (IMEC, document C-69). Our translation.

53. In the 1983-84 lectures (IMEC, document C-69), Foucault distinguishes the enigmatic truth-telling of the prophet, the apodictic truth-telling of wise man, the demonstrative truth-telling of the technician, and the polemical truth-telling of the parrhesiast.

54. Foucault, *Foucault Live*, 390.

55. These expressions are taken from the 1983-84 lectures (IMEC, document C-69).

Chapter 4

1. Michel Foucault, "The Subject and Power," in *Power: Essential Works of Foucault, 1954-1984,* vol. 3, ed. J. D. Faubion (New York: New Press, 2001), 328.

2. Foucault, "The Subject and Power," 329.

3. Everett Reimer, "Freeing Educational Resources," in *After Deschooling, What?* ed. Alan Gartner, Frank Riessman, Colin Greer, Ivan Illich, and Roy P. Fairfield (New York: Harper & Row, 1973), 49.

4. Reimer, "Freeing Educational Resources," 49.

5. Jimmy Carter, "The Crisis of Confidence Speech," Public Broadcasting Service www.pbs.org/wgbh/amex/carter/filmmore/ps_crisis.html (accessed January 5, 2005).

6. Carter, "The Crisis of Confidence Speech," 1.

7. President's Commission for a National Agenda for the Eighties, *A National Agenda for the Eighties* (Washington, DC: GPO, 1980), 84.

8. Noam Chomsky, *Chronicles of Dissent* (Monroe, ME: Common Courage Press, 1992) 105.

9. President's Commission, ii.

10. President's Commision, 84.

11. Jean Baudrillard, "The Violence of the Global," www.ctheory.net/ text_file.asp?pick=385 (accessed on January 5, 2005), 3.

12. Takis Fotopoulos, "Mass Media, Culture, and Democracy," *Democracy and Nature* 5, no. 1 (March 1999): 34.

13. Fotopoulos, "Mass Media, Culture, and Democracy," 34.

14. Fotopoulos, "Mass Media, Culture, and Democracy," 34.

15. David A. Gabbard, *Knowledge and Power in the Global Economy* (Mahwah, NJ: Lawrence Erlbaum: 2000).

16. Michel Foucault, "Governmentality," in *The Foucault Effect*, ed. Peter Miller, Graham Burchell, and Colin Gordon (Chicago: University of Chicago Press, 1991), 92.

17. Foucault, "Governmentality," 93.

18. Michel Foucault, *Discipline and Punish* (New York: Pantheon, 1977), 210.

19. Foucault, *Discipline and Punish*, 210.

20. Foucault, *Discipline and Punish*, 143.

21. Michel Foucault, "Truth and Power," in *Power/Knowledge: Selected Interviews and Other Writings 1972-1977* (New York: Pantheon Books, 1980), 125.

22. Foucault, *Discipline and Punish*, 141.

23. Michel Foucault, "Clarifications on the Question of Power," *in Foucault Live: Interviews, 1961-84*, ed. Sylvère Lotringer (Cambridge, MA: Semiotext(e), 1996), 183-84.

Chapter 5

1. Michel Foucault, "Structuralism and Post Structuralism," in *Aesthetics, Method, and Epistemology*, ed. J. D. Faubion (New York: New Press, 1998), 433-34.

2. Michel Foucault, "Contemporary Music and the Public," in *Politics, Philosophy, Culture: Interviews and Other Writings of Michel Foucault, 1977-1984*, ed. Lawrence D. Kritzman (New York: Routledge, 1988), 314. Originally published in *Perspectives of New Music* 24 (Fall-Winter 1985): 6-12.

3. My reference to "the artworld, broadly construed" is intended to encompass all those who have an interest in artistic production and reception: most obviously, the artists themselves, critics and theorists, and the audiences who experience the artist's work, but also those who nurture the cultural traditions from which specific artistic practices arise.

4. This term, and its counterpart "Eurological," are labels introduced by musicologist George Lewis. They denote culturally distinct traditions of music-making. See George Lewis, "Improvised Music After 1950: Afrological and Eurological Perspectives," *Black Music Research Journal* 16, no. 1 (Spring 1996): 91-122.

5. In my view, the determination of whether a work is taking shape with a particular tradition has nothing to do with the racial, ethnic, or cultural origins of the artist nor can it be *conclusively* determined by reference to formal elements of the work (although these formal elements may aid us in making provisional determinations). Such a determination must incorporate attention to the tradition(s) which the artist is intending to reference. Let me offer an example which shows why I think formal elements cannot be conclusive: that of the work of African-American artist Alison Saar, as discussed by bell hooks in *Art on My Mind: Visual Politics* (New York: New Press, 1995), 10-21. Saar's work, as described by hooks, might initially seem to reference the same traditions which shaped the work of Marcel Duchamp (one of the guiding examples I take up in this chapter). Saar received artistic training within traditional Eurocentric institutions and has done considerable work with "found" or salvaged objects (hooks, *Art on My Mind*, 14), suggesting a similarity to Duchamp's aesthetic trajectory. However, her work departs from his in that her use of found objects takes place within a context of fusion of European, African, African-American, and Native-American artistic/aesthetic traditions and seeks to foreground subjugated knowledges of African-American artists (hooks, *Art on My Mind*, 14). Thus, although critical analysis of her work would clearly involve, and profit from, attention to her cultural borrowings and a residue of Eurocentric pedagogy in her approach to art-making, it would also crucially require acknowledgement of the "aesthetic turn" which brought into her work a commitment to metaphysically influenced folk arts from non-European traditions (hooks, *Art on My Mind*, 14, 18-20). This example problematizes assumptions about easy identification of traditions based on formal elements alone, but also problematizes attempts to categorize works with reference to a

Notes

single tradition (as does the body of work presented by John Coltrane). It is this blending and borrowing of traditions within artistic practices which convinces me that responsible theorizing and criticism needs to take place within a pluralistic context, one which can take note of the fruitfulness of different theories without seeking to collapse them into a single, universal meta-theory.

6. Michel Foucault, "What Is an Author?" in *Aesthetics, Method, and Epistemology*, 205.

7. Foucault, "What Is an Author?" 210.

8. Foucault, "What Is an Author?" 221.

9. Foucault, "What Is an Author?" 222.

10. Foucault, "What Is an Author?" 206.

11. Foucault, "What Is an Author?" 206.

12. Foucault, "What Is an Author?" 207.

13. Foucault, "What Is an Author?" 222.

14. Note that I am here conflating discussion of artistic meanings and aesthetic values. This is done purely for pragmatic reasons of maintaining clarity in a brief presentation of the difference between my views and Foucault's. His interest (in this essay) is in artistic meanings whereas my interests pertain to aesthetic values. While the distinction between meanings and values may obviously be significant in some discussions of artistic practices, I do not believe that anything I say here depends on, or otherwise references, that distinction.

15. Thierry de Duve, *Kant after Duchamp* (Cambridge, MA: MIT Press, 1998), 96-97.

16. de Duve, *Kant after Duchamp*, 98-99.

17. de Duve, *Kant after Duchamp*, 91.

18. de Duve, *Kant after Duchamp*, 97 and 120.

19. Clive Bell, *Art* (London: Chatto & Windus, 1949 [Orig. 1914]), 6-8.

20. Prior to the *salon des refusés* in 1863 France (in which the Impressionist painter Manet showed his first works), would-be painters had to submit their works to a jury charged with determining whether the painting merited exhibition in the *salon*.

21. It should be noted that this "performative" view of music is a compressed statement of a position that I take in a related and highly contentious debate over how musical works ought to be understood. Basically, the distinction I am referencing is this: a "compositional" paradigm implicitly identifies the musical work with a notated score (produced by an individual composer), and demands that the score itself contain distinctive (original) elements in order for the work to be meaningfully differentiated from other works. A "performative" paradigm, on the other hand, takes the performance to *be* the musical work and, in group improvisations, evaluates the work with a focus upon how the musicians find their way out of problems they play themselves into, how they interpret a context for motifs, and how they collaboratively develop an organizing principle for the work "in real time." Although analysis of the merits of "performative" and "compositional" paradigms in music is outside the scope of this discussion, it is an issue that I address elsewhere in as-yet-unpublished work.

22. Ira Gitler, "'Trane on the Track," in *The John Coltrane Companion: Five Decades of Commentary,* ed. C. Woideck (New York/London: Schirmer Books/Prentice Hall International, 1998), 6. Originally published in *Down Beat,* October 16, 1958.

23. Gitler, "'Trane on the Track."

24. John Coltrane, quoted in Frank Kofsky, *Black Nationalism and the Revolution in Music* (New York: Pathfinder, 1970), 227.

25. John Coltrane and Don DeMicheal, "Coltrane on Coltrane," in *The John Coltrane Companion: Five Decades of Commentary,* 102. Originally published in *Down Beat,* September 29, 1960.

26. Henry Louis Gates Jr., *The Signifying Monkey. A Theory of African-American Literary Criticism* (New York/Oxford: University Press, 1998).

27. Frank Kofsky, "Some Thoughts on John Coltrane," www.room34.com/kofsky/jcint.html accessed 27 July 2003 on-line excerpt from Kofsky's *John Coltrane and the Jazz Revolution of the 1960s.*)

28. Kofsky, "Some Thoughts on John Coltrane."

29. Sam Manuel, "Review of two books by Frank Kofsky on the Root of Jazz and the Black Struggle," *The Militant* 62, no. 4 (2 February 1998): 3.

30. Kofsky, *Black Nationalism,* 9.

31. Kofsky, *Black Nationalism,* 10.

32. Theodor Adorno, "Farewell to Jazz," trans. Iain Macdonald, 4. [Originally published as "Abschied vom Jazz," *Europäische Revue* 9, no. 5 (1933): 313-16.]

33. Kofsky, *Black Nationalism,* 9-11.

34. Bob Thiele, quoted in Kofsky, *Black Nationalism,* 54.

35. Ajay Heble, *Landing on the Wrong Note* (New York: Routledge, 2000), 15.

Chapter 6

1. Franco Basaglia and Franca Ongaro Basaglia, eds, *Crimini di pace. Ricerche sugli intellettuali e sui tecnici come custodi di istituzioni violente* (Torino: Einaudi, 1975). Foucault's contribution is entitled "La maison des fous"; reprinted in Michel Foucault, *Dits et écrits,* vol. 2 (Paris: Gallimard, 1994), 693-98.

2. Foucault, *Dits et écrits,* vol. 2, 208-209.

3. Franco Basaglia, *Conferenze brasiliane* (Milano: Raffaello Cortina Editore, 2000), 153, 184-85.

4. Foucault, "Préface," in *Dits et écrits,* vol. 1 (Paris: Gallimard, 1994), 164.

5. Foucault, "Préface," 166.

6. Foucault, "Préface," 164.

7. Michel Foucault, *Le pouvoir psychiatrique. Cours au Collège de France. 1973-1974* (Paris: Seuil/Gallimard, 2003), 14.

8. Jacques Lagrange, "Situation du cours," in Foucault, *Le pouvoir psychiatrique,* 357.

9. Didier Eribon, *Michel Foucault (1926-1984)* (Paris: Flammarion, 1989), 151.

10. Eribon, *Michel Foucault,* 147.

11. Eribon, *Michel Foucault,* 147.

12. Foucault, *Dits et écrits,* vol. 1, 789-821.

13. Michel Foucault, *Histoire de la folie à l'âge classique* (Paris: Gallimard, 1972), 10.

14. Foucault, *Dits et écrits*, vol. *2*, 209.

15. Eribon, *Michel Foucault,* 151; see also Pierangelo Di Vittorio, *Foucault e Basaglia. L'incontro tra genealogie e movimenti di base* (Verona: Ombre corte edizioni, 1999).

16. Foucault, *Dits et écrits,* vol. 3, 148-49.

17. Foucault, *Dits et écrits*, vol. 3, 803.

18. Foucault, *Le pouvoir psychiatrique*, 15.

19. Foucault, *Dits et écrits*, vol. 3, 138.

20. Foucault, *Dits et écrits*, vol. 3, 131.

21. Foucault, *Le pouvoir psychiatrique*, 323.

22. Foucault, *Le pouvoir psychiatrique*, 323.

23. Foucault, *Le pouvoir psychiatrique*, 253.

24. Foucault, *Le pouvoir psychiatrique*, 253.

25. Foucault, *Le pouvoir psychiatrique*, 136.

26. Foucault, *Le pouvoir psychiatrique*, 135.

27. Foucault, *Le pouvoir psychiatrique*, 138.

28. Foucault, *Le pouvoir psychiatrique*, 347.

29. Foucault, *Histoire de la folie*, 623-32.

30. Foucault, *Le pouvoir psychiatrique*, 325.

31. Michel Foucault, *History of Sexuality*, vol. 1 (New York: Vintage Books, 1978 [orig. 1976]), 159. On this point, see also Jacques Derrida, "'Etre juste avec Freud:' L'histoire de la folie à l'âge de la psychanalyse," in *Penser la folie. Essais sur Michel Foucault*, ed. É. Roudinesco (Paris: Galilée, 1992), 139-95.

32. Foucault, *Dits et écrits,* vol. 2, 232.

33. Foucault, *Le pouvoir psychiatrique*, 86. See also Françoise Castel, Robert Castel, and Anne Lovell, *La société psychiatrique avancée* (Paris: Grasset, 1979).

34. Basaglia and Basaglia, *Crimini di pace*, 67.

35. Basaglia and Basaglia, *Crimini di pace*, 67.

36. Basaglia and Basaglia, *Crimini di pace*, 233.

37. Basaglia and Basaglia, *Crimini di pace*, 233.

38. Franco Basaglia, ed., *L'istituzione negata. Rapporto da un ospedale psichiatrico* (Torino: Einaudi, 1968); French edition: *L'institution en négation. Rapport sur l'hôpital psychiatrique de Gorizia* (Paris: Seuil, 1970), 30-31.

39. Franco Basaglia, "La 'Comunità Terapeutica' come base di un servizio psichiatrico. Realtà e prospettive," in ed. F. Basaglia, *Scritti 1* (Torino: Einaudi, 1981-82), 278.

40. Foucault, *Le pouvoir psychiatrique*, 10.

41. Franco Basaglia, "La distruzione dell'ospedale psichiatrico come luogo di istituzionalizzazione," in ed. F. Basaglia, *Scritti 1* (Torino: Einaudi, 1981-82), 257.

42. Franco Basaglia, "Potere ed istituzionalizzazione. Dalla vita istituzionale alla vita di comunità," in *Scritti 1* (Torino: Einaudi, 1981-82), 293.

43. Michel Foucault, *"Il faut défendre la société" Cours au Collège de France. 1975-1976* (Paris: Seuil/Gallimard, 1997), 8-9.

44. Foucault, *History of Sexuality*, vol. 1, 95.

45. Gilles Deleuze, *Negotiations* (New York: Columbia University Press, 1995 [orig. 1990]), 109.

46. Deleuze, *Negotiations*, 98.

47. Foucault, *History of Sexuality*, vol. 1, 95.

48. Arlette Farges and Michel Foucault, *Le désordre des familles. Lettres de cachet des Archives de la Bastille* (Paris: Gallimard-Juillard, 1982).

49. Foucault, *Dits et écrits*, vol. 3, 237.
50. Foucault, *Dits et écrits*, vol. 3, 237-38.
51. Foucault, *Dits et écrits*, vol. 3, 243
52. Foucault, *Dits et écrits*, vol. 3, 240.
53. Foucault, *Dits et écrits*, vol. 3, 239.
54. Foucault, *Dits et écrits*, vol. 3, 238.
55. Foucault, *"Il faut défendre la société,"* 12.
56. Foucault, *Dits et écrits*, vol. 3, 242.
57. Foucault, *Dits et écrits*, vol. 3, 241.
58. Foucault, *Dits et écrits*, vol. 3, 237.
59. Deleuze, *Negotiations*, 150.
60. Deleuze, *Negotiations*, 108.

Chapter 7

1. Giorgio Agamben, *Homo Sacer. Sovereign Power and Bare Life* (Palo Alto, CA: Stanford University Press, 1998); Michael Hardt and Antonio Negri, *Empire* (Cambridge/London: Harvard University Press, 2000).

2. Michel Foucault, *Illuminismo e critica* (Rome: Donzelli, 1997), 72.

3. Michel Foucault, *"Il faut défendre la société." Cours au Collège de France 1975-1976* (Paris: Seuil/Gallimard, 1997), 6-7.

4. Foucault, *"Il faut défendre la société,"* 6-7.

5. Foucault, *"Il faut défendre la société,"* 7-8.

6. Michel Foucault, "Pouvoir et corps," in *Dits et écrits*, vol. 2 (Paris: Gallimard, 1994), 759.

7. Other than Agamben and Negri, see also Roberto Esposito, *Immunitas: Protezione e negazione della vita* (Torino: Einaudi, 2002).

8. Mario Colucci and Pierangelo Di Vittorio, *Franco Basaglia* (Milano: Bruno Mondadori, 2001).

9. Agostino Pirella, "Histoire de la folie en Italie ou la critique de la psychiatrie," in *Penser la folie: Essais sur Michel Foucault*, ed. É. Roudinesco (Paris: Galilée, 1992), 109-20; and Pierangelo Di Vittorio, *Foucault e Basaglia. L'incontro tra genealogie e movimenti di base* (Verona: ombre corte edizioni, 1999).

10. Colucci and Di Vittorio, *Franco Basaglia*.

11. Michel Foucault, "Entretien avec Michel Foucault," in *Dits et écrits*, vol. 3, 140-206; and Pierangelo Di Vittorio, "La parabola della follia," in *Moltiplicare Foucault: Vent'anni dopo*, ed. Ottavio Marzocca, (Milano, Mimesis / Millepiani, 2004), 9-26.

12. Michel Foucault, *Le pouvoir psychiatrique. Cours au Collège de France 1973-1974* (Paris, Seuil/Gallimard, 2003).

13. Michel Foucault, *Les anormaux. Cours au Collège de France. 1974-1975* (Paris, Seuil/Gallimard, 1999).

14. Foucault, "Il faut défendre la société."

15. Franco Basaglia, "Lettera da New York. Il malato artificiale," in *Scritti*, tome 2, 99-101.

16. Franco Basaglia, "Appunti per un'analisi delle normative in psichiatria," in *La ragione degli altri*, ed. Luigi Onnis and Giuditta Lo Russo (Rome: Savelli, 1979), 100-101.

17. Pierangelo Di Vittorio, "Soggetti 'speciali.' I paradossi del governo liberale," *Fogli di Informazione* 194 (2002): 53-68.

18. Foucault, *Le pouvoir psychiatrique*, 199-231.

19. Foucault, *Les anormaux*, 275-303.

20. Foucault, *"Il faut défendre la société"*; and Michel Foucault, *La volonté de savoir. Histoire de la sexualité I* (Paris: Gallimard, 1976).

21. Foucault, *Le pouvoir psychiatrique*, 267-337.

22. Foucault, "Résumé du cours," in *Le pouvoir psychiatrique*, 348-351.

23. Robert Castel, *La gestion des risques: De l'anti-psychiatrie à l'après-psychanalyse* (Paris: Minuit, 1981).

24. Castel, *La gestion des risques*, 75-76.

25. Castel, *La gestion des risques*, 49-53.

26. Foucault, *Le pouvoir psychiatrique*

27. Foucault, *Dits et écrits*, vol. 3, 215-23; Michel Foucault, "La politique de la santé au XVIIIe siècle," in *Les machines à guérir: Aux origines de l'hôpital moderne* (Bruxelles: Pierre Madraga, 1979), 7-18; Foucault, *"Il faut défendre la société,"* 218.

28. Foucault, "La politique de la santé au XVIIIe siècle," 14.

29. Michel Foucault, *Surveiller et punir* (Paris: Gallimard, 1975), 228-43; see also *Les anormaux*, 40-48; and *Histoire de la folie à l'âge classique* (Paris: Gallimard, 1972), 13-24.

30. Foucault, *Les anormaux*, 29-50.

31. Foucault, *Les anormaux*, 29-50.

32. Foucault, *Les anormaux*, 149.

33. Foucault, *Le pouvoir psychiatrique*, 346.

34. Foucault, *Les anormaux*, 147 and 149.

35. Foucault, *Les anormaux*, 300.

36. Foucault, *Les anormaux*, 38.

37. Foucault, *Les anormaux*, 151.

38. Foucault, *Les anormaux*, 151.

39. Judith Butler, *Precarious Life: The Powers of Mourning and Violence* (London/New York: Verso, 2004).

40. Di Vittorio, "Soggetti 'speciali'"; and Robert Castel, *L'insécurité sociale: Qu'est-ce qu'être protégé?* (Paris: Seuil, 2003), 17-24.

41. Pierangelo Di Vittorio, "Marges du pouvoir," *Sud/Nord: Folies et cultures* 20 (2004).

Chapter 8

1. Michel Foucault, "Le sujet et le pouvoir," in *Dits et écrits*, vol. 4 (Paris:

Gallimard/Seuil, 1994), 222-43; Michel Foucault, "La 'gouvernementalité,'" in *Dits et écrits*, vol. 3 (Paris: Gallimard/Seuil, 1994), 635-657; and Thomas Lemke, *Eine Kritik der politischen Vernunft: Foucaults Analyse der modernen Gouvernementalität* (Berlin/Hamburg: Argument Verlag, 1997).

2. See Thomas Lemke, *Veranlagung und Verantwortung: Genetische Diagnostik zwischen Selbstbestimmung und Schicksal* (Bielefeld: Transcript Verlag, 2004); and Thomas Lemke, "From Eugenics to the Government of Genetic Risks," in *Genetic Governance*, ed. Alan Petersen and Robin Bunton (New York: Routledge, forthcoming).

3. The Google search was conducted on 22 December 2004.

4. Lynn Oveson and Mark Yarborough, "The Aspen Report: Ethical Issues in Occupational Genetics." The Ramazzini Institute for Occupational and Environmental Health Research," www.ramazziniusa.org/apr01/geneticprofiles.htm (22 December 2004).

5. Aventis-Institut de France Foundation, "Genetics and Polemics," *Science Generation* en.science-generation.com/biomgene.php (22 December 2004).

6. Aventis-Institut de France Foundation, "Genetics and Polemics."

7. See Dan W. Brock's observation that "[T]he Human Genome Project is likely to affect deeply . . . our conception of ourselves as responsible agents and, more specifically, as morally and legally responsible for our actions, for the lives we live, and for the kinds of people that we become." Dan W. Brock, "The Human Genome Project and Human Identity," in *Genes and Human Self-Knowledge: Historical and Philosophical Reflections on Modern Genetics,* eds. Robert F. Weir, Susan C. Lawrence, and Evan Fales (Iowa City: University of Iowa Press, 1999), 23.

8. See Garrett Hardin, "The Moral Threat of Personal Medicine," in *Genetic Responsibility: On Choosing Our Children's Genes*, eds. Mack Lipkin Jr. and Peter T. Rowley (New York/London: Plenum Press, 1974), 88. "We must admit that if there is one thing a person is not responsible for, it is the genes that were passed on him. . . . We are not responsible as the recipients of errors. But should we not be responsible as the transmitters of errors? If there are some people in society who refuse to take such responsibility, who say *No* for whatever reason, refusing to inhibit their own breeding in spite of the fact they are passing on genes known to be undesirable genes, does not then the issue of responsibility arise in a very acute form? . . . Should individual freedom include the freedom to impose upon society costs that society does not want? . . . We must recognize that this is a finite world. The money we spent for one purpose, we cannot spend on another." See also Sumner B. Twiss, "Ethical Issues in Genetic Screening: Models of Genetic Responsibility," in *Ethical, Social and Legal Dimensions of Screening for Human Genetic Disease*, ed. Daniel Bergsma (New York and London: Stratton Intercontinental Medical Book Corporation, 1974), 225-61.

9. Anne Kerr and Tom Shakespeare likewise distinguish two sorts of responsibility that individuals bear that are found to be at risk for a genetic disease: "The first is to avoid behaviours likely to exacerbate that risk. This starts with consulting and following the advice of medical experts. . . . Second, individuals bear responsibility for informing their genetic kin about their risk." See Anne Kerr and Tom Shakespeare, *Genetic Politics: From Eugenics to Genome* (Oxford: New Clarion Press, 2002), 153-54.

10. Lealle Ruhl, "Liberal Governance and Prenatal Care: Risk and Regulation in

Pregnancy," *Economy and Society* 28 (1999): 103; and Heidi Marie Rimke, "Governing Citizens through Self-Help Literature," *Cultural Studies* 14, (2000): 61-78.

11. Aubrey Milunsky, *Unsere biologische Mitgift: Was man über Erbanlagen wissen muß* (Frankfurt/M./Berlin/Wien: Ullstein, 1982).

12. Aubrey Milunsky, *Choices, Not Chances: An Essential Guide to Your Heredity and Health* (Boston: Little Brown, 1989), xvii.

13. Milunsky, *Choices, Not Chances*, xvii.

14. Milunsky, *Choices, Not Chances*, xvii.

15. Milunsky, *Choices, Not Chances*, xviii.

16. Milunsky, *Choices, Not Chances*, 4-6.

17. Aubrey Milunsky, *Know Your Genes* (Boston: Houghton Mifflin, 1977), 11.

18. Aubrey Milunsky, *Your Genetic Destiny: Know Your Genes, Secure Your Health, Save Your Life* (Cambridge, MA: Perseus Publishing, 2001).

19. Milunsky, *Your Genetic Destiny*, xiii.

20. Milunsky, *Your Genetic Destiny*, xv.

21. For a very instructive discussion of the normative problems see Jorgen Husted, "Autonomy and a Right Not to Know," in *The Right to Know and the Right not to Know*, ed. Ruth Chadwick, Mairi Levitt, and Darren Shickle (Aldershot: Avebury, 1997), 55-68; for an analysis of the juridical cases that were recently decided in the United States see Leonard J. Deftos, "The evolving duty to disclose the presence of genetic disease to relatives," *Academic Medicine* 73 (1998): 962-68; and J. Petrila, "Genetic Risk: the New Frontier for the Duty to Warn," *Behavioral Sciences & the Law* 19 (2001): 405-12.

22. For a striking legal example see *Chevron USA Inc. v. Echzabal*, Case No. 00-1406, U.S. Supreme Court, Washington DC, 2002 and the analysis in Geoffrey Lomax, "Chevron V. Echazabal: A Sobering Decision for Environmental Health Research," *Environmental Health Perspectives* 110, no. 9 (2002): A504-A505.

23. Hans-Martin Sass, a medical ethical philosopher, calls for an "ethos of duty" in handling genetic information. "Leisure time behavior, place of work, or genetic predisposition, or a mixture of all three factors determine the respective individual risks to my health. . . . Some can be eliminated, others reduced, or the stage at which they become acute delayed. The patient becomes the partner in preventing or delaying major health risks. Alongside the doctor's ethics under the Hippocratic oath, with regard to care and outer-determined support, in future will go hand in hand with self-determined and self-responsible ethics of the patient and citizen in healthcare." See Hans-Martin Sass, "Der Mensch im Zeitalter von genetischer Diagnostik und Manipulation: Kultur, Wissen und Verantwortung," in *Wieviel Genetik braucht der Mensch? Die alten Träume der Genetiker und ihre heutigen Methoden,* ed. Ernst Peter Fischer and Erhard Geißler (Konstanz: Universitätsverlag Konstanz, 1994), 343. For a conceptual analysis of the judgment of "genetic irresponsibility" see Judith Andre, Leonhard M. Fleck, and Tom Tomlinson, "On Being Genetically 'Irresponsible,'" *Kennedy Institute of Ethics Journal* 10, no. 2 (2000): 129-46.

24. Evelyn Fox Keller, *The Century of the Gene* (Cambridge, MA and London: Harvard University Press, 2000).

25. See Muin J. Khoury, Wylie Burke, and Elizabeth Thompson, eds., *Genetics and Public Health in the 21st Century: Using Genetic Information to Improve Health and*

Prevent Disease (Oxford: Oxford University Press, 2000). For a popular description see the internet publication "Your Genes, Your Choices" by the *American Association for the Advancement of Science*, that emphasizes the importance of "genetic literacy" www.ornl.gov/TechResources/Human_Genome/publicat/genechoice/contents.html, (3 July 2003).

26. Charlie Davison, "Predictive genetics: the cultural implications of supplying probable futures," in *The Troubled Helix: Social and Psychological Implications of the New Human Genetics*, ed. Theresa Marteau and Martin Richards (Cambridge: Cambridge University Press, 1996), 317-30.

27. Richard Ericson, Dean Barry, and Aaron Doyle, "The Moral Hazards of Neo-Liberalism: Lessons From the Private Insurance Industry," *Economy & Society* 29, no. 4, (2000): 553.

28. John Knowles, the former president of the Rockefeller Foundation, declared in an influential 1977 essay that diseases are mainly the result of a (wrong) life style: "Prevention of disease means forsaking the bad habits which many people enjoy—overeating, too much drinking, taking pills, staying up at night, engaging in promiscuous sex, driving too fast, and smoking cigarettes. . . . The cost of sloth, gluttony, alcoholic intemperance, reckless driving, sexual frenzy, and smoking is now a national, and not an individual responsibility. This is justified as individual freedom—but one man's freedom in health is another man's shackle in taxes and insurance premiums. I believe that the idea of a "right" to health should be replaced by the idea of an individual moral obligation to preserve one's own health—a public duty if you will." Cf. J. H. Knowles, "Responsibility for Health," *Science* 198, no. 4322 (1977): 59. For a still pertinent critique see Robert Crawford, "You Are Dangerous to Your Health – Ideology and Politics of Victim Blaming," *International Journal of Health Services* 7, no. 4 (1977): 663-60.

29. Peter Conrad, "Genetics and Behavior in the News: Dilemmas of a Rising Paradigm," in *The Double-Edged Helix. Social Implications of Genetics in a Diverse Society*, ed. Joseph S. Alper, Catherine Ard, Adrienne Asch, Peter Conrad, Lisa N. Geller, and Jon Beckwith (Baltimore and London: The John Hopkins University Press, 2002): 58-79; and Margarete Bause "Guter Rat ist teuer—humangenetische Beratung unter den Bedingungen der Marktindividualisierung," in *Guter Rat ist teuer: Was kostet die Humangenetik, was nutzt sie?* ed. Jörg Schmidtke (München/Jena: Urban & Fischer, 2000), 96-106.

30. Alan Petersen and Robin Bunton, *The New Genetics and the Public's Health* (London/New York: Routledge, 2002).

31. Mary Douglas, "Risk as a Forensic Resource," *Daedalus* 119, no. 4 (1990): 1-16.

32. Rose Galvin, "Disturbing Notions of Chronic Illness and Individual Responsibility: Towards a Genealogy of Morals," *Health* 6, no. 2 (2002): 117.

Chapter 9

1. Thus, these institutions do not deal with persons who have a "mental illness." These individuals are housed in another type of facility; such facilities will not be the focus of this paper.

2. Norman Daniels addresses health care needs and argues that these should be considered "primary goods" under a Rawlsian scheme of justice. In the case where citizens are no longer "productive," he claims that giving such individuals "care" is an issue outside political justice; however, in the case of older adults, the issue can be framed as one of justice between generations. See Norman Daniels, *Just Health Care*, (New York: Cambridge University Press, 1985). For a recent example of this debate see Dennis McKerlie, "Justice Between the Young and the Old," *Philosophy and Public Affairs* 30, no.2 (2001): 152-77.

3. These are analyses that center on quality of care. For example, how often should a resident who cannot move be repositioned in order to avoid bedsores coupled with considerations of staff costs, etc. These analyses deal with the maximization of care practices; they do not question the practices themselves.

4. One notable exception is the analysis of the concepts of reciprocity and mutuality in two different models of long-term care institutions by Pamela Cushing and Tanya Lewis in "Negotiating Mutuality and Agency in Care-giving Relationships with Women with Intellectual Disabilities" in *Hypatia* 17, no. 3 (2002): 173-93.

5. Eva Feder Kittay, *Love's Labor* (Routledge: New York, 1999); Joan Tronto, *Moral Boundaries: A Political Argument for an Ethic of Care* (Routledge: New York, 1993).

6. See, for example, *Ethical and Moral Dimensions of Care*, ed. Madeleine M. Leininger (Detroit: Wayne State University Press, 1990).

7. Recent publications include: *Caring For/Caring About*, ed. Pat Armstrong et al (Aurora, Ontario: Garamond Press, 2004).

8. It will be established whether the person can dress, feed, and clean herself on her own or with some assistance, whether this assistance is in the form of a prosthesis or a person helping her with these chores. There may also be an evaluation of the person's mental capacity to see to her own affairs.

9. For example, the code of ethics of the institution will typically refer to "residents," not "clients."

10. For critical discussions of the medical model of disability see the writings of Jenny Morris, Jerome Bickenbach, and Michael Oliver, for example.

11. It is interesting to note that there will be a re-creation of society. Social interactions will take place; hierarchies might develop within an institution. Nonetheless, interactions between institutionalized individuals and society "at large" will be difficult.

12. Although there are institutions for particular cultural groups; nevertheless, the criterion for placement in a long-term care facility is the number of hours of nursing care per day required by the particular individual.

13. For example, a feeder is an individual who cannot eat by himself; he needs someone to feed him. Since these needs are what are addressed by the staff, they soon get familiar with the requirements of the residents. There is an identification of the resident by his or her needs.

14. Michel Foucault, "On the Government of the Living, " in *Ethics: Subjectivity and Truth—The Essential Works of Michel Foucault*, vol. 1, ed. Paul Rabinow (New York: The New Press, 1997), 81-85.

15. See Shelley Tremain, "On the Government of Disability," *Social Theory and Practice* 27, no. 4 (2001): 617-36.

16. Margrit Shildrick and Janet Price, "Breaking the Boundaries of the Broken Body," *Body and Society* 2, no. 4 (1996): 93-113.

17. Susan Wendell makes this point in her book, *The Rejected Body* (New York: Routledge, 1996).

18. Even if the resident is mentally apt, her agency is still contrived as she has to manage the various levels of bureaucracy entailed by institutionalization.

19. Even though much has been written about institutionalization due to mental illness, the same cannot be said of long-term care.

20. Long-term care facilities (CHSLD) are government-regulated health-care facilities whereas assisted living facilities are not governmental health-care facilities and may not be subject to the same government regulations and scrutiny.

21. Giorgio Agamben, *Homo Sacer: Sovereign Power and Bare Life* (Stanford: Stanford University Press, 1998).

22. Giorgio Agamben, *Remnants of Auschwitz: the Witness and the Archive* (New York: Zone Books, 1999), 26.

23. Agamben, *Remnants of Auschwitz*, 21.

24. Agamben, *Homo Sacer*, 7.

25. Claudia Card, *The Atrocity Paradigm: A Theory of Evil* (Oxford: Oxford University Press, 2002), 232.

26. For a thoughtful discussion on the appropriation of the paradigm of the Holocaust see Debarati Sanyal, "A Soccer Match in Auschwitz: Passing Culpability in Holocaust Criticism, *Representations*, 79 (Summer 2002): 1-27.

27. Agamben does not look into institutionalization, but he does discuss the comatose patient in *Homo Sacer*.

28. A person can be placed in long-term care against her will. If the person requires too many hours of care work, cannot afford private help, and relies on the public system, she has little choice but to move into a long-term care institution. There is case being fought in the courts in Québec, where a woman with multiple sclerosis is battling against institutionalization.

Chapter 10

1. Pierre Bourdieu and Claude Duverlie, "Esquisse d'un projet intellectuel–un entretien avec Pierre Bourdieu," *The French Review* 61, no. 2 (1987): 205.

2. Pierre Bourdieu, *Die Intellektuellen und die Macht* (Hamburg: VSA-Verlag, 1991), 46.

3. Jean-François Lyotard, "Tomb of the Intellectual," in *Political Writings: Jean-François Lyotard*, ed. B. Readings & K. Paul (Minneapolis: University of Minnesota Press, 1993), 6.

4. Lyotard, "Tomb of the Intellectual," 3.

5. Michel Foucault, *Dits et écrits*, vol. 3 (Paris: Gallimard, 1994), 112.

6. Foucault, *Dits et écrits*, vol. 3, 110.

7. Michel Foucault, *Remarks on Marx: Conversation with Duccio Trombadori* (New York, Semiotext(e), 1991), 160.

8. Foucault, *Remarks on Marx*, 157.

9. Foucault, *Remarks on Marx*, 159-60.

10. Foucault, *Remarks on Marx*, 42.

11. Jacques Derrida, "The University without Condition," in *Without Alibi*, ed. P. Kamuf (Stanford: Stanford University Press, 2002).

Chapter 11

1. David Macey, *The Lives of Michel Foucault* (London: Vintage, 1994).

2. Michel Foucault, "The Prose of Actaeon" [orig. 1964], in *Aesthetics, Methods and Epistemology: Essential Works of Michel Foucault 1954-1984*, vol. 2, ed. James D. Faubion (New York: New Press, 1998): 123-35, esp. 129.

3. Patrick Walberg, "Vers un nouveau mythe? Prémonitions et défiances," Vol. 2, no. 4 (February 1944): 41-44.

4. Roger Caillois, "Préamble pour l'esprit des sectes," in *Approches de l'imaginaire* (Paris: Gallimard, 1974); Frank Pearce, "The Collège de Sociologie and French Social Thought," *Economy and Society* 20, no. 1 (February 2003): 210-11. See also the remarks cited in Hector Biancotti, "Le dernier encyclopédiste: Roger Caillois," *Le Nouvel Observateur* 521 (4 November 1974).

5 Michel Leiris, "Documents sur Raymond Roussel," *La Nouvelle Revue Française* no. 359 (1935): 575-82; Michel Leiris, "Comment j'ai écrit . . . ," *La Nouvelle Revue Française* (1936): 113-15; Michel Leiris, "Conception and Reality in the Work of Raymond Roussel," in *Raymond Roussel: Life, Death, and Works*, Collective edition (London: Atlas Press, 1987 [orig. 1954]).

6. Michel Foucault, "Speaking and Seeing in Raymond Roussel" [orig. 1962], in *Aesthetics, Methods and Epistemology*, 21-32.

7. Michel Foucault, *Death and the Labyrinth: The World of Raymond Roussel* (New York: Doubleday, 1986 [orig. 1963]), 19.

8. Michel Foucault, "A Preface to Transgression" [orig. 1963], in *Aesthetics, Methods and Epistemology*, 69-87, esp. 86.

9. Michel Foucault, "A Swimmer Between Two Words" [orig. 1966], in *Aesthetics, Methods and Epistemology*, 171-74, esp. 174.

10. Michel Foucault, "Theatrum Philosophicum" [orig. 1970], in *Aesthetics, Methods and Epistemology*, 343-68, esp. 343.

11. Michel Foucault and Charles Ruas, "An Interview with Michel Foucault" [orig. 1983], in *Death and the Labyrinth*, 168-86, esp. 181.

12. Ferdinand de Saussure cited in Jonathan Culler, *Saussure* (London: Jonathan Cape, 1976), 39.

13. Michel Foucault, "Sept propos sur le septième ange," (Paris: Tchou, 1970), vi-xix.

14. Jean-Pierre Brisset, *La grammaire logique suivie de la science de Dieu* (Paris: Tchou, 1970).

15. Raymond Roussel, *How I Wrote Certain of My Books*, ed. Trevor Winkfield (Boston: Exact Change, 1995).

16. Foucault, *Death and the Labyrinth*, 15.

17. Foucault, *Death and the Labyrinth*, 19.

18. Foucault, *Death and the Labyrinth*, 66.

19. Foucault, *Death and the Labyrinth*, 63.

20. Roussel, *How I Wrote Certain of My Books*, 16.

21. Leiris, "Conception and Reality," 79-80.

22. Daniel Eribon, *Michel Foucault* (Cambridge: Harvard University Press, 1991 [orig. 1989]): 147.

23. Allan Stoekl, *Politics, Writing, Mutilation: The Cases of Blanchot, Bataille, Roussel, Leiris, and Ponge* (Minneapolis: University of Minnesota Press, 1985), 41.

24. Cited in Macey, *The Lives of Michel Foucault*, xv.

25. Seán Hand, *Michel Leiris: Writing the Self* (Cambridge: Cambridge University Press, 2002): 214-15.

26. Michel Foucault and D. Trambodori, "Interview with Michel Foucault" [orig. 1978], in *Power: Essential Works of Michel Foucault 1954-1984* vol. 3, ed. James D. Faubion (New York: New Press, 2000), 239-97, esp. 241.

27. Foucault, "The Prose of Actaeon," 129.

28. Pierre Klossowski, "The Marquis de Sade and the Revolution" [orig. 1939], in *The College of Sociology (1937-1939)*, ed. Denis Hollier (Minneapolis: University of Minnesota Press 1988), 218-32.

29. Foucault, "Theatrum Philosophicum," 343-68.

30. Pierre Klossowski, cited in Macey, *The Lives of Michel Foucault*, 156.

31. Pierre Klosssowksi, *The Baphomet* (New York: Marsilio, 1998 [orig. 1965]), 164.

32. See the article by A. P. Arendzen, "Gnosticism" in the 1913 *Catholic Encyclopedia*, available online as the *Advent Catholic Encylopedia*, and the disucussions of Gnoticism in Keith Hopkins, *A World Full of Gods: Pagans, Jews and Christians in the Roman Empire* (London: Phoenix, 1999). For many of the Gnostics, Jesus and/or Christ had no human nature and, hence, did not necessarily suffer "the passion" and hence sacrifice himself for our sins. In the *Apocalypse of Peter*, one of the documents recently discovered at Nag Hammidi, is written the following account of the crucifixion: "I saw him apparently being seized by them. And I said, 'What am I seeing, O Lord? Is it really you whom they take? And are you holding on to me? And are they hammering the hands and feet of another? Who is this one above the cross, who is glad and laughing?' The Savior said to me, 'He whom you saw being glad and laughing above the cross is the Living Jesus. But he who into his hands and feet they are driving the nails in his fleshy part, which is the substitute. They put to shame that which examined in his likeness. And look at him, and [look at] me!'" (Elaine Pagels, *The Gnostic Gospels* [New York: Vintage, 1979], 72.

33. Foucault, "The Prose of Actaeon," 127.

34. Foucault and Ruas, "An Interview with Michel Foucault," 181.

35. Foucault, "The Prose of Actaeon," 127.

36. Foucault, "The Prose of Actaeon," 132.

37. Foucault, "The Prose of Actaeon," 129.

38. Foucault, "The Prose of Actaeon," 134.

39. Foucault, "The Prose of Actaeon," 129.

40. Michel Foucault, "The Thought of the Outside" [orig. 1966], in *Aesthetics, Methods and Epistemology*, 147-69, esp. 151.

41. Pierre Klossowski, *Sade My Neighbour* (London: Quartet Books, 1991 [orig. 1947]), 68.

42. Marquis de Sade, *The 120 Days of Sodom* (New York: The Grove Press, 1966 [orig. 1785]), 253.

43. Ian James, *Pierre Klossowski: The Persistence of a Name* (Oxford: Legenda, 2000), 31.

44. Alexandre Kojève, *Introduction to the Reading of Hegel* (Ithaca: Cornell University Press, 1980 [orig. 1947]), 9.

45. Klossowski, *Sade My Neighbour*, 74-75.

46. Klossowski, *Sade My Neighbour*, 75-78.

47. Klossowski, *Sade My Neighbour*, 137-38.

48. Klossowski, *Sade My Neighbour*, 100.

49. Klossowski, *Sade My Neighbour*, 83.

50. Klossowski, *Sade My Neighbour*, 88.

51. These interpretations are associated with the versions of Klossowski's work available when Foucault wrote about his work in 1964. Klossowski would later elaborate the argument that libertines felt that the belief in God produces all arbitrary, perverse, and monstrous behaviour and that, contrariwise, atheistic autonomous reason makes it possible to formulate and maintain the norms of the species in individuals and thereby guarantee the reproduction of the species and of the responsible ego, its self-possession and individual identity. For Sade, however, atheism should oppose such norms and responsibility. If the "language of institutions has taken over . . . what is functional in 'my' body for the best preservation of the species" and if "'I' then do not possess my body save in the name of institutions' then 'the language in 'me' is just their overseer put in me." (Klossowski, *Sade My Neighbour*, 36) What better transgression than the homosexual and heterosexual sodomy depicted in Sade's writings? Transgression is the appropriate word because the complicitous participation of many of the men and (some of) the women in these activities on the one hand by generalizing sodomitical practices renders sodomy in some sense normal–yet the necessarily nonreproductive outcome of the acts means that it cannot exhaust sexual activities within a society–and much of the excitement associated with it still lies in its public condemnation.

52. Michel Foucault, in *Aesthetics, Methods and Epistemology*, 438.

53. Michel Foucault, "Le Non du Père," *Critique* 178 (March 1962): 195-209; a review of Jean Laplanche, "Hölderlin et la question du père," and "Un si cruel savoir," *Critique* 182 (July 1962): 597-611; to its special posthumous issue on Bataille, he contributed a "Préface à la transgression," *Critique* 195-96 (August/September 1963): 751-69.

54. Michel Foucault, "Présentation," in Georges Bataille, *Œuvres Complètes*, vol. 1 *Premiers écrits 1922-1940* (Paris: Gallimard, 1970), 5-6.

55. James Miller, *The Passion of Michel Foucault* (New York: Simon and Schuster, 1993), 45.

56. James, *Pierre Klossowski: The Persistence of a Name*, 38.

57. Bataille, *Literature and Evil* (New York: Marion Boyers, 2001), 111.

58. Bataille, *Literature and Evil*, 115.

59. Bataille, *Literature and Evil*, 117.

60. Georges Bataille, "Hegel, Death and Sacrifice," in *The Bataille Reader*, ed. Fred Botting and Scott Wilson (Oxford: Blackwell, 1997 [orig. 1955]), 287.

61. Georges Bataille, *Erotism: Death and Sensuality* (San Francisco: City Lights Books, 1986 [orig. 1957]), 60.

62. Bataille, *Literature and Evil*, 120.

63. Bataille, *Erotism*, 167.

64. Bataille, *Erotism*, 173-74.

65. Bataille, *Erotism*, 175.

66. Bataille, *Erotism*, 196.

67. Bataille, *Literature and Evil*, 221-51.

68. Foucault, "A Preface to Transgression," 69-87.

69. Foucault, "A Preface to Transgression," 72.

70. Foucault, "A Preface to Transgression," 73-74.

71. Foucault, "A Preface to Transgression," 80.

72. Foucault, "A Preface to Transgression," 86.

73. Michel Foucault, *The History of Sexuality*, vol. 1, *An Introduction* (London: Allen Lane, 1978 [orig. 1976]), 150.

74. Michel Foucault, "Truth and Power," in *Power: Essential Works of Michel Foucault 1954-1984*, vol. 3, 127.

75. Foucault, "Truth and Power," 126.

76. Foucault, "Truth and Power," 132.

77. Michel Foucault, "The Ethics of the Concern of the Self as a Practice of Freedom" [orig. 1984], in *Ethics, Subjectivity and Truth: The Essential Works of Michel Foucault 1954-1984*, vol. 1, ed. Paul Rabinow (New York: New Press, 1997), 281-301, esp. 299.

78. Foucault and Trambodori, "Interview with Michel Foucault," 241-42.

79. Michel Foucault, *The Archaeology of Knowledge* (London: Tavistock, 1974 [orig. 1969]), 38. See also Frank Pearce and Anthony Woodiwiss, "Reading Foucault as a Realist," in *After Postmodernism: An Introduction to Critical Realism*, ed. Gary Potter and Jose Lopez (London: Athlone Press, 2001), 40-50.

80. Michel Foucault, "Two Lectures" [orig. 1976], in *Michel Foucault: Power/Knowledge: Selected Interviews and Other Writings* 1972-1977, ed. Colin Gordon (Brighton: Harvester, 1980), 78-108, esp. 81.

81. Frank Pearce and Steve Tombs, *Toxic Capitalism: Corporate Crime and the Chemical Industry* (Aldershot: Ashgate, 1998).

82. Michel Surya, *Georges Bataille: An Intellectual Biography* (Verso: London, 2002 [orig. 1992]), 517.

83. Georges Bataille, "The Language of Flowers" [orig. 1929], in Alan Stoekl ed., *Georges Bataille: Visions of Excess: Selected Writings 1927-1939* (Minneapolis: University of Minnesota Press, 1985), 10-14.

84. Bataille, "The Language of Flowers," 14.

85. Georges Bataille, "The Lugubrious Game" [orig. 1929], in *Georges Bataille: Visions of Excess*, 24-30.

86. Bataille, "The Lugubrious Game," 28.

87. Georges Bataille, "The Use-Value of D.A.F. de Sade: An Open Letter to My current Comrades" [orig. 1929], in *Georges Bataille: Visions of Excess,* 91-102.

88. Surya, *Georges Bataille: An Intellectual Biography*, 137.

89. Georges Bataille, "The Notion of Expenditure" [orig. 1933] in *Georges Bataille: Visions of Excess*, 116-29.

90. Georges Bataille, "Autobiographical Note" [orig. 1958], *October* 36 (Spring 1986), 109-110.

91. Georges Bataille "Propositions" [orig. 1937], in *Georges Bataille: Visions of Excess,*197-201, esp. 198-99.

92. Georges Ambrosino, Georges Bataille, Pierre Klossowski, Pierre Caillois, Jules Monnerot, and Pierre Libra, "Declaration Relating to the Foundation of a *Collège de Sociologie*" [orig. 1937], in *The College of Sociology (1937-1939)*, 5.

93. Roger Caillois, "Introduction" [orig. 1938], in *The College of Sociology (1937-1939)*, 11.

94. Georges Bataille and Roger Caillois, "Sacred Sociology and the relationships between 'Society,' 'Organism,' and 'Being'" [orig. 1937], in *The College of Sociology (1937-1939)*, 73-84.

95. Taken from Bataille and Caillois, "Sacred Sociology and the relationships between 'Society,' 'Organism,' and 'Being,'" 73-84.

96. Georges Bataille, "The Psychological Structure of Fascism" [orig. 1933-1934], in *Georges Bataille: Visions of Excess*, 131-60, esp. 142. On p. 160 he cites and comments, Emile Durkheim, *The Elementary Forms of Religious Life* (New York: Free Press, 1995 [orig 1912]), 36.

97. Bataille, "The Use-Value of D.A.F. de Sade," 116-18.

98. Bataille, "The Use-Value of D.A.F. de Sade," 94.

99. Georges Bataille, "Attraction and Repulsion" [orig. 1938], in *The College of Sociology (1937-1939)*, 106.

100. Bataille, "Attraction and Repulsion," 122.

101. Georges Bataille, "The Structure and Function of the Army" [orig. 1938], in *The College of Sociology (1937-1939)*, 139-44, esp. 144.

102. Georges Bataille, "Joy in the Face of Death" [orig. 1939], in *The College of Sociology (1937-1939)*, 325-28, esp. 328.

103. Georges Bataille, "The College of Sociology" [orig. 1939], in *The College of Sociology (1937-1939)*, 333-41, esp. 339.

104. Georges Bataille, *The Accursed Share*, vol. 1 (New York: Zone Books, 1988 [orig. 1967]).

105. Roger Caillois, "Festival" [orig. 1939], in *The College of Sociology (1937-1939)*, 279-303, esp. 284.

106. Caillois, "Festival," 284-85.

107. Caillois, "Festival," 298.

108. Caillois, "Festival," 288-91.

109. Caillois, "Festival," 300-301.

110. Caillois, "Festival," 294.

111. Caillois, "Festival," 299.

112. Pierre Klossowski, "Marquis de Sade et la Révolution" [orig. 1939], in *The College of Sociology (1937-1939)*, 218-32, esp. 223-24.

113. Klossowski, "Marquis de Sade et la Révolution," 223-224.

114. Klossowski, "Marquis de Sade et la Révolution," 224.

115. Klossowski, "Marquis de Sade et la Révolution," 224-225.

116. Klossowski, "Marquis de Sade et la Révolution," 225.

117. Evelyne Lever, *Marie Antoinette: the Last Queen of France* (New York: Farrar, Strauss & Giroux, 2000): 119.

118. Michel Leiris, "The Sacred in Everyday Life" [orig. 1938], in *The College of Sociology (1937-1939)*, 24-31.

119. Michel Leiris, "Leiris to Bataille: Paris, July 3, 1939" [orig. 1939], in *The College of Sociology (1937-1939)*, 355.

120. Bernard-Henri Lévy, *Adventures on the Freedom Road: The French Intellectuals in the 20th Century* (London: Harvill, 1995), 210.

121. Georges Bataille, "Nietzschean Chronicle" [orig. 1937], in *Visions of Excess: Selected Writings 1927-1939*, 208.

122. Marina Galletti, "Comunautés morales, communautés politiques," *Les Temps Modernes* 54 (January/February 1999): 153-67, esp. 163.

123. Surya, *Georges Bataille: An Intellectual Biography*, 239.

124. Allan Stoekl, "A commentary on the Texts," in *Georges Bataille: Visions of Excess*, 263.

125. Marina Galletti, "The secret and the sacred in Leiris and Bataille," *Economy and Society* 20, no. 1 (February 2003).

126. Maurice Blanchot, *The Unavowable Community* (Barrytown, NY: Station Hill Press, 1988).

127. Bataille, *Literature and Evil*, 117.

128. It is worth a short diversion into German literary history. In the late nineteenth and early twentieth centuries Alfred Schuler, Ludwig Klages, Karl Wolfskehl and the poet Stefan George were all key members of a semisecret society, "The Cosmic Circle." They shared a commitment to a mystical history which valorized the pagan over the Christian, the male over the female, homoerotic bonding over more conventional heterosexual relations, and a reverence for the Swastika symbol. In 1902, Stefan George had found a beautiful new "*protégé*" in the person of the fourteen-year-old Maximilian

Kronenberger, and in the following year during Carnival the two of them attended a "Dionysian" private pageant in honour of the Roman *Magna Mater,* a spirit who supposedly had presided over orgiastic and sacrificial rites, including the sacrifice of children. In 1904 "The Cosmic Circle" disintegrated as a result of internal conflicts and a few months later Maximilian was to die of meningitis. George's response to this tragic and unexpected early death was to develop the cult of Maximin. While admiring Nietzsche, George criticized him because he had not been a loyal disciple of Richard Wagner and he had failed to recruit his own disciples—George believed himself to be a natural leader and consciously cultivated disciples. George was "inspired" to develop a cult which intimated that Maximilian had effectively been sacrificed and symbolically transfigured in order to make possible the divine figure of Maximin, and George, his priest, shared in his divinity. Subsequently George became a more and more significant cultural figure; there is little doubt that there was an elective affinity between his beliefs and those of the Nazi Party, and there is good evidence that he was a strong Nazi sympathizer. Cf. R. E. Norton, *Secret Germany: Stefan George and His Circle* (Ithaca and London: Cornell University Press, 2002). Ironically, in some ways, Stefan George may have had more success in unleashing aspects of the sacred because doing so requires both the prior existence of sets of collective rituals, beliefs, and identities, (George's own practices), as well as an unpredictable event, (the unexpected but inevitable death of Maximilian). Thus the sacred may need as one element of its genesis a sense of "the iron hand of necessity shaking the dice box of chance." Cf. Friedrich Nietzsche, *Daybreak: Thoughts on the Prejudices of Morality* (Cambridge: Cambridge University Press, 1982), 130).

129. Michel Foucault, *Discipline & Punish: The Birth of the Prison* (New York: Vintage Books, 1979 [orig. 1975]), 188.

130. Foucault, *Discipline & Punish*, 222.

131. Danica Dupont and Frank Pearce, "'Foucault contra Foucault': Rereading the Governmentality Papers," *Theoretical Criminology* 5, no. 2 (May 2001): 123-58.

132. Frank Pearce, "The *Collège de Sociologie* and French Social Thought," *Economy and Society* 20, no. 1 (February 2003).

Index

abuse, 98–101

accountability, 37; and high-stakes testing in schools, 47–48

Acéphale, 115, 136

Acéphale, 57, 115, 116, 129, 131

Adorno, Theodor, 8

Aesthetics, 51–52; avant-garde, 53–56; of existence, 31; formalism, 51–53, 55, 58; jazz, 54, 56–58

African-Americans, 57, 58

Agamben, Giorgio, xii, xiii, 16, 71, 93; and "bare life", 99–100, 101–102, 103, 104; and bio-politics, 100; and Primo Levi / "grey zone", 94, 100, 101

America, 6–9

Americanization, 7

Les anormaux, 73, 76, 77

anti-psychiatry movement 61–67

The Archeology of Knowledge (L'archéologie du savoir), 72

asylum, xiv

Austin, John L., 112–113

author function 51–53

"bare life", 99–100

Barnes, Mary, 63–64

Basaglia, Franco, 61, 62, 66, 72, 75

Bataille, Georges, xiv, 115, 116, 119, 124–126, 127, 128–129, 130, 131–132, 135–136, 137

Baudrillard, Jean, 42

Beckett, Samuel, xii, 52, 58, 120

Bell, Clive, 55

Benjamin, Walter, 18

Bentham, Jeremy, 40

Bentley, Arthur, 6

bio-politics, 71, 74, 75, 100; and bio-security racism, 78–80; and the generalization of social danger, 77–78; and the pathologization of crime, 76–77; and the professionalization of doctors, 76

bio-power, x, xii, xiii, 16–17, 18, 26, 45

bio-security and racism, 78–79

Birth of the Clinic, 72

Blanchot, Maurice, 115, 116, 119, 126, 127, 136

Boulez, Pierre, 51

Bourdieu, Pierre, 107–109, 113

Butler, Judith, 79

Caillois, Roger, xiv, 115, 116, 130–131, 132, 133, 135, 136

Card, Claudia, 101

Care, 93–94; and bio-politics, 96; as a commodity, 93; as an enabling practice, 103; institutionalization of, 94–95, 102–103; instrumental value of, 96; as medical procedure, 96, 97; technologies of, xiii–xiv, 95-98; as work, 102

Carter, Jimmy, 39

Charcot, Jean Martin, 65, 66, 69, 74, 77

Chicago School, 6

Chomsky, Noam, 13–14

Classical Age, Classical era, 62

College of Sociology (*Collège de sociologie*), xiv, 115, 116, 128, 129–130, 133, 135–136

Coltrane, John, 52, 54, 56

Community Mental Health Center
    (CMHC), 73, 74, 75
Cooper, David, 62, 63, 64, 66, 67
conduct, 77–78, 83
control, 3, 5–8; functionality and
    conflict, 23; and discipline 23;
    as free of institutions, 23–24,
    27; nondisciplinary 30, 32; and
    power 23; as product of institu-
    tions, 23–24, 25, 27; as vaga-
    bond entity 23; and sovereignty
    24
coppertops, 41, 44, 45; students as
    47

dangerousness, 26
deinstitutionalization, 25, 27; and
    pantopticism 28; and the state
    28
Deleuze, Gilles, 6, 24, 29, 70, 116
Derrida, Jacques, xiv, 112–113
Dewey, John, xi, 6, 8
disability, 95, 96; and bio-politics
    96; medical model of, 95–96;
    social model of 96
discipline, xi, xii, 19, 23–28, 41,
    44–45, 76
Discipline and Punish, x, xii, 4, 11,
    14, 19, 21, 23–27, 30, 32, 43,
    72, 76
dominant social paradigm, 42–43,
    46
Dreyfus Affair, 108
Duchamp, Marcel, 52, 53, 54–55
Dumézil, Georges, 115
Durkheim, Émile, 5, 10

economization, 43
education, 38
enclosure, 41, 44, 47, 49
enclosure movement, 41
Enlightenment, 4, 10, 11,
European Union, xi, 9–10, 11,

Feudalism, 24,
Ford, Henry, 7

Formalism, 51–53, 55, 58
Fotopoulos, Takis, 42–43
Frankfurt School, 4, 8
Freud, Sigmund, 5; and Freudo-
    Marxism 5, 65, 72

Gates, Henry Louis, Jr., 57
genetic responsibility, 83, 84–85,
    89–91; as moral discourse, 85–
    89
Gitler, Ira, 56, 57
Google, 83
Gorizia, 66–68
governmentality, xi, xii, xiv, xv, 3,
    6, 28, 43, 79–80, 83; and dis-
    ability 96; of others x, 24, 30,
    32; of the self, 24, 30
Grimm, Dieter 9–10
Groupe d'information sur les pris-
    ons (GIP), ix, 61, 67, 71
Guantanamo Bay, 79

health care, 93–94; and bio-politics,
    96; as a commodity, 93; as an
    enabling practice, 103; as medi-
    cal procedure, 96, 97; as
    work,102; institutionalization
    of, 94–95, 102–103; instrumen-
    tal value of, 96; technologies of,
    xiii–xiv, 95-98
Heble, Ajay, 58
Hegel, G.W.F., 25, 122–124, 126,
    131, 133
Heidegger, Martin, 30
high-stakes testing in schools, 47–
    48
History of Sexuality I (Introduc-
    tion), x, 3–4, 5, 16, 24, 29, 68,
    76
History of sexuality II (The Use of
    Pleasure), x, 24, 30
History of sexuality III (The Care
    of the Self), x, 24, 30
Ho, Fred Wei-han, 58
Hobbes, Thomas, 18
Horkheimer, Max, 8

Husserl, Edmund, 17, 34

institutionalization, 27, 98; and the
  state 28
intellectual, xiv; general role of the
  107–113; specific, 109–112;
  universal, 109

James, William, xi, 6
juridicism, xii, 19–20
justice (*jus*), 13–15

Kelsen, Hans, 3
Kittay, Eva Feder, 94
Klossowski, Pierre, xiv, 115, 119–
  126, 128, 130–131, 133
Kofsky, Frank, 56–57
Kojève, Alexandre, 122–124, 126,
  131

Laing, Ronald, 62, 63, 64, 66, 67
law, 14–15, 17–18, 21, 22
legal legitimacy, 18
Leiris, Michel, xiv, 115, 116–119
Lenin, Vladimir, 19
lettres de cachet, 25, 26, 68, 69
Levi, Primo, 100
Lippmann, Walter, 8
Lyotard, Jean-François, 107, 108–
  109

madness, 61, 62, 63, 64, 65, 66, 77;
  freedom of, 64
Madness and Civilization (*Histoire
  de la folie*), xiii, 61, 62, 63, 65,
  69, 72, 111
Manuel, Sam, 57
market, 42;; as dominant social
  paradigm 46; as virus 42
marketization, 43
Marx, Karl, 4, 5, 8, 10, 14, 19, 126,
  131; and Freudo-Marxism 5,
  65, 72; Marxism, 3, 4, 5, 17, 19,
  32, 68, 72
The Matrix, xii, 40–42, 44–45
Matza, David, 10

Mead, George Herbert, 6, 10
Mills, Charles Wright, 6, 8
Milunsky, Aubrey, 85–88
Mutt, Richard, 54

National Institute for Environmental Health Sciences, 84
A Nation At Risk, 46–47
Negri, Toni (Antonio), 71
neoliberalism, x
Nietzsche, Friedrich, xiv, 14, 115,
  119, 120, 124, 126, 127, 129,
  130, 131, 136
No Child Left Behind, xii, 47–48
normalization, xi, xiii, 24, 26, 27,
  28, 76, 79

Oppenheimer, Robert, 110
The Order of Things (*Les mots et
  les choses*), 72, 121

panopticism, 4, 19, 24, 45; and
  deinstitutionalization, 28
Panopticon, 40
parrhêsia, parrhesiast, 29, 34
Pinel, Philippe, 62, 64
Le pouvoir psychiatrique, 61, 63,
  64, 73
power, 13–15, 16, 17–22; and the
  role of philosophy 37
President's Commission for an a
  National Agenda for the Eighties, 39
pre-socratics, 30
Price, Janet, 96
psychiatry, 61–69; anti-psychiatry
  61–67; psychiatric expertise 74,
  77, 78; psychiatric power 74,
  76; psychiatric Reform Law
  180 73, 74
public sphere, 9–10

racism, and bio-security, 78–79;
  neo-racism, 79
Raulet, Gérard, 51
Reagan, Ronald, 8

Reimer, Everett, 38
resistance, 62, 66, 68, 69, 70
risk management, xiv
Rorty, Richard, 6
Ross, Edward A., xi
Rousseau, Jean-Jacques, 5, 8,
Roussel, Raymond, 116–119

Sade, Marquis de, xiv, 115, 116,
    121–125, 127, 128–129, 133–
    134, 136
Sartre, Jean Paul, xiv, 107
Schmitt, Carl, 16
schools, 37, 38, 39–40, 42–49
self: technology/technologies of
    the, xi, 30-31
Shildrick, Margrit, 96
society: controlling, 23, 24; disci-
    plinary, 23, 24, 29; feudal, 24;
    liberated, 29; panoptic, 24, 28
"Society must be defended" (*Il
    faut défendre la société*), 68, 73,
    76

sovereign, 16–17; and *lettres de
    cachet* 25
sovereignty, 18, 20, 79–80
Spinoza, Baruch, 14–15, 18, 21, 22
state, 3, 5, 6, 7, 16, 17; and deinsti-
    tutionalization 28
subjectivization, x, 37, 111
surveillance, xi, 26, 76
Szasz, Thomas, 62, 67

Tocqueville, Alexis, 5
Trieste, 67
Tronto, Joan, 94

La volonté de savoir, 73

Weber, Max, 8
"What Is an Author?", xii
Wirth, Louis, 7

Zola, Emile, 107

About the Contributors

Alain Beaulieu, Ph.D. Philosophy
Professor at the Department of Philosophy, University of Sudbury (Canada). Research and teaching interests: Contemporary European Philosophy, Sociology of Mental Health. He recently published: *Gilles Deleuze et la phénoménologie* (Mons/Paris: Sils Maria/Vrin, 2004), "Les sources heideggériennes de la notion d'existence chez le dernier Foucault," *Revue philosophique de Louvain* 4 (2003); and contributions to *Abécédaire de Michel Foucault* (Mons/Paris: Sils Maria/Vrin, 2004)..beaulieual@hotmail.ca

Mario Colucci, Ph.D. Psychiatry
Psychiatrist affiliated with the Dipartimento di Salute Mentale di Trieste and associate professor at the Faculty of Philosophy, University of Trieste (Italy). Research and teaching interests: French Philosophy, Psychoanalysis, and History of Psychiatry. He is a member of the Forum Psicoanalitico Lacaniano and of the École de Psychanalyse du Champ Lacanien. Recent publications include: (with P. Di Vittorio) *Franco Basaglia* (Milano: Edizioni Bruno Mondadori, 2001); "Il vetro dell'acquario. Michel Foucault e le istituzioni della psichiatria," *Revue Aut Aut* (1998); editor of *Follia e paradosso. Seminari sul pensiero di Franco Basaglia* (Trieste: Edizioni "e," 1995). mario.colucci@tin.it

Pierangelo Di Vittorio, Ph.D. Philosophy
Associate professor in the Department of Philosophy, University of Bari (Italy). Research and teaching interests: Modern and Contemporary Philosophy, Contemporary Political Philosophy, Critique of Psychiatry and other Systems of Power, Minority Rights. Recent publications include: "La parabola della follia," in *Moltiplicare Foucault: Vent'anni dopo*, ed. O. Marzocca, (Milano: Mimesis/Millepiani, 2004); coeditor (with R. Finelli, F. Fistetti, and F. R. Recchia Luciani) "Politiche della verit," in *Globalizzazione e diritti futuri* (Roma: Manifestolibri, 2004); (with M. Colucci) *Franco Basaglia* (Milano: Edizioni Bruno Mondadori, 2001); *Foucault e Basaglia: L'incontro tra genealogie e movimenti di base* (Verona: Ombre Corte Edizioni, 1999). arnaldo.divittorio@tiscali.it

David Gabbard, Ed.D. Educational Foundations
Professor in the Department of Curriculum & Instruction of the College of Education, East Carolina University (USA). Research and teaching interests: Pedagogy, (De)schooling. Recent publications include: coeditor (with E. Wayne Ross) *Defending Public Schools: Education under the Security State* (Westport, CT: Praeger, 2004); (with K. J. Saltman) *Education As Enforcement: The Mili-*

tarization and Corporatization of Schools (New York: Routledge, 2003); editor of *Knowledge and Power in the Global Economy: Politics and the Rhetoric of School Reform* (Mahwah, NJ: Lawrence Erlbaum, 2000); *Silencing Ivan Illich: A Foucauldian Analysis of Intellectual Exclusion* (San Francisco: Austin & Winfield, 1993). gabbardd@mail.ecu.edu

Monique Lanoix, Ph.D. Philosophy
Postdoctoral fellow at the Department of Philosophy, Dalhousie University (Canada). Research and teaching interests: Contemporary European Philosophy, Applied Ethics. monique.lanoix@dal.ca

Christian Lavagno, Ph. D. Philosophy
Associate professor in the Department of Philosophy, University of Osnabrück (Germany). Research and teaching interests: Critical Theory, French Philosophy, Enlightenment. His publications include: *Rekonstruktion der Moderne: Eine Studie zu Habermas und Foucault* (Würzburg: Verlag Königshausen und Neumann, 2003); *Negative Dialektik und Kritische Ontologie: Eine Untersuchung zu Theodor W. Adorno* (Würzburg: Verlag Königshausen und Neumann, 1992). alavagno@uni-bremen.de

Thomas Lemke, Ph.D. Political Science
Research fellow at the Institut für Sozialforschung in Frankfurt/Main (Germany) and assistant professor of sociology at Wuppertal University (Germany). Research and teaching interests: Theory of Society, Political Theory, Sociology of Organization, Biopolitics, Genetics, Reproduction Technologies. His publications include: *Veranlagung und Veranwortung: Genetische Diagnostik zwischen Selbstbestimmung und Schicksal* (Bielefeld: Transcript Verlag, 2004); "Foucault, Governmentality, and Critique," *Rethinking Marxism* 14, no. 3 (2002); (with K. Türk and M. Bruch) *Organisation in der modernen Gesellschaft: Eine historische Einführung* (Wiesbaden: Westdeutscher Verlag, 2002); coeditor (with U. Bröckling and S. Krasmann) of *Gouvernementalität der Gegenwart: Studien zur Ökonomisierung des Sozialen* (Suhrkamp: Frankfurt/M., 2000); *Eine Kritik der politischen Vernunft: Foucaults Analyse der modernen Gouvernementalität* (Hamburg/Berlin: Argument Verlag, 1997). lemke@em.uni-frankfurt.de

Dario Melossi, Ph.D. Sociology
Professor of Criminology with the Faculty of Law, University of Bologna (Italy). Research and teaching interests: Sociology of the State, Law, Deviance, Social Control and Punishment, Security. His publications include: "Theories of Social Control," in *The Blackwell Companion to Criminology*, ed. C. Sumner and W. Chambliss (Oxford: Blackwell, 2003); "'In A Peaceful Life': Migration and The Crime of Modernity in Europe/Italy," *Punishment and Society* 5, no. 4 (2003); *Stato, devianza, controllo sociale: Teorie criminologiche e società tra Europa e Stati Uniti* (Milano: Bruno Mondadori Editore, 2002); "Introduction" (pages 9-46) to the Transaction Edition of G. Rusche and O. Kirchheimer, *Punishment and Social Structure* (New Brunswick: Transaction Publishers, 2002);

The State of Social Control: A Sociological Study of Concepts of State and Social Control in the Making of Democracy (Cambridge, UK: Polity Press and New York: St. Martin's Press, 1990). melossi@giuri.unibo.it

Warren Montag, Ph.D. Comparative Literary Studies
Professor of English and comparative literary studies at Occidental College (USA). Research and teaching interests: Marxism, Spinoza, Althusser, French philosophy. Recent publications include: *Louis Althusser* (London: Palgrave, 2002); "Toward a Conception of Racism without Race: Foucault and Contemporary Biopolitics," *Le Pli: The Warwick Journal of Philosophy* 13 (2002); coeditor (with M. Hill) of *Problematizing the Public Sphere: Masses, Classes and Counter-publics* (London: Verso, 2000); *Bodies, Masses, Power: Spinoza and his Contemporaries* (London: Verso, 1999); Preface to E. Balibar, *Spinoza and Politics* (London: Verso, 1998); coeditor (with T. Stolze) of *The New Spinoza* (Minneapolis: University of Minnesota Press, 1997); "The Soul is the Prison of the Body: Althusser and Foucault 1970-1975," *Yale French Studies* (Fall 1995). montag@oxy.edu

Tracey Nicholls, Ph.D. Philosophy
Teaching Assistant in the Department of Philosophy, McGill University (Canada). Research and teaching interests: Aesthetics, Feminist Theory, Philosophy of Improvised Musics, Philosophy of Law. tracey.nicholls@mail.mcgill.ca

Frank Pearce, Ph.D. Sociology
Professor in the Department of Sociology, Queen's University (Canada). Research and teaching interests: Classical Sociological Theory (Marxism, Radical Durkheimianism, Foucault), Sociology of Sacrifice, Sociology of Law, Crime and Deviance. Recent publications include: "Off with their heads: Caillois, Klossowski and Foucault on Public Executions," *Economy and Society* 32, no. 2 (2003); "Multinational Corporations, Power, Crime and Resistance," in *The Blackwell Companion to Criminology*, ed. C. Sumner and W. Chambliss (Oxford: Blackwell, 2003); (with T. Woodiwiss) "Foucault as a Realist," in *Realism after Postmodernism*, ed. J. Lopez and G. Potter (London: Athlone Press, 2002). pearcef@sympatico.ca